# Where Angels Fear to Tread

*One man's journey in starting his small business*

## GEORGE H. SEABERG

WESTBOW
PRESS
A DIVISION OF THOMAS NELSON

ISBN: 978-1-4497-3038-3 (e)
ISBN: 978-1-4497-3039-0 (sc)
ISBN: 978-1-4497-3040-6 (hc)

Library of Congress Control Number: 2011960330

WestBow Press books may be ordered through booksellers or by contacting:

WestBow Press
A Division of Thomas Nelson
1663 Liberty Drive
Bloomington, IN 47403
www.westbowpress.com
1-(866) 928-1240

Printed in the United States of America
WestBow Press rev. date: 11/11/2011

**Picture of ARI pyramid in back part of Tully's Automotive - 1974**

Top row: (left to right) David Dayton, Larry Gainer Middle row: Dennis Flockhart, George Seaberg, Dan Mansuer Bottom row: Jim Fleck, Mark "Rocky" Robinson, Craig Kinzer, Fred Hurt

# Endorsements

In my experiences working for and with a variety of companies, I have concluded that being an entrepreneur is the most challenging. Starting your own business and making it a success takes skill in the chosen field, determination, eternal optimism, and an attitude of doing whatever it takes. George Seaberg is a true entreprencur and graciously shares his experiences of the challenges, ups and downs, and rewards of starting his own business. His story is a true inspiration for all who are or who would like to start their own business, as well as for the rest of us.

Bill Ligon, manufacturing executive and consultant

I wanted to give this book a quick scan. I couldn't do it because I found it too informative and interesting. I had to slow down so I could savor this amazing blend of practical business management advice, Christian worldview, and family values. Seaberg has done many things well over his lifetime, and now he has added book writing.

Perry Pascarella is the former editor-in-chief of Industry Week magazine and vice president-editorial of Penton Publishing Co. He has authored seven books, the most recent of which is Christ-Centered Leadership.

Mr. Seaberg spells out in detail how his management style, and more generally his approach to life, resulted in the successful startup and growth of his manufacturing company. In thirty-six chapters, he is able to successfully use his personal life experiences as examples of his principles for dealing with all of the institutions and people associated with starting and running a business. This book is a must-read for anyone wanting to start a business in today's economic and social climate. I highly recommend it.

Timothy J. Lowe, PhD<br>Tippie College of Business<br>University of Iowa

It is an honor and a privilege for me to endorse George Seaberg's book. I had the pleasure of being introduced to George in 2008, and his influence on my life has been immeasurable since that time. His deep faith in God, love of family, and dedication to his community and country are manifest in everything he does and says, and this book is a prime illustration of those commitments and principles. Chapter 4, entitled "Ethics? Morality?" perfectly encapsulates George's ethics and morality and highlights why his leadership created a successful company. I wish George every success in publishing this wonderful book and hope it receives the widespread distribution it and he deserve.

Hubert J. Pries LTC, SF, USAR (Ret.)

George Seaberg has written a frank and enlightening book about his personal journey starting and operating a specialty manufacturing business. He provides an excellent, well-organized guide to anyone considering a similar path. As a small business entrepreneur myself, I found Seaberg's insights and recommendations to be right on target.

Tom Hanson, managing partner (retired), Fleming Hanson Sales<br>Metro Mechanical Services, Chicago, CEO (retired)<br>Radford Trane Mechanical Contractors, Winston-Salem, NC

It is clear to see the belief in and application of Christian principles has served as the catalyst for George's success—as a businessman, family man, and friend. If you want to improve your chances for success in business and achieve peace and sense of purpose in your life, read this book!

John P. Byrne, PhD<br>Professor and chairperson, marketing department<br>College of Business, St. Ambrose University, Davenport, IA<br>2005 Leadville, CO, trail hundred-mile finisher; 2008 Ironman finisher

This book brings into focus all the things necessary to make a business, large or small, successful. George has the focus and personal attributes that are critical to ensure that a new business can grow and succeed over time. He clearly shares these experiences with the reader. Some of these attributes he shares are:

- Be a mentor to others in the organization

- Develop a detailed business plan
- Carefully select and develop team players
- Understand your role in the organization very well
- Accept the fact that attitude is everything

These attributes and many others outlined in the book will be invaluable to any aspiring business owner.

Michael Plunkett
Plunkett Business Background
Senior VP Engineering, Technology,
and Human Resources Deere &Company
Member Board of Directors Deere &Company
Member Board of Directors Hon Industries

This book is for the person who has a vision for starting a business but lacks capital and resources. You will learn how to succeed by having a strong faith in Jesus Christ, a willingness to sacrifice and take risks, a supportive family, and a humble spirit that leads to surrounding yourself with good, competent employees who are loyal and trustworthy. In the book of Proverbs, we read that a wise person seeks counsel from many people. George Seaberg often networked to get the help needed to solve problems and move forward with often trendsetting ideas.

Ted Brolund, Retired CEO W. A. Whitney Company,
an Esterline Technologies Company

I met George Seaberg in the 1980s when we were both active in our local chapters of ASME and SME. He was building up his company while I was a mid-level engineering supervisor at the US Army's Rock Island Arsenal. We found that we not only shared an enthusiasm for our profession, having both graduated from the University of Iowa, but that we also shared strong religious and political values (though I still don't agree with him on mandatory term limits).

Over my career, I've unhappily watched a lot of guys (a whole lot, in fact) start their own businesses and flounder. George was one of the able few who actually pulled it off. I've also unhappily encountered too many ethically challenged managements and managers. George was one of the nice guys who really did finish first. Happily, he has shared with us how he did it.

George has always been a good guy to have a cup of coffee with, and now he's written a good book to read.

Stephen Robinson, PE
Director- Science and Engineering
US Army Rock Island Arsenal
Retired

# About the Author

George Seaberg was born and raised in Moline, Illinois, along the banks of the Mississippi River.

After graduating from high school, he attended the University of Iowa on a basketball scholarship that enabled him to go to college. When he graduated with a degree in mechanical engineering, he served in the army as a helicopter pilot.

When his service was over, he worked as an engineer for several manufacturing companies before becoming a consulting Professional Engineer.

He and his wife reside in Riverdale, Iowa, and attend a local Lutheran church. They have three married children and seven grandchildren.

# Preface

My main reason for writing this story is to explain how a small manufacturing business succeeded in the latter twentieth and early twenty-first centuries' competitive world market. My research came from the notes and diary I kept as I ventured through the startup and then growth of my small machining and fabricating company in the period from 1972 into 2006. I also used the writings of eminent authorities in the business world, as noted in this story.

# Acknowledgments

For me, it all starts with thanking those who I call *family*. I thank my deceased parents, siblings, many business friends, and past and present employees of Seaberg Industries for helping me to live the dream of starting, owning, and operating a manufacturing business.

For years I didn't fully realize how much my parents had instilled an entrepreneurial spirit in their children, each of whom has either married a small businessman or worked for and started at least one business. Maybe it was because we kids used to sit at the kitchen table talking about how we would improve Ecklund's small drug store, which was located just a few blocks from our home, if we owned it.

Thank you to my former fellow employees, especially Craig Kinzer and Harold Paget. I thank the first men to mentor and guide me in taking my business baby steps to keep me out of the hazards out there: Bill Hampton, Ray Brown Jr., Don Martin, Don Shewry, Wes Bracken, and Julian Weigle. Harry Conn and Ted Brolund of W. A. Whitney Corporation and I almost became partners early on, and Harry, in his wisdom, felt it was best for us to just be good friends. Dick Sabo was of more help than he could realize. I want to thank Dave Hocamp, my IT wizard, who kept me from pulling out my hair in frustration while working through the challenges of understanding what I wanted my computer to do while working on this project.

And I especially want to thank my wife of fifty years, Sue Trissel Seaberg. We both know that without you at my side as editor, proofreader, and encourager, I would not have built a successful manufacturing business, nor would I have been able to write this story.

# Contents

# Background

I always wanted to run some kind of enterprise or be in charge of whatever work I was involved in doing. My parents encouraged me to be willing to assume authority and to be responsible for my actions.

My paternal grandfather, Severin Seaberg, influenced me through his engineering successes and in the kind, steady way he conducted his life. He was an inventor and one of the founders of Eagle Signal Company, as well as the most significant developer of the vehicle traffic light.

The week before Christmas in 1973, I was suddenly fired from my job as assistant to the president of a small metal fabricating company. Our children's presents had been bought and paid for. My wife, Sue, always my strongest supporter, said, "You always wanted to run a business. Now you might as well get it out of your system." While I thought about what to do, I knew it was most important for Sue to remain as a stay-at-home mom for our three young ones and not have to get a job outside the home.

A deep motivating force behind my desire to start a company was that I wanted to prove that a tiny manufacturing company in America could outperform Japanese companies. At that time, the media and the Japanese themselves were saying, "Japan, Inc., is going to buy America." Japanese companies had already bought much of the real estate of Hawaii, and one group had just bought the Pebble Beach Golf Course in Carmel, California, as well as businesses in the United States. As was to happen several years later, these Japanese companies lost the golf course and most of the land back to American owners. Not once did I ever lose a competitive bid to a Japanese company, even when the part prints were made in Japan. Our cultural differences required me to have a Japanese translator explain the nuances that were part of those drawings.

The other desire I had was to be a net contributor to the wealth of our economy in the only endeavors that would do it: Farming, Mining or Manufacturing. I chose Manufacturing.

It was during a time when going to work as a registered professional engineer, which I was, for a large company would have been fairly easy for me to do. Instead, I wanted to try starting and running my own business. After thirty-three years, I finally "got it out of my system" when I sold the company in 2006.

In 1972, I began with a drawing board and a small blacksmith's vise in our basement, plus a station wagon and $2,400 in our savings account—and no customers.

# Introduction

I wrote this book for one reason: to help those who want to know more about how a small (less than 150 persons) American manufacturing concern can operate and survive in today's business climate. The largest part of my work life has been spent helping the company I began in 1973 survive and grow in the metal machining and fabricating business. I speak from that perspective. At times my views may seem somewhat narrow or parochial, but this kind of focus and intensity was required of me for the company to succeed.

When I was working as a professional engineer consultant for an architectural/engineering firm in the late 1960s and early 1970s, I had the opportunity to observe many companies that our firm either worked for or from whom we were seeking to obtain contracts. This gave me a larger view of the business and manufacturing world. I relied heavily on this part of my work experience not only to help start and keep our company going in the earlier years of its existence but also to help it continue to grow after I sold it to my managers in 2006.

The principles stated in the Bible are the basis on which I've tried to build a successful company, and these shaped or were the most significant factors in the business decisions I've made. This philosophy is really no different from those of the men who started Hobby Lobby, J.C. Penney's, Phillips Oil, Servicemaster Corp., The Lincoln Electric Company, and numerous others.

Most of the incidents I wrote about that happened before 2000 are from diary notes I made as those events occurred.

Many of my thoughts on small company management come from one of my benchmark institutions, The Lincoln Electric Company, Cleveland, Ohio. John Lincoln founded the company in 1895, and his younger brother, Jim, joined the firm in 1907. Their moral upbringing in an itinerant minister's home was the basis for their company's operating philosophies. In this book, reference is made to the use of those principles.

I do now, and have since I started working in my chosen vocation, feel pitifully short in knowledge of my career subjects. This must be why successful and long-established company heads have often mentioned how the people who supported the leader of that company gave him or her the support he or she needed. Even a mechanical genius like R. G. LeTourneau, the father of modern earth-moving equipment, needed to have some of his engineers make drawings from the sketches he literally made in the dirt floor of his Peoria factory before putting them onto engineering drawings.

Seaberg Industries, Inc., has been certified as a manufacturing supplier to Caterpillar for many years and for almost forty years has been a successful parts supplier to manufacturers. And like most businesses, Cat's quality requirements have necessarily increased each year to keep their hard-earned high reputation. Anyone who has tried for a supplier certification from Boeing, Ford, Deere and Company, or other similar companies realizes what an accomplishment it is to become one of their certified suppliers. One of my business friends who owned a very well-thought-of Midwest company told me it took his firm four years to earn its quality certification. Another company, having been a Caterpillar supplier for some twenty years, took six years of concerted effort to become fully certified, and as quality requirements continued to increase, they've had to redouble their efforts to retain that certification.

Chapter 1

# Fragile but Strong

---

Why would anyone think a small enterprise could be fragile? After all, small businesses make up over 90 percent of the nongovernment employment in America.

A small company fits the description of being fragile, while at the same time being very strong. This dichotomy usually comes from not having very much financially but also having a very strong commitment and a will to succeed in spite of difficult circumstances. When there is nowhere else to go, you just have to dig in and tough it out. I have only read of a small number of companies that ever had a smooth, trouble-free beginning.

My best description of *"fragile but strong"* comes from looking at something as simple as a chicken eggshell. The weight of the shell is very light, but it can resist any relatively large structural forces that are gradually applied on the exterior. However, if it is dropped a short distance, or if a sharp instrument punctures that shell, it will then collapse quite easily. In engineering terms, the shell is a strategic enclosure. Similarly, most businesses have a strategic business plan. If an unplanned calamity or force happens to a business, like the sudden withdrawal of a small company's only client, the business likely will fail. If an egg is dropped four feet onto a concrete floor (strategic force), we know the egg will burst apart when it hits the floor.

But if a business has as part of its strategic plan the gradual withdrawal of its only customer, it very likely will survive. And if an egg has a fairly small and gradual force applied to it, the strategic enclosure of the shell should be able to withstand that pressure.

## Weaknesses

A small startup can collapse from too little cash flow or not having a versatile and competent staff to handle many of the serious threats to its sensitive early survival. For example, we had to fabricate just about anything in the early days before we found our best niche, which was making machined and fabricated metal parts. The list of our products included the three-hundred-foot-long catwalk that hangs from the University of Iowa's Carver-Hawkeye Arena ceiling and supports all the lighting and sound systems for the floor and seating areas, two truck-mounted, eight thousand–pound oil well workover rigs, factory hoist lifting components, specially designed wheeled trash containers, and small dies the size of an egg carton. Since having started a venture of my own, it is easy for me to understand why fifty percent of small business startups fail in their first year and 80 percent fail within the first five years. According to what my friend Harry Conn, past successful CEO of W. A. Whitney Corporation, once exclaimed to me, "George, you needed more guts than brains to survive!" He was right, in spades. But I had a dream that just wouldn't go away.

I can remember only too well my first job of any size. I furnished complete machined parts drawings to a large local company one month after my wife and I decided to give starting a business a try. After I successfully completed the work, the company buyer paid me out of his petty cash fund since my bill was for less than $1,000. I didn't say anything, but I was thinking that this was a house mortgage payment and food money for the next month. Incidental cash to one business can be almost everything to another!

The frailty or strength of a small company logically revolves around whatever cash reserves it has available for operations. If you don't have the money on hand or available, most of the time you should wait until you can afford whatever it is you may need. Buying with cash was easier for me to talk about than to learn the hard way from experience. Companies usually go bankrupt from not carefully watching the cash flowing in and out of the firm.

For example, when Bandag, Inc., now Bridgestone Bandag LLC, headquartered in Muscatine, Iowa, was a small foundry established by Roy Carver, he had serious cash flow problems. People may find it hard to believe now that the company is a financial success. There was a time when Mr. Carver offered stock to suppliers as payment for large foundry material purchases. When he died at the latter end of the twentieth century, he left an estate with a net worth approximating $300,000,000. By not breaking but persevering when his company was bent, he ended up financially successful.

Most of the time it takes years to overcome a lack of financial inertia and get out of the cash flow binds inherent in starting an enterprise. In order to appreciate this fact, one only needs to look at how frequently the local restaurants in your town open and a short time later, for a number of reasons, close their doors.

Any economic downturn on the part of the client, no matter how slight to them, can have dramatic effects on the subcontractor working for the larger firm. Recently a former buyer for a large local manufacturing company was complaining to one of their subs that his company's sales had gone down 20 percent. But he said the company wasn't doing badly because they were using up inventory to handle orders. What this person did not realize was that the subcontractor he was talking with had to contend with sales that plunged some 70 percent because of the necessary steps of reducing inventory the manufacturer had taken. An analogy to this is that if a firm such as General Electric or General Motors catches an economic sniffle, most of their suppliers get pneumonia because these little guys have to maintain certain minimum inventory levels to meet any sudden increases in customer orders and have much fewer financial resources to work with.

The agricultural and construction equipment industries suffered a severe recession in the early 1980s, causing International Harvester, a firm founded in 1831 by Cyrus McCormick, to cease operations. Several Quad City small businesses also closed down as a result. Seaberg Industries was in the same fix as these firms, with personnel layoffs and other unpleasant problems caused by a falling economy. Our existence was severely tested, but we were able to hang on. At the time, we incurred a negative net worth, which stretched us dearly. But we didn't, and wouldn't, break. It just caused us to become more efficient with our employees and other resources at hand.

In 1982 we faced a major downturn in business when a major client went on an extended strike; another customer was in the process of going out of business; and the economy was down in the rest of the agricultural equipment market, as I previously stated. In the Quad Cities, where my company was located, the conditions were like the former automotive Big Three of General Motors, Ford, and Chrysler all shutting down in Detroit at the same time. People may recall that the upper Midwest was called the Rust Belt instead of the Corn Belt at that time.

The situation became so desperate at my company that I was seriously planning to lay everyone off but my wife, who was my part-time bookkeeper, and me. We had about twenty-five employees on the payroll then. My most valuable employee, Craig Kinzer, was about a week away from signing a contract to build a home with a fellow employee. Suddenly a job we had quoted on at a large foundry came in, and we were able to call our employees back to work.

Along with economic and emotional friability is a "feast or famine" feeling with the little guy. In the late 1970s and very early 1980s, companies in the US oil business were feasting on super-boom times. Even our northwestern Illinois firm was doing work for small and medium-sized oil patch firms in central and southern Illinois, Oklahoma, and Texas. Our oil customers told me, "This boom is going to last for years."

For those in the oil business, it is usually boom or bust. I'll never forget a telegram (this was before the advent of the Internet) I received in 1982. It was from the president of Cooper Manufacturing Company, a respected Tulsa, Oklahoma, firm. We had just shipped a parts order to the company the previous week. This fine company was trying to adjust to the fast-changing market but still didn't react fast enough to the catastrophic reductions in going from a high of fifty oil well workover rigs per week to only one. These units were selling for $150,000 each ($350,000 in 2011 terms) at the time.

I laughed out loud in disbelief that the message said that the gates were locked, *no* shipments would be received, and *all* freight trucks would be turned back at the gate. However, I didn't laugh too much when I tried to collect an outstanding bill from them of $20,000 over the next year and a half. Unfortunately, the company went bankrupt a year after I finally collected all that was owed. This was a fine company with a very good product and ethical people running it, but they ran into a market that literally evaporated overnight.

What wasn't so funny was that I had to reduce the two top wage earners' wages in early 1983 for a short time. Harold Paget, my maintenance manager and confidant, got his back several weeks later. Craig Kinzer, our other top-earning employee, had his wages restored the following week. My pay was about what I earned some five years previously, but all of us were paid something every Wednesday.

Our oldest daughter, Susan, was at the University of Iowa then and was so committed to helping us stay afloat that she worked sixty hours a week in the summer at Seaberg and a local Payless Cashways lumber yard. And our son, Tom, unbeknownst to us, took out a college loan and applied to join the army ROTC program at Iowa to be sure there was enough money for him to continue going to school. Fortunately, the army program had a full roster. Having two kids in college at once plus having a pay cut made for some interesting financial challenges. It also strengthened my faith when I stepped back to observe how the Lord was still providing for our family.

A Quad City company at that time did one of the most desperate tricks I had ever heard of to try to stay afloat. The company officers allowed a steel service center truck to pull into their plant dock area to unload a flatbed trailer full of steel with the understanding that it was a COD (Collect on Delivery) shipment. When the trailer was emptied, the shop employees asked the truck driver to pull his rig into the street and then come in to pick up a company check. As soon as the trailer cleared the gate, the employees slammed the gate shut and locked all the doors so the driver couldn't pick up the nonexistent check! It should be no surprise that this firm was insolvent a short time later.

## Strengths

Perhaps the greatest collective strength we had in our company was a desire to unashamedly serve Jesus Christ. The front cover of this book is a picture taken in 1975 where all the male employees formed a human

pyramid at the company entrance when it was in the back end of an
auto body shop. The men are: first row, left to right, Jim Fleck, Rocky
Robinson, Craig Kinzer, and Fred Hurt; second row, left to right, Dennis
Flockhart, the author, and Dan Manseuer; top row, left to right, David
Dayton and Larry Gainer, my first full-time employee.

The Scripture verse above them is from Romans 8:28: "And we know
that all things work together for good to them that love God." Since
that time, this verse has been over either the company office door or the
employee entrance, where it is now located.

One of the strongest attributes the little businessman has is his
perseverance and commitment to keep going, no matter what. A book
written entitled *Man's Search for Meaning* by Dr. Viktor Frankl, a Jewish
psychiatrist interred in the Auschwitz, Germany, concentration camp
during World War II, deals with the human motivation to survive. Dr.
Frankl turned his situation as a prisoner into a human behavior laboratory
to explain this strong drive. His thesis, from personal experience as
an inmate, was that the less a man has, the more individualistic he
becomes. In this Nazi concentration camp, a person had only his own
skin—not even his own underwear. Understandably, most inmates went
to extraordinary means to appear healthy to the guards to keep from
being sent to the gas chambers. This is the exact opposite of Sigmund
Freud's theory that says the less freedom one has, the more he behaves
like others.

I think the survival instinct described by Dr. Frankl was so strong for me
when I operated my small business because of the intimacy that comes
from smaller numbers of people working together and being more aware
of what is going on in the company. Malcolm Gladwell, in his book, *The
Tipping Point* (published in 2000), mentions this in his chapter on the
Rule of 150. Mr. Gladwell's point is when a society or group gets larger
than 150 persons, the individuals lose touch with each other and become
less caring about others and what the others are doing.

Nothing seems to work harder against a person's determination and
motivation than when he or she goes about his or her business with
both feet firmly planted in mid-air. Such a person doesn't know if the
company is strong or if it's going to have a layoff, or even if what he or
she does makes much of a difference in the enterprise's outcome.

It was a constant challenge for me to keep my employees informed about company business. This is one of the reasons why I started having short company information meetings each week on company time. The other reason is that I would talk about lessons for us from the Bible. Later on, I would invite fellow employees and speakers from businesses and churches to share a word with us.

In my own personal, family life, I told my kids when they were young that there was no such thing as divorce or bankruptcy in our family. We went from cash in the bank and thirty-day payment terms in 1982 to no cash and as much as 120+-day payments in the span of two very long years. As I told my fellow employees in our biweekly meetings, during that time the bank even owned the underwear I had on. In these cases, you either gave up or you cranked up. I chose to crank the motivational juices up another notch.

Schlumberger is a fine and well-respected oil well service company that has been around since 1920. With principal offices in Paris, Houston, and The Hague, it has a global reach into 80 countries as of 2009, with 105,000 employees and 2009 revenues of $22.7B. It could easily be a stodgy bureaucracy and cumbersome in its operations because of its size. But it isn't the case.

Why has this world-renowned company succeeded through difficult times to become so strong? I can best answer this by relating a conversation I had with several Schlumberger field crew members in a San Antonio hotel elevator several years ago. For starters, the field operations were made up of many small six- to ten-man crews. The men I talked with *knew* there wasn't a better foreman in their company than the one running their crew in southwest Texas. They had heard stories about other Schlumberger crews having outstanding foremen, but *nobody* could be better than their boss. I'm sure that if I talked to another company crew working in Kansas or South America, those men would have bragged to me that *their* crew boss was the best in the company. It's these kinds of feelings and intimacy among employees that gave that company the strength to endure tough times and even prosper.

Schlumberger grew strong by being completely decentralized and trusting each field service crew to be an entity unto themselves. As it was explained to me, these crews used to operate in the United States by going to an area assigned to them by the responsible regional office. If the work ran out, each man in the crew became a salesman, still on the payroll, and went out looking for oil field service work. Obviously, loyalty to their company was unequalled in the oil business, unless someone else did the same thing. In 1983, the company was at the fifty thousand employee level and never had a layoff in its over sixty-year history.

Adaptability in the marketplace is one of the best strengths of a world-class small manufacturer. In the early 1990s, we received a faxed drawing from a client that needed an emergency turnaround for a somewhat complicated part. We quoted the work in the morning; were awarded the quote that same morning; cut the steel and welded and machined the part during the day; and shipped the work late that afternoon. This is a clear example of our plant being fully in tune with what the office needed to have done. And it was completed with a minimum disruption of the other work currently in process.

Being in a small business gives you a sense of true security. You create the work yourself because nobody but you is going to get many of those important tasks done. And as you start completing work like this, you gain recognition and self-confidence. And this gives everyone around you that same sense of security, significance, and self-respect.

There are other small business strengths I will mention throughout this book as they relate to specific subjects. I wanted to state at least a few of them in the beginning to give the reader a better feel for what it is like to run an operation that can stand few errors without ceasing to exist.

# CHAPTER 2

# Does Everyone Have to
# Think and Act the Same?

Our new small business usually had a wide range in the ages of our employees because of market conditions and the fact that the wages weren't competitive with similar, more-established firms. Most of these older men at the time were either not very skilled or didn't have the stamina necessary to work in a larger factory.

Varying ages among our personnel was a frequent occurrence in the early years of our existence because I couldn't afford the wages for the more-experienced people I wanted to hire. We also had a relatively low level of manufacturing knowledge and ability because manufacturing jobs were in high demand at that time in our area. I had to hire just about anyone who showed up at our door, which was located in the back end of Tully's Auto Body Shop. The cover picture of this book was our plant entrance at that time. As we became a more mature company, we were able to pay higher wages and attract older and more-experienced people.

Fortunately, having a spread of ages let me communicate with men with different life perspectives and thus have the advantage of a wide range of job experiences. I have seen the value of someone who fought in World War II, who took a more conservative approach to problem solving, working alongside another who protested in college in the 1960s against the Vietnam conflict who was a little more innovative in his thinking. Diversity of views usually helped to bring out more ways to finding a solution to a problem in the office or on the floor. It brought a better insight to the work we did because of these different cultural views. We could then choose the best way from many alternatives rather than looking at only one or two choices. Until I sold Seaberg Industries in 2006, while we looked for the best person for a particular job, we still hoped to keep a balance in the ages of our employees.

All of us relate to our early childhood environments, for better or worse. Mr. Gladwell in *The Tipping Point* mentioned how the older hands lend an air of stability to the workplace and serve as teachers to the younger ones without lording it over them, as can sometimes happen. One of our youngest machinists in our early years was training and working as an inspector and ran out of work one day. He asked around to see what else he could do and went and operated a machine to fill his time productively. Conversely, the older employees who had worked at other places were too inhibited to act because of a fear of what their peers might think. But this young man didn't know any other way and started a good precedent of working *wherever* he could be useful. Because of that kind of work attitude, he shortly became one of the highest-paid hourly workers in the company.

At Seaberg Industries, we hired people whose ages ranged from their teens to their late fifties or early sixties. The last time I did an age profile was in the 1990s and 37 percent were eighteen to twenty-nine years old; 22 percent were thirty to thirty-nine; 23 percent were forty to forty-nine; and 18 percent were ages fifty to fifty-nine. A few years earlier, we had several men working on the floor in production who were in their sixties.

Once we hired a man who was over seventy years old. His name was Herman Buchwald, and we nicknamed him "The Human Crane" because he was so strong. There wasn't a job he was afraid to do. He was what you would call "old country" because he gave a full eight-hour shift and outworked younger guys. When he first walked in the shop door with his pastor, Herman was a bitter man because of the wrongs done to him at a large company where he worked most of his life. He remained a quiet person all the time he was with us but eventually started smiling and relating to me why his previous working conditions caused his bitterness. I came to love Herman and the kind of person he became at the company before he had to quit working because of his diabetes.

His illness made being on his feet all day impractical. He passed away shortly after leaving our shop.

We have never had a retirement ceiling, and the present owners adhered to that same policy. The 2006 age breakdown approximated what it was in 1991: 30 percent for the eighteen to twenty-nine age group; 23 percent for thirty to thirty-nine; 20 percent for forty to forty-nine; 21 percent for fifty to fifty-nine; and 6 percent for sixty years old and above.

It's a given in small businesses that many of the employees in their thirties, forties, and fifties came from other businesses, both large and small, making parts in the agricultural and construction industries. Usually, but not always, these persons have been downsized at the larger companies. And many times the men and women just want to work where they don't feel like a number punching a clock and know they are now making a significant contribution.

We have also found that the majority of these people we hired brought a good work ethic as well as discipline, high moral standards, and many fine ideas for productivity to the company. Of course, if we didn't feel any of them would be a net contributor, we would not have hired them in the first place.

I might add that most of the new men/women felt this was about the first time in their careers they were able to make, and install, their own productivity suggestions and improvements without being ignored or discriminated against. They sensed that their contributions were significant in affecting the company's bottom line.

The benefits of the different age ranges and work backgrounds of people is fully explained by Morris Massey, author of *What You Are Is Where You Were When*. His landmark videos have some of the following key learning points:

1. Understand how to motivate and work with different age groups.
2. *Ask* people and *listen* to what they say.
3. Accept that other people's values are just as valid as your own.
4. Put your own values on hold.

We have employed legal immigrants from Asia, Afghanistan, and other countries. Perhaps the most unusual one was Lee Fong Heu, who worked in the Vietnam highlands as a silversmith, where all the Hmong tribe lived. Centuries earlier his countrymen lived in Mongolia before they were driven into China. His grandfather was a Mongol warrior who later had to immigrate to Laos to escape Chinese persecution. This short, rugged man with a thick shock of black hair also worked for the CIA and had to escape the Viet Cong during the Vietnam War. Lee Fong grew up in Laos. At the end of the war, his family fled the Viet Cong and tried to get to the American lines. The Viet Cong were shooting at them as he paid black market prices for a place for his family on an open, overcrowded boat. A sad note about his family was that one of his two young children fell off the boat as they were crossing the Mekong River and drowned.

After being flown to America, the small Hmong community settled in the Quad Cities, and Lee Fong found employment at Seaberg as a welder. A happy note about his family was that their surviving Vietnam-born son went through Rock Island public schools and was valedictorian of his graduating class at Rock Island High School. One of the highlights of my career was the last thing Lee Fong said to me as the entire Quad City Hmong community was preparing to move to Ottumwa, Iowa, at the turn of the century. In his heavy accent, he said, "George, you are like a brudder (brother) to me." I felt the same about him and told him so.

Our company was intentionally "rainbow" in the cultural and racial makeup of our personnel, including former hippies, one of whom was raised by a sixty-person commune. This man appreciated having rules and organization in his work life because he was raised without any of that in a chaotic lifestyle. Other hires were: wannabe hippies resulting from the antiwar philosophy toward the Vietnam conflict, and whites, blacks, Hispanics, etc. Each person's unique background and different views actually added to our corporate strength for competing in a worldwide market because of the variety of talents they brought.

Our diverse backgrounds have helped us to realize what Samuel Gompers, founding president of the American Federation of Labor (AFL) said in a speech in Chicago in September, 1893. "We want more school houses and less jails; more books and less arsenals; more learning and less vice; more constant work and less crime; more leisure and less greed; more justice and less revenge; in fact, more of the opportunities to cultivate our better natures...."[1]

But if I had a choice of an employee to hire, it would first be a farmer who grew up knowing what work was and how to figure out problems on his own. Second, I then preferred former military personnel because they had good work standards drilled into their psyche.

Another quote from Mr. Gompers that I agree with which shows his depth of understanding how business operates is, "The worst crime against working people is a company which fails to operate at a profit."[2] I never took advantage of any employee to gain a better profit. Too many times I did just the opposite and gave raises and bonuses when financially I shouldn't have done so.

1    A New Labor Movement for the New Century, by Gregory Mantsios, 1998.
2    Bionomics: Economy as Business Ecosystem, by Michael Rothschild, 1990.

# CHAPTER 3

# Good Business Friends

One of the best things I did at my company within its first year of existence was to form an advisory group of two company owners and friends I respected for their business sense. I couldn't afford the liability insurance for a board of directors, but I was able to do the next best thing. These men generously gave of their talent to help guide me in making company decisions. This was a key part of helping ARI Industries, as it was called in its first two years, grow during those first fragile, exciting, and sometimes frightening times.

One of the finest services these men did was whenever I asked them to meet with me on a project or proposed plan, they would set aside time and serve as "devil's advocates" to offer objections and encourage me to come up with the best plan possible for whatever subject we were discussing. They disapproved or modified so many of my early thoughts that I sometimes wondered if I could ever do anything original. When they were doing this, they were tactful and careful of my feelings while forcing me to think through my challenges and opportunities more logically and clearly.

An excellent example of the compassion, adaptability, and flexibility that people in a small business can have was shown to me in 1973. That was the day I was fired from my job, one week before Christmas. My employer, John Tailor, was a chemical engineer and member of the Mensa Society, with an IQ of 170, but he was a pitiful money manager. Because of this fault, his bank forced him to hire me as his company assistant in 1972 to help get him on a good financial footing. After working for him one week, I sat in the small root beer stand across the street from Tailor & Company one lunchtime and wondered why I had agreed to work for this man. But I was determined to live up to my commitment to work for him. After six frustrating months on the job, I walked into John's office one day and politely asked him if he would just let me help him in running the business, I would easily make him a millionaire in six months without even trying hard. But he just couldn't let anyone else have some control of the business.

My employer had never fired anyone before, which made my dismissal even more surprising. After being there a year, John did it in a letter that was delivered to me by his secretary after he went out the office door and told everyone there that he was going on a two-week business trip to Russia. John earlier told the plant manager that he was "going to get rid of the Christian." A few years after I was fired, John Tailor lost the business and died alone in a small apartment, a pauper and thirty days from being evicted. It was such a needless waste of talent and engineering ability.

After reading my dismissal letter, I immediately went to see my older World War II–era friend, Bill Hampton, at his Bettendorf, Iowa, crane and erection service company a few blocks away. Bill was right in the middle of some work, but he stopped what he was doing to listen to me explain my situation. Bill knew what it was like to face tough times himself, having once been blown off a mammoth tank he was welding on in a riverside fuel tank farm years before. Understanding my situation and knowing I was still in shock from the experience, he made up some work for me to do right then. I didn't realize it until later, but he created this job for me to do, putting a hydraulic system on a portable metals shear, to keep my mind off the dismissal. He was also ready with good advice for me, which was to forget what just happened and to go about getting on with my life.

Later, after consulting with my wife, Sue, I decided to start a business. My work as a consultant making detail drawings for whoever I could sell my services to. I put three old drafting tables in our family room and had several friends who could do drafting work come to our home after their workday to make detail drawings for me. I did this work for about six months while I was also working to start what I had dreamed of doing: operating my own manufacturing company.

Late that winter, when I was easing into manufacturing instead of continuing on as an engineering design service, Hampton rented me a 10 foot x 10 foot space in the corner of an old unheated corrugated metal building with the necessary electrical power for a buck a day so I could do flame-cutting and welding work. The price of $30 a month was right, and it turned out to be a wonderful temporary home where I was able to do quite a bit of work.

In the spring of 1974 as I was looking for more space to rent, I called on a Caterpillar Engine Remanufacturing plant that was moving into a vacated building in our city. In my naiveté, when I walked in and introduced myself to the plant manager, Wes Bracken, I asked him if I could rent some of his space. Wes was a gentleman and neither laughed at me nor shooed me out the door. We became friends, and a few days later on a Saturday, he drove me 120 miles to Morton, Illinois, to visit the Caterpillar Parts Depot where he had just left as the assistant plant manager. Wes did this kind thing while he was living in a motel with his family, building a home, and in the middle of union negotiations. He gave me a tour of the facility and asked the purchasing department to let me quote work to see if I was good enough to become a Caterpillar supplier. I was so green and busy trying to find work that I didn't realize that the Midwest economy had tanked. Obviously, God's hand was on me and taking care of me and my family.

Another person who helped me in early 1974 when I was just getting started was Don Shewry, owner of a good-sized company, Tri City Fabricating, in Davenport, Iowa. I landed a contract with an East Moline company to form ¼ inch stainless steel angle iron bars into four-foot-diameter rings for their line of industrial clothes dryers. I asked Don if I could use his equipment. He said yes. I would buy the steel at a local steel service center and haul the straight iron to Don's shop in my older yellow-and-white Plymouth station wagon whenever his shop doors were open, and he had someone to teach me how to use his large angle iron rolls machine. He then let me use his equipment without thinking of charging me for the use. And he didn't even require me to have any insurance coverage. It was a case of another Good Samaritan helping me along the way.

A few months later, I moved next door from Hampton's yard to the back half of Tully Body Shop and bought an old railroad car spring compressor that Bill Hampton generously sold to me for only $250. I took some measurements, sawed up some cold-rolled steel bars for the way guides and forming supports, and converted it into a four-foot-wide press brake. I also bought a blacksmith anvil for $50 that I later realized Bill hated to part with, but he did it out of a deep concern for my welfare. Also during this time I would scour the want ads looking for machinist tools of deceased workers that were for sale, such as metal scales, dial indicators, calipers, and micrometers. I would go to the widows' homes and bargain for a fair market value for the tools I wanted.

Bill's friendship didn't stop there. Later in the spring, I spotted an old turret lathe sitting outside under a canvas tarpaulin in Bill's company yard. I got his permission to use it and landed a contract to turn down eight-inch outside diameter by two-inch inside diameter graphite cylinders and cut them into quarter-inch-thick rings. I have worked in some very dirty places in my career, notably inside the dirty air side of a dust collector for carbon dust, but this was the worst of all. Even though we were outside, we couldn't escape the gritty, abrasive dust we made from that cutting. But sometimes you have to take work where you find it.

The next person to be of invaluable help to me was a man Sue and I met, with his wife, at a neighborhood gathering. Rainsford (Ray) Brown Jr. was a very sound financial man who owned a local Mack truck dealership as well as several other businesses. It seemed that for the first few years of my entrepreneurial venture I was in Ray's office four out of every five days for anywhere from five to fifty minutes seeking, and getting, help on how to run my business and avoid financial trouble. In fact, our first accounting and financial statements had a definite Mack Truck flavor as Ray so graciously let me talk with his controller about the necessary accounting details for operating a business. Along with this help, he made sound suggestions on managing my fledgling company.

One man who was another unexpected help to me was Julian Weigle, owner of the area's biggest tool and machine shop, Swan Engineering. I met Julian when I worked at Tailor & Company, just a block away from Swan. Our friendship seemed to grow from the fact that the original owner of Swan Engineering, Mel Swan, worked for my Grandpa Severin Seaberg before starting out on his own.

After I started my manufacturing business, I would need a tool on short notice to complete a job. Julian would let me come into his plant at any time it was open to borrow various tools and gages I didn't have. I would only borrow them once because by the time I needed that tool or gage again, I had purchased it. My dad taught me to borrow only once so I wouldn't wear out my welcome. He learned this from his days as a tool and die maker. To the best of my knowledge, Julian never let anyone else into his plant to borrow like this, and I felt truly blessed by his kindness.

Another friend came along about seven years after we had started in 1973, and by then we had relocated to a bigger building across the Mississippi River in Moline, Illinois. Don Martin was a CPA who had just taken early retirement from John Deere and Company. At one time, he managed all financial operations in Europe and Africa for John Deere before returning to their headquarters in Moline, Illinois, where he did corporate planning and served on the board of directors for John Deere-Australia. I think he initially felt sorry for me and offered to help with the planning and financials for a manufacturing firm. Don was able to quickly see solutions to financial problems in clear, logical terms. He would briefly look at only a few of our figures and then make estimates and projections many times that proved to be fantastically accurate after following standard accounting procedures. He had a wisdom I didn't have at the time.

At Don's suggestion, I put a desk for him in my small office so he could get a better grasp for how a small company functioned as compared to a Fortune 500 company like Deere where he worked after an early career at Arthur Anderson and Company as a certified public accountant. He showed me what a few key financial figures properly utilized could do to obtain a clearer picture of how well the firm was doing. And just as importantly, he saw clearer ways through some of my manufacturing and marketing challenges that I hadn't noticed.

Because our business relationship had become so close, Don became a mentor to me during those earlier growth years. His being ten years older plus his excellent business experience were invaluable to me in my dealings in the marketplace. Don and I joked together many times over the years about how we seemed to disagree about everything, including how the Iowa Hawkeye basketball team was coached, and then laugh about it. But his contrary views were invaluable to me in conducting company business.

At one time, Don told me he believed the main reason why Seaberg Industries succeeded when others had failed is that I used to spend an hour in prayer and Bible study before the workday. This came from a hard-headed, aggressive executive with a Christian heart of gold. Before he died, he had become one of my two best friends outside of my family. And I know I will see him again someday.

## Special Friends

How can you repay persons who gave of their time like these men did? The only answer for me is that I try to do the same service to others who may be in similar circumstances as I was when I began my company. What they did for me expresses a most mature form of love, the kind that builds up and endures.

The book of Proverbs, 11:14, in the NKJV Bible states, "Where there is no guidance the people fall, but in an abundance of counselors there is victory." In Proverbs 19:20 ESV it says, "Listen to advice and accept instruction, that you may gain wisdom for the future." These verses have been confirmed to me time and time again by these tough-minded, caring men: Bill Hampton, Wes Bracken, Don Shewry, Ray Brown, Julian Weigle, and Don Martin.

# CHAPTER 4

# Ethics? Morality?

My definition of success is, "Happiness and peace of mind." It is very simple. It has nothing to do with money but everything to do with how you feel about God, yourself, and others. I have seen it in people from all walks of life and experienced it myself. The happiest and most fulfilled times in my life haven't had a thing to do with what I owned or was recognized for.

Unless you try to treat your fellow human beings as you want to be treated, I don't see how you can experience the byproduct of genuine happiness in your life. Seeing a project successfully through that is legal, ethical, and moral, especially if others are involved, *is* very fulfilling and a source of continued contentment for me. Galatians 5:22 in the New Testament says, "But the fruit of the Spirit is love, joy, peace, patience, kindness, goodness, faithfulness, gentleness and self control." To me, this describes what happiness really is.

For that peace of mind in any of my business dealings that surpasses human understanding, I have used four sections from the Bible. The first section is the Ten Commandments, which are a mirror that helps me look at how I conduct my life. The second is the book of Proverbs because it gives practical advice on how to best live my life with others. The third is Matthew 7:12 (commonly paraphrased as the Golden Rule) because it instructs me on how to treat my fellow man. Last I've used Romans 12, what I call the management chapter of the Bible.

If I knew I had done my best and didn't knowingly mistreat anyone, I could go home at day's end with a peace of mind I wouldn't have if I had practiced "dog-eat-dog" and "me-first" business ethics, thinking only of getting ahead, whatever that means.

In the mid-1970s when I started the venture, there were hitchhikers on all the interstates, and occasionally I would pick up someone while traveling between sales calls. Of course, today there are rarely men with their thumbs out because it is too dangerous, when one considers the highway crimes that have been committed by hitchhikers.

But once during that period, I was alone and gave two young hikers a ride in eastern Iowa on my way back to the shop from a business trip. After we went a short distance, I asked them what they were doing. They told me that they were running away from the Hell's Angels biker gang in California. They said that running away was the only way to leave the gang alive, and they decided to go to a place called "Yipsi" in Michigan. (I'm sure they meant Ypsilanti, but I didn't feel comfortable correcting them.)

It was about noon, and I asked if they were hungry. They were, so we stopped at a truck stop, and I bought them lunch. As we pulled into the lot, I asked them what they had been doing recently. The wilder-looking one said he had just got out of prison, and the hideous grin I saw on his face in the rearview mirror, even though I was thirty-seven years old and physically fit, made me wish I hadn't picked them up.

After we finished lunch, we got in my yellow International Travelall (forerunner to the SUV), and before pulling back onto the interstate, I asked them if they knew about Jesus Christ. They said that they knew a little about Him. I then explained more of the Lord to them, and to my *great surprise,* I was able to lead them into a prayer of accepting Jesus Christ into their hearts! Immediately their countenance dramatically changed from a frowning cynicism to bright smiles and laughter.

The three of us were so excited about their new lives that I brought them into our shop in downtown Bettendorf at that time and introduced them to everyone there as new born-again Christians. The young men wanted to get going, and I drove them back to Interstate 80 so they could continue on their way east. I gave them my business card so they could keep in touch if they wanted, but I never heard from either one, so I guess I'll have to wait until I get to heaven to know how they turned out.

It has been said that everyone can be bought for a price. I disagree. The principled ethical and moral person will not sell his or her self-respect at any price. I believe it depends on the value system one uses if one can be bought. The above parts of the Bible let me keep my thoughts going in the right direction and not fall into a trap where I knew I shouldn't be.

In December of 1975, I had a cold and the flu off and on for about one month. I got over this in early January only after I had given my financial burden for the company and the employees to Jesus Christ. When I made that decision, I was finally able to put a two-year-old problem behind me that I hadn't at first realized that I had. Just as soon as I made that decision, the cold was gone and I surrendered myself to the point where I said, "Lord, if you want me to lose my home and have to move the family again, that's certainly all right." From that time on, I had a great peace come over me. Most of the tensions I felt just disappeared. Of course, the carryover from that was that the employees seemed to feel more relaxed about their work.

## Guest Speakers

On Good Friday in March of 1976, I started to invite outside pastors to come in and give us a devotion to go along with our semi-monthly Friday noon business meetings. These lasted just thirty minutes, all on company time. After they spoke, they usually stayed to listen to the rest of us discuss the business of the past week and the forecast of what we would be doing the next week and beyond.

The purpose behind having guest pastors speak was twofold. First, it was to bring the Word of God to the people at ARI Industries (a symbol for Joseph of Arimathea, who buried Jesus Christ in his tomb) as it was called then. Many times Sunday was just not enough time to receive His Word, plus there were several who didn't go to church and this became their church time. Second, it gave the pastors a chance to see people in their work environment without Sunday clothes on, which gave them a better feel for understanding the things their congregations did in their vocations. A real blessing from this was that it was nondenominational and wouldn't be looked on by others as self-serving. The first three ministers were Lutheran, Four Square Gospel, and Nazarene.

## Morality in Congress

When the first President Bush was in the US House of Representatives, the former congressman from Iowa's first district, Jim Leach, was an aide working for him. One day Jim told me about Mr. Bush's aboveboard, high ethical standards. For example, whenever a woman from outside his office had an appointment with Mr. Bush, he either kept his office door open or had an aide present in his office during the meeting. This way he avoided any possible rumors of impropriety. Instances like this have helped make him the effective leader he was as president, especially when he needed to put a seventeen-country coalition together for Desert Storm in 1991.

History has a way of exposing people as they really are. For a contrast between sound and unsound ethical standards, I'd like to look at the two leaders of Texas's fight for independence from Mexico in the 1840s. Santa Ana (the one who introduced chewing gum to the Americans) was, among other things, president for life and general of the Mexican Army. He even called himself "The Eagle," as is shown on the Mexican flag. He practiced what we today call situational ethics and a strong "me-first" attitude, caring only for himself. Santa Ana was ruthless in the pursuit of his personal goals. He would change allegiances on the spur of the moment to suit his needs, usually at others' expense. This was all too clearly shown at the pivotal Battle of San Jacinto where he lost the Texas war. As a result of lifelong selfishness, he later died in abject poverty in a Mexico City hovel. He so embittered his exploited countrymen that no monument has ever been erected commemorating any of his early achievements.

Conversely, Sam Houston, otherwise known as the Raven (a highly respected name bestowed on him by the Cherokee Native American tribe), has had innumerable statues of him erected and institutions named after him. He was a brilliant and courageous military leader like his adversary, Santa Ana, with but a few important differences. These differences are that he was loyal to his high standards of treatment of others, and he was consistent in carrying out his commitments. History has placed this man who became governor of two states, Tennessee and Texas, in a place of high honor because of his high ethical and moral standards.[3]

In my personal and business life, my priorities are based on biblical ethics and morality. My God is first, family is second, Seaberg Industries was third while I was the owner, and others were fourth in my dealings. Many times it seemed to me and other people that my priorities were company, company, company, and company! Yet I always made the time available to support and be at our children's activities. In fact, I only missed two high school events of our three children in my years owning the company. I encouraged our employees to do the same thing in participating in family activities. My observation has been that however well a person performs at work, about 50% of the way he or she performs is caused by what his or her home life is like. If things are fine at home, it usually shows up in better performance and relationships at work.

As part of these priorities, we discouraged personnel from working or traveling on Sunday because the Lord promoted that day as a family and rest day. We told our clients that we would be willing to work on a Sunday only if it was absolutely necessary. We ran a three-shift operation and could usually complete any necessary work without coming in on a Sunday. Since starting the company in 1973, and until 2006 when I sold it, I had only traveled or worked on two Sundays, and I was tired all the following week after working on those two Sundays. I have been concerned about my peers who worked for large companies and routinely had to start their work week on Sunday afternoon if they were traveling outside the office. How can we expect Americans, especially our leaders, to be efficient and effective if they don't have time to enjoy their families and get proper rest?

## Practicing the Golden Rule

We worked at practicing the Golden Rule, much like Jim and John Lincoln, founders of The Lincoln Electric Company in Cleveland, Ohio, used when they began company operations at the turn of the twentieth century. Part of that rule had to do with absenteeism. It was a disgrace to be absent from work. As such, if an employee missed work, he or she

---

3    James A. Michener, *The Raven and the Eagle*, Tor Books, 1991.

had to apologize to two fellow workers and also have a written excuse if it was for an illness. That is the tough, and the good, side of what "Treat others as you want to be treated" is all about. It is no accident that this well-run company has for years been the highest-paying hourly employer in the industrial world.

J.C. Penney, founder of the company bearing his name, believed so strongly in the Golden Rule that he named the first store he owned, in Kemmerer, Wyoming, the Golden Rule Store. That was a statement that left no doubt in anyone's mind where he stood on treatment of others.

A wealthy man once chuckled when he told me, "I'm being paid too much, and it's still not enough." This is nothing more than a reflection on the "me-first" mentality that is so damaging to our nation's moral fiber. A person like this may never be content in his or her work because he or she has the mistaken feeling that he or she never has enough material things. Perhaps this is where the bumper sticker "He Who Dies with the Most Toys Wins" comes from.

My feelings about never having enough can best be described by the accountant of a billionaire who had just died. When the accountant was asked how much Mr. Smith left behind, he replied, "When Mr. Smith died, he just left it all." A saying from the Bible that helps me deal with this temptation is, "Beware and be on your guard against every form of greed, for even when one has an abundance his life does not consist of his possessions."[4]

In the early 1980s, we were on the verge of bankruptcy. Proof of this is that after looking over our financial statements, a retired corporate controller told me I was technically bankrupt. I knew what he was saying was true, but I just couldn't, and wouldn't, accept that. Maybe this thinking came from my "I'll show you!" stubbornness about not quitting a project I once started it if I believed in doing it.

During then and one other time, I was tempted to declare bankruptcy and start over again. As stated previously, the only thing to stop me was that bankruptcy, like divorce, was not an option in my life. How could I then face those who had trusted me to pay them for their trust and services? It wasn't right, so I didn't see a bankruptcy lawyer. Even if I

---

4    Luke 12:14.

had to spend the rest of my life repaying debts, that would be better than quitting on people who had trusted me with their assets.

On December 21, 1983, I called a Davenport bank that was interested in loaning to our company, this being the first time I had ever applied for a Small Business Administration (SBA) loan. The bank had seen my SBA Loan Application and turned it down because they had withdrawn their offer to purchase the folded Security Bank where I had my previous loan.

I was at a loss of what to do. It was earnest prayer time again.

So I called Jim Thompson, then assistant director to the local SBA office, for advice. He called the Cedar Rapids, Iowa, regional office on my behalf. After that, he called my congressman, Jim Leach's, office and asked if his office would call the SBA on my behalf. I then called Gary Marti, the SBA loan office in Cedar Rapids, who gave me names of men to call at my local area banks.

This is when I learned not to totally trust any *one* bank to be loyal when adversity struck a business or individual. I remembered that thought as over my career at ARI and at successor Seaberg Industries, I ended up doing business with seven banks.

Last I called my Jewish friend Julian Weigle of Swan Engineering. I asked his advice, and he recommended a bank where he was a director. I went into his bank at peace in my heart, claiming to myself that Jesus would take care of my needs. I was confident as I showed a vice president my SBA application and he said his bank would review it. It was a "coincidence" that SBA officer Gary Marti would be in this bank at the end of the week and that Brad would go over it with Gary. Looking back, I now know that my friend Julian had decided to help his young Christian friend—again.

When a bank is evaluating whether to make a loan to a small business, the officers many times will use a rough guide that is called the Five Cs of Loaning: Character, Capacity, Credit, Collateral, and Conditions (local business environment). My reason for including these Five Cs of Loaning in this chapter is that banking is really a people business, where an astute banker's loan judgments are ultimately based on the loan applicant's personal qualities and not necessarily what his business may look like. I don't envy the job of being a banker, for it always seems they have to be looking right through the financials at the lender to examine his true ability to repay his loans and debts. In reality, it is a people business and not a numbers business.

Let's look at these *Five Cs of Loaning* a little more closely:

Character: Does the person have integrity? Is she diligent? What kind of work ethic does she have? Is her word good when she makes a promise? No one likes to have bad financial surprises. If one is known for her truthfulness, diligence, and sound business judgment, she can be more readily trusted with the use of a bank's assets for her business.

Capacity: This is a person's ability to handle the business undertaking. For instance, it would be ridiculous to think a one-man machine shop could do $1B annual sales no matter what size loan the business owner wants. What kind of skills does he have? Is he competent to do the work he's seeking a loan to perform? How much experience does he have in this field? Just being highly qualified in one area doesn't make him an expert in another. Will he tend to get in over his head, a common malady in startups? Are the facilities he has or wants able to produce the financial returns he is proposing?

Credit: Does she pay all her bills on time or at least consistently? Has she had a bankruptcy in the past? Does she have a good Dun and Bradstreet rating? What kinds of payment terms is she used to having with her suppliers?

Collateral: What's left if the venture goes bad? (One banker where I live would make no loan unless he knew ahead of time that he could collect all of the loan if the debtor defaulted.) In the early 2000s, this banker might have been a little more lenient because of the poor-quality loans made by banks that were encouraged to do so by Congress.

Conditions: What is the present state of the local economy to support the venture? State, national, and even international business conditions should also be considered. For example, if a farmer has a sizeable loan and grain prices suddenly go south, can the bank still liquidate the farm and recover their investment? This happened in many instances in Iowa in the 1980s and earlier in the 1920s where a bank could have had 50 percent of the collateral on a farm. And if the lending institution had too many farm loans at 50 percent of the value, and the land value declined 50 percent, catastrophe resulted. When enough farmers couldn't make payments, both the farmer and the banker ceased business operations.

A parting note in this chapter comes from London House, Park Ridge, Illinois, as quoted in *Industry Week* magazine back in the July 1, 1991 issue, "whose recent survey revealed that ethical executives are happier, more responsible, and less stressed than those willing to tolerate unethical behavior. Those execs with high scores on ethics tests were also less likely to foster feelings of hostility, anxiety, and fear."

Thomas Alva Edison, inventor of the incandescent light bulb, put it very well when he simply said, "There is no substitute for hard work." By the way, it took some six thousand experiments before Edison successfully invented the first electric light bulb.

## CHAPTER 5

# There Is No Free Lunch

There once was a king in ancient Persia who desired to know all the wisdom in the world at that time, so he called in his wise men to give him this wisdom. After a year, they came back with a volume of books to fill the throne room. The king said, "Condense this wisdom. Make it smaller." After another year, they came back again with it condensed into one medium-sized book. "No, no!" cried the king. "Make it smaller yet." Two years later, the wise men returned with a single piece of paper. The king asked them to read it to him. It said, "There is no free lunch." And the king was pleased.

Perhaps when a man's life is to be accounted for, it comes down to others knowing if what he did was significant. If he was self-sufficient and helped others on their way, he learned that he had to work for the rewards he received in this life. There are many things we can't control in life—where we were born, our parents, etc.—but hard and intelligent work is something we can control and is usually at the top of the list of people who succeed in their businesses. The Bible had something to say about this in the New Testament in 2 Thessalonians 3:10: "If a man will not work, he shall not eat."

I'm reminded of an experience from my youth I had about earning my way. In 1960, I graduated from college, and I had a chance to visit the jungles of British Guiana (now named Guyana) in South America. There was just one catch to this. Being a student, I had no money, and my expenses were figured out to be $800 ($6,100 in 2011), which was a lot of money for me that I didn't have. The trip was to start three months after I was invited to go, and I did raise the cash, and other than selling my car for $200, I still wonder how I was able to raise the finances at that time. What I do remember is that I wasn't going to allow anything to prevent me from making that trip. By working hard at any job I could find, plus receiving a few monetary gifts from relatives, I was able to go on the adventure.

While visiting in British Guiana, I had the privilege of being flown to visit an aboriginal Indian tribe living deep in the Amazon jungle at the equator. The Wai-Wai people were now Christian, and the few Wycliffe Bible missionaries who lived with them rightly encouraged them to retain their culture and self-respect while writing their first written word from the book of John in the Bible. While I was there with my two friends from Iowa City, Rev. Roy Wingate and Dave Baskerville, I contracted severe dysentery and just made it out of bed before my bowels let loose all over the wood tree house floor.

At almost the exact same time back in Moline, Illinois, my mother suddenly was awakened in bed and told my dad, "Rube, George is sick!" When I got back home a little over a week later, Mother surprised me by repeating to me her story about knowing I was very sick on the day and time when God woke her up. I now know that she had been praying for my safety while I was in South America. This was another confirmation to me of the awesomeness of our Lord and Savior—being able to let someone know of a loved one's distress from thousands of miles away.

Sometimes we think that if we were guaranteed a job for life that we'd be motivated to want to continue improving in our job because of that security. But the reality is that if we feel "entitled" to that job for life without any incentive for advancement, we will most assuredly slow down in our efforts. It may not even be consciously done.

There has been a true story circulating on the Internet about a college professor in a class at the beginning of the semester stating that everyone in the class would receive the same grade at the end of the term. After the first quiz in the course, the A students tried hard and did well, while the less-motivated ones scored average and a few did poorly. When the test scores were posted, everyone got the same grade—a C. As the semester progressed and all the students continued to receive the same test grade, the students quit studying for the tests. At the semester's end, all the students failed the final. The professor flunked the entire class, something he had never done before. The lesson is that when one loses motivation, one performs poorly no matter what the class or work project or even a concentration camp job might require.

In the late 1980s, an employee had a tragic accident where he worked in the Quad Cities. He almost lost one of his legs and severely damaged the other one. The manager of that company felt so bad about the mishap that he told this man as he was recovering that he had a job for the rest of his life at the firm. Several years later, the company was sold and the new owner terminated the disabled man. Another employee felt that the permanently injured one was let go because he had "lost his edge" and became too lax in his work since the disabled man thought he still had a guaranteed lifetime job.

When "Good King Hezekiah" was told by God that he would get well from his sickness and live prosperously for another fifteen years, he relaxed so much that he forgot about others' welfare and turned into a poor ruler after that. I suppose it was because King Hezekiah had his life taken care of as God had promised him, and he probably felt he didn't have to work to preserve his prosperity and health any more.

One of the nineteenth and twentieth centuries' most recognized leaders was Thomas Alva Edison, the inventor of the electric light bulb. He said, "The three great essentials to achieve anything worthwhile are hard work, stick-to-itiveness and common sense."

Most achievements in life are gained by our own efforts. These successes could be social, emotional, physical, vocational, etc. At Seaberg Industries, this was the reason why no one had a vacation until he had been employed for one year. After a year working at SI, he *earned* two weeks' vacation. Another example of earning your way at Seaberg is that when the company reached a certain monthly sales goal, a free meal was served to all the employees on every shift as a thank you for their efforts. Bonuses were also given if the balance sheet warranted it.

Malcolm Gladwell, who I referred to earlier, wrote in his recent number-one best-seller, *Outliers*, published in 2008, that if a person would spend ten thousand hours on one subject, by the time she was twenty years old, she would be an expert in that subject. The Beatles rock band playing in Hamburg, Germany; Bill Joy, founder of Sun Microsystems and Java software; Bill Gates, founder of Microsoft; Canadian and Czech professional hockey players; and Mozart are examples of people who have unconsciously and intensely followed this rule. From Gladwell's book, "Ten thousand hours of practice is required to achieve the level of mastery associated with being a world-class expert – in anything."[5] I am sure it is the same case for Rory McIlroy, the twenty-two-year-old 2011 US Open golf champion.

As far back as I can remember, I always wanted to have full responsibility for a company's future. But I wanted to come in a little down the company ladder and work my way to the top because I didn't want the task of working to overcome the inertia I thought was required to begin an enterprise. When I did begin work on my own, I still didn't know how hard it would be to create something from nothing without any guarantees that there would be any financial success for all the effort needed. When you begin a business from zero, no one has a vested interest yet, so no one really cares if you fail. That innocent indifference by others was scary for me because I've always wanted to feel I was doing significant work in my life.

In fact, I tried to hide my fear of failure by seeking my first work from out-of-town companies. That way, if I failed, my embarrassment would be from people who were not from my hometown area, the Quad Cities.

In 1987 we had a handful of customers who operated approximately fifteen assembly lines for which we were making parts. We were behind in delivery every day. We got into that pickle because many quotes we turned in were awarded at once, plus several current jobs had large quantity increases. Every morning at 7:00 a.m., I had to make phone calls to see what lines we were responsible for were about to be shut down. Then we would have a mad scramble in our plant for the next twenty-four hours, hoping none of our machines would break down in the meantime. Not only did we have to make parts, but we also had to make the time-consuming tooling that was necessary to make the parts! I felt we were busier than one-armed wallpaper hangers. We knew we were getting extremely busy and tried to at least slow down the orders, but we really didn't have much choice in the matter. The alternative to

---

5    Malcolm Gladwell, *Outliers* (New York: Little, Brown, and Company, 2008), 40.

completing the orders was to lose customers from whom we had worked so hard to get business.

The choice one of our more-demanding customers gave us at the beginning of 1987 was to take all the work at once or not take any of it. The problem with this one client was that he literally wanted the next twelve months' worth of orders to be completed in one month instead of being spaced throughout the year. We did not want to see this profitable business go out the door, but this agricultural equipment company had us in a bind we couldn't possibly fulfill, and they chose to go elsewhere. In hindsight I believe I could have handled the situation more diplomatically and possibly saved a customer for us.

Thank heavens for those understanding men and women at our other client companies who helped us solve our difficult delivery challenge. Before 1987, I thought not having enough work was the worst thing that could happen to a company, but I learned it wasn't the case. This was by far my most stressful and anxious year up to that time.

During that year, my wife, Sue, stood firmly by me. I think she knew better than me how much I wanted to prove that I could start and operate a successful manufacturing business. She blessed me by never complaining about the seemingly crazy thing I was doing. If she hadn't supported me like she did, I know that at some time I would have had to close the doors. And I was tempted to do just that more than once.

According to economist and business guru Peter Drucker, there are only three endeavors that build any economy: farming, mining, and manufacturing. I wanted to be a net contributor to our national economy. Drucker's comment was a major reason why I chose to become a manufacturer as my vocation.

In retrospect, one of the neat things that Sue did to help make ends meet in the early going of my new career was to sell corn husk doll kits out of our home. I would build the small plywood boxes out of quarter-inch oak-stained pieces that displayed the beautifully handcrafted dolls. Meanwhile, Sue would process the corn husks, buy the other kit components, and put everything together into individual kits. She would then get a group of women together and teach them how to make corn husk dolls from the kits. She sold these kits for $3.50 each, and it did a lot to help feed the family. Now whenever we're out shopping and see these kinds of kits in store windows, I get a little nostalgic thinking of how much Sue helped Seaberg Industries grow during its first few years.

When I was recovering from a heart arrhythmia in 1981, my cardiologist couldn't understand why I still got so tired in the afternoons. The only explanation I have is that I felt I had to be so intense and concentrate so hard on company matters that by the afternoon, I was just worn out. But if I could squeeze in some running or play a game of racquetball at noon, I would be fine the rest of the day. Sometimes meeting a weekly payroll in a small company does strange things like this to your body. It is amusing now when I think about meeting those long-ago payrolls, but eventually when your company grows bigger, this kind of stress does lessen.

Family Instances of Paying for Their "Own Lunch"

I mentioned earlier that my priorities were Christ, family, company, and others. Rather than ever lose my family, I would easily have chosen to lose my company. I'm reminded of an experience from the time when I was employed by the Pillsbury Company in Springfield, Illinois. I was on a business trip that several of us took to visit a small company in Wisconsin. The owner of the small company was using an idea unique to the food industry to improve his processing and make a better food product. In the course of our conversations, he told me that his work took so much time that he had to make a decision between staying married or keeping his work. He chose the company. I was disturbed by his comments and felt sorry for this man who chose business over family.

I feel fortunate that our three children worked in the business for various periods of time as their contributions to helping the company grow. My wife worked for me part time as the bookkeeper for over eight years before she retired, at her request. There is no way I can repay this wonderful person for the sacrifices she made for me except by trying to show my deep love for her.

Tom, our oldest child, started working during the summers when he was twelve years old. He swept floors, painted the building walls, and did other nonproduction, miscellaneous jobs necessary to the operation. When he was in high school, he began operating machines, starting with a small Logan engine lathe. This hands-on work continued while he was in a co-op his first two years as an engineering student at the University of Iowa. This experience enabled him to work as a co-op student his last two years in college for a local Alcoa plant. He excelled in sports and academics in high school, earning Academic Sports Athlete of the Year his senior year. But I am proudest of his work experience when in junior high school he missed only one day, due to illness, during the two years he delivered newspapers by himself. He got up at 5:30 a.m. every morning to do so.

Susan (now Sue Sampson), our next oldest child, started working at the company when she was ten, emptying waste containers and doing other office jobs. She continued to work part time at Seaberg in the summer while going to college until after she was married. One of our buyers remembers seeing Susan smartly and correctly answering the phone when that person came for her job interview in 1980 even though Susan was only fifteen years old. Some special moments for me were when she was chosen as homecoming queen in high school and when she set a school record that still stands in the 880-yard run. But I was proudest of her when I saw her happily serving food, in hairnet and uniform, in the dorm cafeteria at the University of Iowa her freshman year as a way to help pay for her education.

Our youngest, Anne (now Anne Atkinson), followed the pattern of her siblings by working during her junior high years doing office cleaning duties. Her high school and college summers were spent helping out in the office doing filing, answering the phone, and other similar duties, as well as working at other local businesses. Even though she was a high school all-American sprinter, I was proudest of her when she positively asserted her position without being intimidated on an issue in a classroom at the University of Kentucky when one of her professors discriminated against her.

We tried to have a positive home environment for the children to grow up in, and we encouraged them to form friendships with classmates who had the same kind of positive outlook on life.

Through all of their experiences at the company, our children learned the value and rewards that productive work brings. Through these family experiences, I've enjoyed seeing the self-esteem and self-confidence our kids developed that comes from them earning their own way in this world.

**Early 1980's picture of Seaberg Family at home.**
**l. to r. Anne; Sue, the mother; Susan; Tom;**
**top, George, the father.**

# CHAPTER 6

# Five Factors That Dominate a Business

In 1972, before I started ARI Industries, I went to a seminar conducted by the Metal Fabricating Institute at Purdue University in Lafayette, Indiana. At this conference, Harry Conn, then chairman of W. A. Whitney Corporation, explained five factors that would help guide a business if used properly. These five factors are: *cash, time, space, equipment,* and *skills.* One of these five will be the dominant priority of a company at any given time and take up most of top management's time. In an aside, he preached having a PMA (positive mental attitude) and using OPM (other people's money). When Harry passed away in 2001, I felt the deep loss of a good and trustworthy friend.

## Cash

*Cash* is a necessary ingredient for running a business. For me, cash has been money, assets, and goodwill because when properly used, these three will increase the value of a business. Several months after starting the company, I needed to borrow $8,000 to purchase a small Bridgeport vertical mill and a welder machine and for working capital. When the bank made a six-month loan and I had the money, I thought I had all the money I'd need because I had made what I thought was a sufficient cash flow projection. Little did I realize it would be different when the note came due and I *assumed* that the bank would renew the note. However, the bank wasn't interested in renewing the note! This was a surprise and jolt to me, especially since I previously did graduate-level work in a corporate finance course and thought I knew a lot about using money properly. I had no problem going to another lender for a loan, but it was a good experience for me to be refused that money from my first bank. I learned to not *assume* other institutions' intentions.

After several years and more loans, at my insistence I would visit my small bank weekly for their review of company cash needs so I could better learn the bank's future intentions concerning my company. To properly know how to make the most judicious use of my loan money, I used my banker as a financial consultant since I was concentrating 95 percent of my time and effort on trying to grow the business. (Before opening the doors, I had written a business plan that I was relying on to help keep the company fiscally sound.) This growth not only included getting more sales but also learning my own machining and welding skills via OJT (on-the-job training—I also called it "running scared"); hiring the best people I could afford; training the work force; figuring out what I could do best; and most importantly, overcoming the inertia of getting a business up and running.

Working with the bank, and through several friends' advice, I was able to obtain cash to move the business from my home. Then I rented a ten-by-ten-foot unheated work area. Then I moved to the back end of an auto body shop and then to a twenty-five thousand-square-foot area in an older unused factory. When we did the last move, I thought I was in "hog heaven" because we moved into a place devoted solely to our manufacturing needs.

Because of my close business relationship with our local Bettendorf banker, in 1981 I purchased a $250,000 metal plasma cutter-punch machine. At the time Seaberg Industries was the smallest company to ever purchase this large of a machine from W. A. Whitney. I learned later from then president of Whitney, Ted Brolund, that the company officers personally guaranteed my purchase, unbeknownst to me. I remember our bank officer, Harold Abdo, literally sweating in front of me, wondering if this was the right thing to do. He was wondering how he was going to present this loan request to his board of directors for approval. But there was no doubt in my mind that this machine would be a big help to our marketing and manufacturing efforts. As it later turned out, having this state-of-the-art machine probably was the most important factor in keeping us from going out of business during the Midwest's economic depression of the early 1980s. We had found this to be a unique manufacturing service that a company with low overhead could offer to their clients.

By the middle of 1984, we had an opportunity to purchase a new, well-designed production building to house our expanding company. We were getting the facility at about 50 percent of its construction cost. We had been looking for a permanent home of our own, and I felt that it was well suited to our needs. Unfortunately, we would have to carry a total debt load approaching $1,000,000 ($2,300,000 in 2011). This may not seem like much, but this amount was also not very far from our annual sales figures at the time. In retrospect, it would have been better to work out a little better financial package to keep the debt more in line with sales and profits.

The biggest danger for small businesses in dealing with banking institutions is not in getting too little cash to borrow but in getting too much. Sometimes bankers become so comfortable with their customers that they let the debtors have more than can be paid back.

## Time

This is something we are all given an equal amount of. There is just no way of getting more than twenty-four hours out of any one day. When first getting started, you may need to sacrifice sleep, family time, and friendships for a while. The important thing is to think about how long that "while" might take.

For some people, they never really plan to work less than eighty hours a week, take a vacation, or be with their family. These tend to be the people who later have ulcers, strokes, or heart attacks, lose their kids' love, get divorced, or wonder why they're alone and unhappy with life after they have become wealthy.

The best way I handled my work time was as follows:

1. I set yearly goals and reviewed them once a month to be sure the ship stayed the course.

2. At night before bed, I thought about the next day in general terms. For example, what would I need to be wearing tomorrow? Would I need to wear shop clothes or be dressed in a suit and tie for visiting client firms?

3. First thing in the morning I had devotions and sorted out that day's challenges, followed by a thirty-minute cardio and stretching workout.

4. Next, I became much more specific about what I was going to be doing while I shaved. In fact, some of my best organizing thoughts have been done there.

5. On my way to work or to a customer, I would fine tune my thoughts and priorities.

6. Then I looked at my long-term list of priorities in my organizer to see if I'd overlooked anything that needed to be done now.

7. I then quickly wrote down the day's priorities and when I would do them.

8. If I was driving out of town to a customer, I found that some of my best planning thoughts occurred when I was driving on the road because I had no office or production distractions.

Even though I was sometimes distracted by the normal, inevitable emergencies that happen in a small business, I could usually continue through the day following the priorities I had set that morning. But there were days when I, like most everyone, hadn't even gotten the first priority done. The important thing was to keep the self-discipline to repeat my habits each work day.

One thing I relied on was to have routines and good habits for handling most of my circumstances so my mind didn't get cluttered with constantly organizing details I regularly did during the week. This left me with the time to bore into a project that needed maximum concentration.

# Space

How much is just enough space? This is an especially difficult question for the small business executive to answer for any of the following reasons:

1. The primary reason may be that the owner doesn't have the cash reserves to recover from errors in making brick-and-mortar building decisions. For example, 10 percent profit on $1,000,000 is $100,000, which is a lot more money than a 0.5 percent profit on $10,000,000, which is $50,000. The implication is that the larger sales will require more space. If the owner builds a $300,000 addition to his plant for anticipated higher sales and it turns out to be a total failure, he loses that cash that could have been used for payroll, equipment, an unplanned financial opportunity, or a sudden need.

2. The owner also has to plan several years down the road, but forecasting many times seems to be a dark science at best. He might get by with pole barn type structures rather than more permanent structures. But pole barn types of buildings may not be in the firm's best interests, short or longer term. This is especially so since these temporary buildings have a habit of becoming permanent structures that wear out over time and eventually become liabilities.

3. His manufacturing needs may change dramatically in a short period of time due to opportunities or setbacks to his business, like the severe national recession of 2008.

4. He wants to preserve the integrity of his operation. If he has several manufacturing units of ten to fifteen employees each, his overhead and transportation costs could be too high in this spread-out condition. Control would be much better if these ten- to fifteen-person units were in one building. As an example of cost savings, one quality assurance person would serve one facility instead of having one at each site. Or the owner/president could much more easily monitor the processes under one roof versus traveling half the time to observe and coordinate multi-plant operations.

The good news about manufacturability in the twenty-first century is that rapidly increased technology reduced space needs while increasing productivity. When our company moved from a twenty-five thousand-square-foot building designed for continuous processing of candies to a 16,500-sqare-foot one that was designed for machining and fabricating of metals, our productivity dramatically improved. In fact, sales in the new smaller building tripled in six years because of our space efficiencies.

The reasons why we could carve added space out of the smaller plant were:

1. We reduced inventory by over 50 percent. This included *not* buying enough extra raw material to allow for scrap like we had to do in the past. We were making the first piece right instead of having a "first piece scrap" problem.

2. The "bone yard" where we put rejected or reworkable parts remained the same size with the increased sales, rather than getting bigger, as one might think. Using newer quality assurance methods brought this savings about.

3. Work-in-process was greatly reduced. We used to be proud of our turning inventory ten times a year in the 1980s while the industry standard was three to four turns. And we thought we were doing a good job. At last count in 2006 when I sold the company, we were turning plate inventory well over twenty times. Castings and forgings had fewer turns because it was more economical to purchase these special items in large quantities.

4. The length of time from when a part was started in process until payment from the customer for that finished part remained about forty-five days. That is the time required to schedule the order, procure material, fabricate, machine, heat treat if necessary, machine, paint, ship, and get paid.

5. Improved software has enabled us to reduce obsolete spare parts. This could be a false "security blanket" left over from old, bad habits I hadn't discouraged strongly enough.

6. The quality assurance staff remained the same because of more staff quality training and having a certified apprenticeship course taught through a local junior college for our welders

and machinists that has put more quality control in the hands of the people making the parts.

It is very simple. The best way to solve space problems was for management to fully explain what we needed to do. Then management had to get out of the way of these intelligent people in engineering and production so they could figure out as a team how to best complete the project.

## Equipment

When I started the business in 1973, the common wisdom of machine tool experts was that the economical useful life of mills, lathes, and other such equipment was about five years. Charts were brought out to prove that improved technology, increasing maintenance costs, and reduced accuracy made it imperative to "purchase new." There was also the conventional wisdom among job shops, and I was definitely part of this, that bigger (especially with more "bells and whistles") was "better for you." I should have looked closer at what "better" was and who the "you" was. I think the "you" was the tool salesman.

In the years since then, and closer to when I sold the business in 2006, I have come to disagree with both notions of newness and bigness. The best example of this thinking concerns one of the first machines I purchased. In March of 1974, I bought an old, durable, heavy, belt-driven five-spindle drill press for $125 at an auction. I kept trying to justify selling or junking this machine for about five years, but there always seemed to be a constant need for this old clunker. Our machine operators thought it still had useful life, and in early 1991, they persuaded me that they should add six-inch channel iron skids under it and that an electrical quick disconnect switch should be added to make it easy to move around the plant floor. As a result, on only *one* production run of some five hundred pieces of a small machined flat plate, they reduced manufacturing costs *30 percent!* And the two principal machine operators were mad as hornets that they hadn't done better! I guess proving the old man wrong was fun for them. But this is also what happens when management steps out of the way and lets the workers show what they are more than capable of doing if we just trust their judgment.

Another example of sometimes using old equipment in a proper way is from one of the tours I had of The Lincoln Electric Company by Dick Sabo, former assistant to the CEO. I saw mostly old equipment being used for long runs that made for, in all probability, the most efficient manufacturing company in the world. Later, in the twenty-first century, the plant was totally retooled to just-in-time manufacturing standards. This was because the company found they could do even better with shorter runs with less inventory versus long runs with only three or four raw material inventory turns per year.

The lesson here is that the biggest, newest, and fanciest equipment your company can afford isn't necessarily always the best choice. It's all a matter of choosing the proper equipment to best meet the customers' needs.

## Skills

I've often wondered what made Seaberg Industries stand out from our competitors. Our physical plant could be replicated fairly easily by a large company anywhere in the free world, so bricks and mortar didn't seem to be the answer. What it came down to is that we couldn't replicate the people who work in a so-called capital intensive business where your most important asset walks out of the building at the end of each shift.

Knowing that our competitive edge lay in the skills of our employees, we spent much time working to help each one hone his or her abilities.

When do *skills* become the dominant feature of the *five factors* mentioned in this chapter? I have found it to usually be when we're in a crisis mode, for then it tends to show where our personnel shortcomings show up. What kind of crisis am I talking about? The obvious kind would be when sales suddenly surge and overtime, or subbing out the work, won't absorb the work overload. What about when a present client wants you to make a part a little bit out of your capability range so you can win that lucrative contract? Or what happens when a key employee resigns or gets sick for an extended period of time?

One crisis worth considering is what to do when sales suddenly sag and people don't have enough work to keep busy. In December of 1990, this very thing happened to us, again like in past years. Only this time around, we handled it differently than at any time in our past. It was normal to have a slight holiday dip in orders in the metals manufacturing business, but the drop off of sales this time was much more severe.

Instead of wondering who to lay off like we did in past years, we tried a different approach, quite frankly with a lot of prayer for guidance. Knowing how important each employee was and how expensive it was to train new hires, we instead went into an extensive training program on the floor and in the plant classroom, and we did it without the cash reserves we would liked to have had. The training consisted mostly of how to work as a team and how to be a better supplier to your in-house customers, whether they are the Seaberg shipping and receiving technician or a Seaberg vertical machining center machinist. We also did it with an unusually small backlog of work that would normally translate into L-A-Y-O-F-F.

In the following January, an interesting thing happened. We suddenly received many new orders for work, and at the same time, we completed major maintenance that we normally did during a one-week summer shutdown. In fact, we did such a good job of balancing new work and major maintenance that we avoided having any maintenance shutdown the following summer.

In 2011 I talked with Iowa National Guard Staff Sergeant Jacob Pries, who was home on leave from duty in Afghanistan. He said that by far the best men and women he saw on assignment there, and verified by superior officers, were those who came from the upper Midwest. They repeatedly were given the most difficult assignments, which is sort of a backhanded compliment. I was pleasantly surprised when he told me his observations in his military experience. In general, these Midwesterners work harder, follow orders better, use more initiative, and are better disciplined that their counterparts from other areas of the United States.

The five words *cash, time, space, equipment,* and *skills* were displayed on the white board in my office in various order of importance depending on the company's current situation for over twenty years. Until I walked away from the business in 2006, they helped me to better prioritize my challenges.

*A final note.* Shortly before Harry Conn died in 2001, I spent an enjoyable afternoon in his Rockford, Illinois, consulting office reminiscing over stories from past manufacturing experiences. Until I sold the company, I often tried to think of what Harry would say on a venture I would be considering.

# CHAPTER 7

# Get Your Head in the Game!

My Moline high school basketball coach, Jack Foley, was inducted into the Illinois High School Basketball Hall of Fame in the 1960s because he focused and paid close attention to the details that built a winning tradition for him at Moline. Few people knew of the emphasis he put into the grade school basketball program. His love for kids had him working with the grade school principals to provide basketball as a wholesome outlet for boys. Also, he made sure that his junior-high coaches were always invited to any function where the high school team was to be honored wherever he was to be speaking. Jack felt so strongly about these coaches that he wouldn't go to any dinner or speaking event unless these coaches were included. He not only kept his head in the game of running a successful program, but he was always anticipating what to do next with the basketball agenda. His outstanding record at Moline plus the successes of his former players is a testimony of how well he had his head in the game of life and how well he coached his players to always have their heads in the game.

Coach Foley also cared that his players acted like gentlemen off the court. One piece of evidence for this was when each year he showed all his new players how to fold a dress shirt to keep its press in a suitcase for our overnight games. He would lay the shirt flat and explain what he was doing as he neatly and carefully made three folds in the shirt. I used his advice on shirt folding throughout my college career, and to this day I still fold my shirts this way before I go on an overnight trip.

I heard the highest compliment I ever received as a player when I was over seventy years old. Jack had mentioned to one of his teacher friends, Jack Dye, that he wished he had given "more playing minutes to George" during my senior year at Moline High School. What hardly anyone remembers is that *eight* of my fellow seniors went on to play college ball, *five* of whom played Division 1 basketball. Whitey Verstraete, Johnny Myers, and junior Ken Anderson always started, and getting playing time for the other two spots was a struggle.

When I played for the University of Iowa in the late 1950s, if I was in a close game in the last few minutes, I was more focused and usually felt very confident I could make the baskets then even though defense was the strongest part of my game. We played in the Queen City Invitational Tournament in Buffalo, New York, in December of 1957. In the title game, I was fouled in the last minute by a Niagara University player. I needed to make both free throws to win the game and had no doubt I would make them. I did, and we won. It seems that as I concentrated more on the game, I was able to elevate my level of play, especially since I felt the coach and teammates needed my efforts. I tried to project that same feeling to my fellow employees in the work place at Seaberg Industries of getting your head in the game.

One thing that really upset me was having someone "asleep at the switch" (i.e., not paying attention to their work, especially at a critical time). I used to tell this to my children when they needed to pay attention to something they were doing, and I passed this on to our employees, particularly the newer ones. Examples of inattention were: wrong order entries, mis-counts, or making a run of bad parts instead of catching the error in the first piece.

## Keystone Kops

An incident happened in 1976 that is funny now, but at the time, it was anything but funny. My boyhood friend, Dale Schweinberger, in whose wedding I served as best man several years earlier, had just bought a new car. He wanted me to see his silver blue Mercedes-Benz 450 SLC, not even a week out of the dealer's lot. Dale drove it over to Bettendorf and parked in our tiny parking area that also served as a materials storage area and walked into the shop to see me. While he was just inside the door talking to me, one of my men accidentally backed our four thousand-pound fork truck into this shiny new expensive auto and "autographed" it with a terrible scratched-up dent. The fork truck driver, one of my best employees, obviously didn't have his head in the game.

We were only fifteen feet away when we heard the crash, and horrified, we ran out to the car to see what happened. My landlord, Jim Tully, was in his body shop next door and came over to see what needed to be done to repair the mishap.

Jim had to remove the fender to do the repair because the damage was so severe. Fortunately, to my immense relief, he was able to completely erase the dent perfectly and match the fender paint color. It was a severe test of Dale's friendship to me.

How well we work with this inattention problem is by positively encouraging our employees to be alert when they step into the plant. To help ensure this, the first thing we do is try to hire people who have a positive mental attitude. Second, our small company has extensive ongoing training programs geared not only to make employees more competent in what they do but also to encourage them to have a good feeling about Seaberg Industries. Then we say that what they do and how they do it is very important to the company, or they wouldn't have been asked to join us.

In the 1990s, Standard Forwarding Company in East Moline, Illinois, had a state-of-the-art overnight freight delivery system. This company used to be able to hold an average of one hundred less-than-truckload (LTL) and full truckload (T/L) loads overnight for second-day delivery (overnight plus one day). Then just in time (JIT) came into vogue where manufacturers required quicker delivery and to points closer to the actual point of assembly. This resulted in earlier deliveries to new "point-of-use" truck docks. A further step in delivery the industry developed was line side delivery using curtain-sided trailers so product could be off-loaded from the sides of the trailers rather than the back end. Now the line assemblers could roll up the trailer curtains and pull off the parts directly onto the harvester combine, bulldozer, etc., assembly line directly and more quickly. That led to a vehicle traffic congestion problem with large highway eighteen wheelers driving inside the plants.

In the 2000s, supply chain management, at customers' urging, evolved to "a plan for every part" (PFEP) where specific parts called point-of-use stock were delivered as needed, where needed by smaller factory fork trucks to the point of use on the factory floor. There are other names or phrases for supply chain risk management (SCRM) such as 5S/visual factory, turbo flow, lean enterprise, lean logistics, lean six sigma logistics, and A3 thinking, but these will not be discussed further.

Perhaps the most recent revolution in factory parts delivery and assembly is the Volkswagen factory in Dresden, Germany. This VW Phaeton facility is a transparent factory where customers can order their car, watch it being assembled, and even help assemble it. This ultraclean and modern factory is a place where parts move via robotic transports and sleds to the exact place at the exact time, thanks to German engineering.

Goal Setting

A good way, and my opinion the only way, to keep up with changing business conditions and sometimes be ahead of what is coming down the road is by having realistic goals to strive to reach. And in order to do that, we need to know the basic elements that make up our goals. These basic elements are: *specificity, achievability, measurability,* and *visibility.*

One of the best ways for someone to know what's going on is to encourage employees to have personal short-range company goals every day. It may be to complete a certain number of quote requests mistake-free today or to have the setup piece be a good part, instead of the old, old idea that it is okay for the first piece to be scrapped out.

A goal that starts with, "Someday I'll …" probably will never get beyond the wishful thinking stage. The first step in goal setting is to be specific in what you want to do. An example of specificity would be, "I'll start my daily second and third shift scheduling by 2:15 p.m. and finish no later than 2:45 p.m."

I always tried to set goals that would give me satisfaction of a job well done. By setting standards *with* an employee, like making all good parts on a short production run, we prevented unnecessary frustrations or discouragement. If the goals were set too high, he would either not even try, give only a half effort, or quit trying when he realized the unattainability of the goals. In other words, goals have to be *achievable*. This also meant for me to respect the abilities and efforts of honest work.

A goal has to be *measurable*. How else will you know if you've reached your target? For example, knocking ten strokes off your golf score over a season is a solid number that lets you form a good mental picture of what the target is.

Last, a goal has to be *visible*. We put our monthly sales goals on a thermometer chart for our employees to see how we were doing in the current month. Because the chart was there for everyone on the Seaberg team to see, it served as a self-motivator for the personnel.

One of my sons-in-law is a stock broker. A brokerage house where he used to work used to post the brokers' sales and commissions for all the salespersons to see. I never said this when Bryan was at the firm, but I thought this kind of visualization was embarrassing and de-motivating to those who weren't the top dollar-getters. It seemed too focused on short-term results and created undue competition in the office. This then created some envy among the brokers that could lead to unnecessarily buying and selling of their clients' assets for the brokers' increased commissions, or what is called "churning" in the business. His present brokerage firm doesn't follow the above practice, and my observation is that this office has a better and more relaxed and productive working-together atmosphere among the brokers and technicians.

Contrast that kind of visibility with what Aaron Rodgers, MVP quarterback of the Super Bowl XLV Champion Green Bay Packers, said about goal visibility. He said the single best lesson he learned about football he learned from his sixth-grade coach. He was told to visualize how a play he was going to call would look in his mind before starting the play. Can you think of a better way to show how a visible goal is beneficial to an outcome, in this case the completion of a pass, lateral, or other function in a game?

When we published our company *annual plan*, it had specific, achievable, measurable, and visible goals for our managers to examine and help implement for the coming year.

Specificity includes stating *exactly* what you want to do and the time frame in which you are going to do it. An alcoholic not taking a drink for the next hour is one example of this. Achievability means the goal has to be something you can do. If I said I was going to do the Ironman Triathlon next month, I'd never even start training because I know it would be impossible to do. However, if I said when I was younger that I was going to run the Bix seven-mile run in Davenport in two months, I know I would be able to do so and would adjust my training to suit the goal. Measurability speaks for itself. Make the goal visible! Step out in faith, and publish it on a wall or bulletin board or at least in your computer. If you've never done this before and try it, you'll be surprised how much of a motivator this becomes.

# CHAPTER 8

# Success Isn't an Accident

Our company mission was *to create a customer and satisfy his or her needs*. We used to say that our company goal for each employee was to constantly and continually improve the quality of his or her work. This was an error because we couldn't fully quantify the goal. We later called this statement our company attitude and for each person to have the attitude to "constantly and continually improve the quality of my work." These statements were put on the bottom of the *"I care about quality"* cards that we gave to each new employee as part of his or her orientation, on company time, before starting to work at the job for which he or she was hired. Our mission and attitude statements were also displayed in the company classroom.

Harold Paget, a former Seaberg employee, learned how to put a car engine together in his backyard in the mid 1930s so he could have a car to drive. He was one of eleven children in his family, so he had to teach himself how to make most of the things he wanted to use or go without. This kind of success carried over to his later work life where he developed a knack for figuring out mechanical and electrical problems that no one else could solve. Harold didn't know it when he was young, but he was training himself to be self-sufficient the rest of his life. One time when we were fishing for northern pike on a lake we had flown into in a remote part of Canada, he told me he could live right where we were with just an axe. There is no doubt in my mind that he could have done just that! I was so blessed to be able to work alongside him at Seaberg, where he was the maintenance manager before his retirement.

## Basic Strategic Plan

The first thing a successful enterprise needs to do is develop a *basic strategic plan*. It took me some seventeen years to write this down because I didn't know how to go about creating this kind of plan. I knew that our company was a manufacturer of metal products. I also knew we made machined and fabricated parts. I also had short-, intermediate-, and long-range goals without having a laid-out way to reach them. But that was about it. It took a business friend, Randy Fellerhoff, president of Hagerty Bros. of Peoria, Illinois, to help me learn how to develop a basic strategic plan (BSP). What such a basic philosophy does is help keep the company ship on course in the turbulent seas of everyday business living. Opportunities may come along that look good for the company at the time, but if they don't fit the basic strategy, the ideas will dilute your company's efforts to succeed. Look at Fortune 500 companies that have lost markets to see if they have a clear strategic concept like Diamler Benz's, *"The best engineered car in the world,"* a company giant that has existed for almost one hundred years and endured two world wars in Germany.

After teaching my managers how to develop a basic strategic plan, we set about making our own BSP for Seaberg. To work out our plan, there were four questions that we answered:

4096. What is our key strategic business concept? For Seaberg Industries, it was "Manufacturers of machined and fabricated products." This is simple, yet it sets the direction we wanted to go.

4097. Where should we compete? Only in Illinois, Iowa, Wisconsin, Missouri, and Nebraska.

4098. How to compete? Telemarketing with one-on-one contact by mail. (This was before the Internet. Now it's all email and Twitter in all its various forms.)

4099. How aggressively should we expand? Add a salesman before a market is established or use a new salesman to penetrate a new market?

After answering these four key questions that comprise the basic strategic plan, we then developed our *annual plan* that was used throughout each year.

## Annual Plan

Part of being alert and ready to act on any challenge that comes along is for the small firm to have an annual plan. The plan serves as a guide for the current year's sales and profit performance. It needn't be elaborate or very sophisticated. Well-run large companies have personnel who may do only planning, whereas the president of a small enterprise usually does it, with the help of his in-house accountant or an outside accounting firm.

When writing my annual plan, the first thing I did was spend time with our clients, seeing what their plans and projections were and how Seaberg could best accommodate those plans. This might be called "getting to know their culture." For instance, Dell may be planning to introduce a special PC next year, and as a special supplier of keyboards, I may need to partially or completely retool my shop to meet the anticipated demand.

Second, I made phone calls and/or visits to friends throughout US industry and finance to get a feel for how they viewed the economy in our kind of business for the next twelve months. This all took place throughout the year, but for us it was more intensely done during the October through December period. It was also more focused then than normal because I wanted to set my corporate and personal goals for the next year in December of each year. The company annual plan began in January, and I liked to have that phase behind me by December 28 of each year so I could be ready to implement the plan on January 1. I also wanted to concentrate on other important parts of the business. Throughout the next year, I met with my managers and other fellow employees on an informal basis for their feedback in making out the following year's annual plan. This same cycle was consistently repeated every year.

Third, I looked at past goal setting I had done to see how well this compared to my intermediate-and long-range goals. My goals at the time I sold the business in 2006 were substantially different than when I started the company, but because I was constantly adjusting these goals a little at a time, the final result has been relatively easy to adapt to any outside conditions beyond my control.

Fourth, I made a written statement about current business conditions and the plans we had for the next calendar year. This statement elaborated on what I found in my investigations during the year. It also served as a philosophical mind-set and checklist of things we needed to examine to arrive at our best annual plan. It is modified every year to adjust to new internal and external business developments.

The main parts making the annual plan were: *planning, forecasting,* and *the annual plan.* (See Appendices A and B for the complete format and outlines.)

Fifth, I worked out our forecast expenses. I also factored in funds for special projects, such as plant additions and other large capital purchases.

Now I was ready to summarize my findings and assumptions. I created a three-row sales plan with a row of *plan* profits. An example is shown below:

## SALES by $1,000s

|       | Jan. | Feb. | Mar. | Apr. | May | Jun. | Jul. | Aug. | Sep. | Oct. | Nov. | Dec. |
|-------|------|------|------|------|-----|------|------|------|------|------|------|------|
| Best  | 700  | 700  | 800  | 900  | 800 | 800  | 800  | 500  | 700  | 900  | 900  | 900  |
| Plan  | 600  | 600  | 650  | 750  | 650 | 650  | 650  | 300  | 600  | 750  | 750  | 800  |
| Worst | 500  | 400  | 550  | 600  | 550 | 550  | 550  | 250  | 400  | 600  | 600  | 550  |

Actual Sales (fill out here as each month was completed during the year—to be used as next year's guide)

| Profits | 40 | 40 | 45 | 55 | 45 | 45 | 45 | 20 | 40 | 55 | 55 | 60 |
|---------|----|----|----|----|----|----|----|----|----|----|----|----|

Actual Profits (fill out here as each month was completed during the year—to be used as next year's guide)

In a growing economic cycle, the previous year's actual becomes the next year's worst. And in a negative growth cycle, the previous year's actual becomes the next year's best. It was very interesting to see how close our company normally came to functioning according to plan. In the years of good growth (1974 and 2005), we were under strong pressure to keep up with customer demand and weren't always successful. In our biggest recession (1983; I sold the company in 2006, before the 2007–2008 recession), the planning kept us from having to close the doors. You think you are ready for such highs and lows, but the suddenness of the heights and depths can still be staggering.

The last thing I did before implementing the annual plan at Seaberg was to revise our intermediate-term (two to five years) and long-term (six to twenty years) goals.

## Results

Month to month, we obviously couldn't follow *plan* as it was written. The only other choice was to do no planning and act like we were playing the lottery. However, over the course of a year, most of the time we came fairly close to our targets set a year earlier. Even when we didn't hit our goals, having a plan to follow gave the company leadership stability when unforeseen events happened. One success in planning tended to lead into other successes.

This is somewhat similar but not nearly as chaotic as a military operation. If you followed any of our country's battles against Iraq and Muslim terrorists, you witnessed the extreme detail the military planners did. But after the war was engaged and enemy contact was made, the plans were rapidly changed to meet battlefield conditions. Similarly, we make our plans for the coming year and react to whatever the changing conditions require us to do.

In the latter 1990s, we were using electronic data interchange (EDI) and bar coding with several clients to speed up and clarify our purchase order receipts and product invoicing. This was a quantum leap over the snail mail we had been using. Worse yet was having to go through reams and reams of computer paper daily to keep up with client schedule changes.

In 2000 we installed visual manufacturing software, which automatically told us of daily changes without any hard copies. Seaberg is still using it, with the periodic upgrades from the supplier.

# CHAPTER 9

# You Can Make It, but Would You Buy It?

General Dwight D. Eisenhower is one of my heroes. I've studied the background of this World War II military leader and later president and have come to admire his character and many of his accomplishments. One of his phrases that particularly impressed me came from his experiences as commander of European Allied forces: "That which is not inspected, deteriorates." To me, this means that you have to continually be alert to seek circumstances or production parts that don't measure up to company standards. It doesn't mean that you have inspectors piled on top of inspectors examining the same part over and over. It means once you have an effective process in place, you still need to keep monitoring it to be sure people keep or exceed established standards. This is one of the reasons I spent so much time in our manufacturing areas—to help make sure that our processes stayed up to the high levels our customers expected. And when our standards were exceeded, I found ways to reward the people involved.

" Throughout my manufacturing career I've believed that good quality begins with production, and this is best accomplished by instilling a habit of constant and continuous improvement in the quality of the product being made. If you haven't got something good to sell that customers want to buy, you'll soon go out of business. And in today's market, customers change allegiances very fast if they feel they are not getting the quality they expect.

One of our CNC machinists told me a story about the large company where he had previously worked before that plant was closed. Bob said to me one morning during his shift, "You know what I like about this place, George? It's that we make the part right, first. Then we go for speed." Bob then proceeded to tell me about the foreman in the department where he had worked who used to stand behind the men at their machines and berate them because they weren't producing enough.

"I was even timed going to the bathroom," Bob said. His department was operating at a 52 percent production rate, and the union steward told the foreman to just spend one day doing bookwork and stay away from the men. That *day* the production rate shot up to about 86 percent. The next day, the foreman came on the shift and shouted, "I knew you guys were screwing me, and you just proved it! Now get to work!" Not surprisingly, production after that tirade dropped off even lower, to a 46 percent level, and stayed there.

At Seaberg Industries, the burden of proving quality rested with the maker of the part. It could be me, a technician, an office worker, a machine operator, a machinist, a welder, an engineer, a programmer, a team leader, or a subcontractor. It is more complicated than one realizes, and one can see how a tiny mistake could be made that would sour our customer relations. In a positive sense, these valuable persons had that opportunity and satisfaction of proving their quality and their workmanship.

Naturally, the employee would like to know that his work is excellent rather than having the internal customer (the next person in the production process) remind him that his work wasn't up to Seaberg standards of excellence. At one of our company meetings, I once showed everyone a rather simple part that was a small, rectangular 2" x 1" x 4" steel bar stock with two 5/8" drilled and tapped holes. I then had people line up representing each step in our entire process before the product was shipped and invoiced. It took *fourteen* persons to completely process that small piece in our plant, from engineering processing, ordering material, and receiving the bar stock, all the way to invoicing the customer. Almost all the employees hadn't realized how complex making a simple part was.

A word of caution here is that I was striving to show Seaberg excellence, not perfection. This demonstration gave them an understanding of how important it was to prevent quality errors and costly mistakes. I wanted our personnel to be careful to prevent small mistakes without being careless or paranoid about always being perfect, which is an impossibility. We believed work was enjoyment, not punishment.

People tend, consciously or unconsciously, to move toward their focal points. For several years I religiously plotted reject costs weekly and made a graph for all our company people to see. But the costs were never reduced. In fact, they started to get worse. It took our then quality assurance and training manager, Rhett Bicknell, to correct this approach. My focus was entirely wrong. I was concentrating on mistakes instead of correcting the process and using charting to prove that we could improve. I quit the charting, and the rejects started disappearing. Throughout his 2008 bestseller, *Outliers*, Malcolm Gladwell stated that you should focus on what you want and not on what you want to avoid.

At Seaberg, we are constantly aware of our continued need to keep furnishing better quality to our clients. In the 1970s' and 1980s' quality goals, we built product around the phrase "conformance to customer specifications."

## 1980s Quality

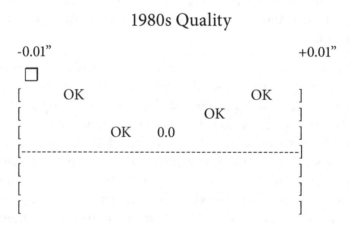

In the above example, the OK marks meant that the part was "OK" or acceptable so long as the hole tolerance was within drawing specifications. I attended a seminar where a former vice president at International Harvester Corporation confessed that it was usual to set rejected parts aside on the assembly line, and then if no replacement parts had arrived by the end of that shift, the rejected parts were *jammed or forced onto the assembled unit* and the completed assembly was sent out the door to the dealer.

If a part hole tolerance was + or − 0.010", the part was always satisfactory if all the holes were made within that tolerance range. No consideration was given for improving the accuracy beyond the called-out tolerance. If the part hole size was at the low end of the tolerance range and a mating part to be inserted into the hole was made at the high end of the tolerance range, you could have a piece that couldn't be assembled even though they were both made within their called-out tolerance. Similarly, I owned a 1951 Plymouth coupe when I was in college, and the driver's door would always rub against the car door frame when it was opened or closed. This was normal and accepted for most cars made at that time and one reason cars were sometimes called "rattle-traps." This kind of acceptance by Americans went on until the 1990s.

In the 1990s, new quality goals were set and met by instituting a phrase called *"reduced variability around the target."* These new quality goals most likely happened because of the higher quality of foreign cars being sold in America.

## 1990s Quality

| -0.10 | | 0 | | +0.10 |
|---|---|---|---|---|
| Poor | Better | Best | Better | Poor |

Now, if a part tolerance was + or − 0.10", we continued to reduce the quality variability around the target (best) to the point where we had no measureable variability. We than had excellent part fitups on the customer assembly line that kept improving the longer the run kept going.

One method we used to achieve our excellent quality was to furnish each new employee with a *quality attitude* card, given out at their beginning quality class. The card read as follows:

# SEABERG INDUSTRIES QUALITY ATTITUDE
## "I CARE ABOUT QUALITY"

1. I must set up and run to the planned method.
2. I have all proper available gages, process sheets, and print(s) on the job at setup and available throughout the operation.
3. I check gages to the print at the beginning of each shift or setup to make sure they are right.
4. I measure all my measurable operation's characteristics of the setup piece or first piece of the shift and know it is right before taking it to quality assurance.
5. I check and gage my work often enough to be sure I am running quality work.
6. I must be sure piece part is located properly.
7. I set aside and identify parts that are not to print and inform quality assurance.
8. I *never* put a bad piece in the load.
9. I fill out my time card and reject report properly each day.
10. I—no one else—am responsible for the quality I am producing.

## "I ALWAYS DO THE BEST I CAN."

Mission: Create a customer and satisfy his or her needs.
Attitude: Constantly and continually improve the quality of my work.

---

One of the ways we improved quality was to have each person sign off on a process card for the work he or she did. If he was a welder, he marked his work with his own personal metal stamp. In the office, everyone, me included, who wrote a report signed or initialed under the work he or she did. These practices are common to most businesses, but we sometimes forgot the impact this had on improving quality. Employees have told me more than once, "If my name is on it, it's going to be right." Maybe it's all about taking the right kind of pride in one's workmanship. See Appendix E for a sample process card.

In the 1970s and 1980s, our company was interested in reducing rejects to less than 1 percent. This was no longer the case beginning in the late 1990s. At Seaberg, we were then involved in a program called 6 Sigma, which is defined as a quality rate of 3.4 parts/million. Each internal process on every machine in the plant went through a 6 Sigma certification process.

At the turn of the century, we met at least weekly as a quality review team. The team members were the president, vice president of manufacturing, quality assurance and training manager, and manufacturing engineering manager. I served as the secretary where unresolved problems and customer complaints were formally discussed. However, we did most of the quality problem solving informally in the hallway, at the workbench, at the machine, or anywhere where the problem could best be addressed.

## Caterpillar Certification

The Caterpillar certification process was normally conducted at a supplier facility in the following way.

The obvious first step was to have a product or perform a service that Caterpillar needed. In that market niche, competency in what you did became the determining factor if you were to be considered for certification. It was not based on sales dollars to the company but rather on how critical your work was to the manufacturer of a world-class product. If the buyer you were dealing with perceived your company's work as an asset to Cat's guidelines and goals of quality, delivery, price, and schedule flexibility, he would then request a supplier audit.

The supplier audit was a detailed, lengthy examination of your company by a team of two or more Caterpillar employees. They would visit and look at your plant in detail. The obvious first thing to be tested was your quality assurance system. When I first started doing work for Caterpillar, I didn't have much money, and I put it all into tools and machinery. I naively didn't feel that I needed to "get those essential gages." Then one day one of my Cat clients asked if I wanted to make fence posts or Caterpillar parts. That ended the argument about gaging, and ever since I have purchased all necessary quality assurance equipment. In the 1990s, in most cases if you didn't have a computerized numerical control

(CNC) coordinate measuring machine installed in a temperature- and humidity-controlled laboratory, you wouldn't be considered for certification. These machines started at $20,000 or $50,000 in today's figures, for recording measurements on a inch-long piece, up to several million dollars for a unit used to measure a completely assembled bulldozer.

Because larger companies have strived to reduce their supplier base since then, they could devote more time with the remaining suppliers to help make better equipment. More detailed analysis of significant suppliers was partitioned into management, finances, engineering, manufacturing, quality, and materials. What this kind of rating system did was tie those things that affect the supplier-client relationship together into one package for a more thorough and complete review.

These subjects can be further broken down as follows:

1. Management. Capability and overall performance, depth of staff, and responsiveness to client needs. For instance, how well or how fast could the supplier react to design changes that the consumer requested? How committed was the supplier to help keep production lines operating, even when there were occasional short-dated needs that had to be met?

2. Financial. Was the supplier able to manage his finances well enough to keep up with planned growth of the client? Or how well could he withstand temporary market slowdowns? How well did he measure up to the Five Cs of Character, Capacity, Credit, Collateral, and Conditions as explained in Chapter 4?

3. Engineering. What did the supplier need to do to enhance his own research and development? What facilities did he have to conduct joint development engineering work? Could his computers link properly with Cat's for design or development?

4. Manufacturing. What facilities, machines, and equipment did the supplier have to support the client? Could the client download software directly to his machines? Did he have space available for expansion? If so, how much and where?

5. Quality. This is mostly covered earlier in this chapter. Additionally, was the supplier providing training for his personnel so the company could keep up with changing standards as well as with

short- and long-term needs of the customer? How well was the supplier moving toward 6 Sigma process capability (3.4 defects per million)?

6. Materials. Was that priced-right, normal quality part being delivered on time? How well was the subcontractor responding to the client's changing requirements? Was the supplier delivering only the exact quantity that was needed?

7. Pricing. What was the supplier doing to reduce prices and/or hold their pricing? Was the pricing policy consistent, or did it go all over the price map?

The Caterpillar certification ceremony used to be conducted at each supplier's facility that was being approved because Caterpillar wanted the contractor employees to know how important quality was to Cat and to have them share in the special moment. This approach made the entire certification process very personal to suppliers' employees and let them feel how important they were to this customer.

This certification not only opened sales doors in the United States but abroad as well. One European company that contacted us wanted a snapshot taken of our Caterpillar plaque and sent to them as proof of our quality before negotiating any further.

The Caterpillar certification was earned annually. Out of the years we have been certified, there have been several where the re-cert has been delayed until a few questionable items were clarified to customer satisfaction.

## Deming Quality

The Seaberg manufacturing and quality managers and I have attended various courses where Dr. Deming's fourteen principles of quality have been taught. I also taught these principles to every new employee in our eight-hour beginning quality assurance course. We obviously agreed with Dr. Deming, but once in a while we have had strong differences of opinion on interpreting the obligations.

Many books and articles have been written about the obligations of top management. The fourteen points are listed here as a reminder of what good quality should be in a company and how to achieve high productivity. These obligations are as follows:

## Obligations Of Top Management
## by Dr. W. Edwards Deming

1. Create constancy of purpose toward improvement of product and service with a plan to become competitive and to stay in business. Decide to whom top management is responsible.
2. Discard the old philosophy of accepting defective products.
3. Eliminate dependence on mass inspection for quality control; instead, depend on process control through statistical techniques.
4. End the practice of awarding business on the basis of price tag. Instead, depend on meaningful measures of quality, along with price. Eliminate suppliers that cannot qualify with statistical evidence of quality.
5. Use statistical techniques to identify the two sources of waste— system or process (85 percent) and local or operator faults (15 percent). Strive to constantly reduce this waste.
6. Institute better, more thorough job-related training.
7. Provide supervision with knowledge of statistical methods; encourage use of these methods to identify which defects should be investigated for solution.
8. Reduce fear throughout the organization by encouraging open, two-way, nonpunitive communication. The economic loss resulting from fear to ask questions or report trouble is appalling.
9. Help reduce waste by encouraging design, research, and sales people to learn more about the problems of production.
10. Eliminate the use of goals and slogans to encourage productivity, unless training and management support is also provided.
11. Eliminate work standards that prescribe numerical quotas.
12. Remove barriers that stand between the hourly worker and his right to pride of workmanship.

13. Institute a vigorous program for retraining people in new skills, to keep up with changes in materials, methods, product designs, and machinery.
14. Make maximum use of statistical knowledge and talent in your company.

### The Three Truths of Quality

At the Wallace Company, the 1990 Small Business Category winner of the Malcolm Baldridge Award, they have what they call "The Three Truths" of quality:

1. Quality is not only a word.
2. Everyone can attain a higher level of quality.
3. Quality works when you get 100 percent quality from 100 percent of your people, 100 percent of the time.

This company was right on target. In the spring of 1991, I listened to one of their executives in Chicago talk about their company. Before Wallace became committed to quality, the company president never seemed to venture off the executive floor, didn't know anyone's name, and generally gave the impression that he didn't care how they felt about anything they did. As a result, the employees didn't care what kind of work they did.

By the Wallace Company's executives' own admission, it was hard to believe how arrogant and insensitive this company became. Then the officers came to their collective senses, decided they wanted to remain in business, and made the dramatic turnaround they did. An example of how quality conscious they have become came from their valve department. Wallace didn't make any of their own valves for the south Texas chemical industry where they're located. However, they rework their competitors' valves to tougher QA standards for the resold valves than what the valve maker supplies. Wallace just rebuilds those valves in their own shop that don't meet what they think are proper standards. In the long run, Wallace found out that it saved on field replacement costs and kept customers coming back.

Seaberg's quality assurance conference room used to be the most highly people-populated area at the company. But with our improved QA practices, it has become one of the least-used areas of the plant. In fact, I started calling our QA manager "the Maytag Man" because no one ever showed up anymore to have a questionable part examined. There are few questionable parts, and most of the inspecting we do is properly done where the parts are made, except that for the first part of a run, which is given a thorough inspection in the quality lab or the fixture is certified before being issued to the shop floor. This leaves more time for the QA manager to look for potential problems on the floor.

# Chapter 10

# There's Got to Be a Boss

My parents were simple, honest, unsophisticated folks. They were very loving to each other and their children, never playing a favorite, though I suspected that I *was the favorite*. This is a joke among us children because Mom and Dad" made each of us feel we were so special that each of us felt we were our parents' favorite.

This kind of upbringing gave me a lot of self-esteem and self-confidence, which enabled me to willingly tackle difficult challenges later on in my life. It also made for a happy childhood. There was no doubt who was the boss: Dad. Because of this family order of Dad, Mom, and then the four kids, my mother felt confident and very secure in her life even though we had very little money. We weren't poor; we just didn't have any money or even a car. But we did have a lot of love.

The joke in the family as we got older was that the boys either had haircuts and holes in their shoes (temporarily covered with cardboard from a Wheaties cereal box) or new shoes and long hair. But no matter how bad things got, there was always enough good food on the table for the kids. I might add that we never felt we had to do without anything, except that when I had holes in my shoe soles I learned how to cross my legs so the shoe bottoms couldn't be seen by my school and neighborhood friends.

Dad died six months after I started my company. In the early months when I first began making fabricated light gage machine guards, I persuaded Lyle Efflandt to let me use his equipment and coach me

69

on some of the machine operations. His one-man sheet metal shop in Moline was located at the time between Sixteenth and Seventeenth Streets on Fourth Avenue. As I made a few of the machine guards for a new customer, I would run them over to my parents' house for my Dad to see. He was dying from throat and lung cancer, and he couldn't leave the house then. Even though I was thirty-six at the time, I still wanted his approval of my workmanship, and he did approve of the quality of my work.

I contrast my family upbringing with that of one of our young employees. He was raised in a commune during the 1960s where there were sixty parents, a result of the "flower power and peace" generation that protested the Vietnam War. Don told me that he never had any guidance, never knew if he was doing anything right or wrong, and grew up totally confused. The fact that his father started feeding him drugs when he was five years old didn't help matters either. Fortunately, when he was drafted into the army, he met a wonderful, more traditionally raised woman, whom he married. And he had a faith-changing experience that started to put some order into his personal life. When he was at Seaberg, he was a very good father who spent time with his three happy children, and he was a gentle and orderly head of the household.

Don's dysfunctional childhood hurt his academic advancement in our certified apprenticeship training program. His ability to concentrate and discipline himself to study was hard for him. It was to Don's credit he had such a winner's attitude that he kept improving in his scholastic and vocational work. However, the scars from his childhood have been hard for him to cover over and move on.

Family orderliness is necessary in operating a business. Someone's got to be in charge or else you have chaos. And where you have too little control (hippie flower power) or too much control (autocrat, arrogant, abusive), the productivity fails to reach its full potential. The management style most likely to cause insolvency is the one without a boss. This is a workplace where the one in charge doesn't want to take responsibility or is too interested in the social welfare of his employees and forgets about running the establishment. It's interesting to me that women I've observed running small businesses are less likely to be this way than men. I suppose that it's because they have something to prove or are too fearful of losing control, all to their credit.

In the late 1970s when I had the company going a few years, a retired executive from John Deere who was then doing volunteer work through the local Service Corps of Retired Executives, otherwise known as SCORE, spent some very productive time helping me. He told me my main job was to "review and direct" operations, even though we only had some twenty employees at the time. It was helpful advice because I was repeatedly taking a direct hand in plant operations even though I was not directly involved on a day-to-day basis anymore. You can imagine how this screwed things up a little and unsettled some of our people. Shortly after I started the SCORE sessions, I saw the error of my ways and stopped this poor over-managing practice.

When I sold the business in 2006, I felt that a better and more appropriate phrase should be "review, direct, and lead" operations. This implies working closely with our people but not interfering with what they're doing. If we hired the right kind of person, she would be doing her job better than I could hope to do since she would be at that job every day and know what to do much better than anyone else. But more than that, it means that the leader should set the example for other company people to follow.

Part of setting a good example occurred in the early fall of 1991 when I put Craig in charge of plant operations. He spent good plant floor time "building a chain of customers" by helping others do their jobs more easily by getting tools or other necessary items for them, running a press brake, driving a fork truck, and welding some parts (he was AWS certified with his own weld stamp). He did this after I told everyone that we had a certain cash flow deadline to meet. When his "customers" in-plant saw how helpful he was to them, it seemed that everyone picked up the productivity a notch. And this was happening just as I had announced a possible layoff due to a shortage of future work. What a wonderful crew we had. Morale was high and awesome to me, even in the face of looming company layoffs.

## CHAPTER 11

# Who Takes the Heat?

---

Someone once told me that everyone who wants to be a manager should have the chance to meet a payroll. After starting and operating a business, I can say that I wholeheartedly agree with that comment. Having direct responsibility for another's weekly paycheck puts backbone in your spine that never used to be there, at least consciously. If your employee cannot pay for food, clothing, and shelter for his family because you failed to pay him for his services, how can you feel comfortable when looking in the mirror? That person trusts *you* to come up with the money if *he* comes up with the productivity.

There have been many times in the early years of our company's existence when I didn't take a paycheck just so others could have their pay. I don't have any regrets about my decision, but I have felt bad that my wife, Sue, had to do without. Thank heavens she had a great attitude about those missing or delayed checks. I couldn't have made it without her support.

When I hired my first full-time employee, Larry Gainer, in March of 1974, Sue sobered me with the remark that I was hiring a family, not just a person. That was like a bucket of cold water being splashed on my face because I was only thinking of possibilities, not responsibilities. The pressure of financial responsibility quickly overcame the small euphoria I felt, which was that I was finally on my way toward operating a company when I hired a full-time person. Ever since hiring that first person, I often think about, and appreciate, the over five hundred people who I asked to join the Seaberg Industries family over the thirty-plus years I owned the company.

When I took on the stress that goes with being responsible for a small company's success, I had to make good decisions that weren't necessarily popular with the troops. These decisions usually fell into the discipline category. (The topic of discipline is fully covered in chapter 12 and will not be further discussed here.) This really isn't too much different for me than being the father in my own home, where I am morally and ethically required to provide for and protect those living under my roof.

When I described my job function, I used the phrase of being a "benevolent dictator." I listened to and took part in discussions about various subjects relating to company operations. And I almost always tried to have unanimous agreement on whatever the decision might be, whether it was buying a machine, hiring a new employee, or looking at a new market for us. But when there was no agreement among those involved, it was up to me, as president, to make a decision so the company could go forward and proceed to attack other challenges. Peter Drucker, the only man I ever called my management guru, once wrote that if a manager makes the right decision 33 percent of the time, he is equivalent to having a major league baseball All-Star's batting average. Being decisive after the facts were shown gave the firm continuity in its culture and helped to let our employees know where the company stood on issues, which in turn gave them a feeling of stability in the firm.

Having one person in charge prevented a situation from arising where one person might feel he was working for two people. An example could be where a second-shift CNC machinist received machine operating instructions from the first-shift team leader, but the second-shift team leader was responsible to the vice president of manufacturing for the CNC machinist's work. Another case of serving two masters is where one of our employees wanted to work at Seaberg and also make parts for us in his home workshop. I didn't allow this to happen because of the conflict-of-interest problems that would occur from him thinking about his own home problems while at our plant or maybe compromising any internal secrets we had.

When things got really stressful and exciting, I compared my situational thinking to "earning my flight pay." This was a holdover from my army days as a helicopter pilot when I would occasionally fly into a dangerous situation I had to quickly work my way out of.

The best industrial likeness to this is when I had to appease a client who was angry at the company for something he might have thought we caused or failed to do. In that case, I would stop whatever else I was doing, and if the situation was serious enough, I would personally travel to meet with the client to find out what we might have done to cause the unfortunate incident.

One time when I worked at Ralph Hahn & Associates, I was in charge of moving a chemical company from Missouri to Kentucky. I had just arrived back at the office in Springfield, Illinois, from a trip to the new plant where the move and construction was thought to be complete. I got a phone call from a very irate CEO of Hadley Adhesive telling me that one of the pumps critical to the process wasn't working and that if I didn't *immediately* drive the 350 miles down there to solve the problem, the firm I worked for, and I, would be getting a big lawsuit. I was on-site the next morning, and when I looked at the system, I opened the pump and found a cardboard spacer in the inlet that the company installing the pump had forgotten to remove before starting the system. I removed the piece of cardboard and quietly told the construction supervisor what I did. After the system was running as specified, I called the CEO and explained, to his relief, that everything was working as it should. Quick reaction to a potentially difficult problem prevented a very serious litigation issue.

Beginning in March through mid-April of 1983, we had two stressful incidents that tested my Christian faith because Caterpillar, our largest customer, was on strike. The first was the proposed contracts we made with International Harvester Farmall Works in Rock Island at a time when our local economy was in a recession. My concern was whether these proposals would be accepted because of the Caterpillar strike. Would we lose part of them, or would the entire contract be voided? Fortunately, IHC signed all the orders for us that we bid to do.

The second test was that on the first of April, we couldn't make our utility payments. This was the first and only time in our history this happened. But I put my trust in the Lord to keep the gas and electrical power from being shut off. The utilities were kept on even though we made the payments six days late!

Facing these kinds of problems was just part of the job. Peter Drucker said something to the effect that managers should not feel comfortable and if they did feel comfortable, they weren't doing their jobs. Some may call this management by crisis (MBC), which is another term for constantly putting out fires. I tried to keep those crisis problems to an absolute minimum so they were not a distraction to my employees.

Another area where the small company chief executive takes the heat is in pay raises. I deeply desired to make my employees the highest-paid shop workers in the part of the country where we lived. After all, I would probably be more popular with my fellow workers and have many fewer disgruntled people if they were the highest paid around. However, I could only make those raises from profits we generated or we would go out of business. I talked to our employees often about their income and pay compared to higher wages in the Quad Cities offered at the large corporations and federal government shops at the Rock Island Arsenal. Generally speaking, the larger companies with proprietary products did pay higher wages.

A Proper Way to Deal with the Heat of Making a Payroll

Eventually I wanted to make our pay raises similar to how The Lincoln Electric Company inaugurated them in 1932, during the Great Depression. James Lincoln Sr. stated at that time that he would be very willing to give out pay raises. However, they had to be based on three ideas: 1. A lower price to the customer; 2. A benefit to company shareholders; and 3. Retained profits for the company to grow on. When these conditions were met, the employees could have their increased pay. The Lincoln people did their part, and Mr. Lincoln did his part. As far as I have been able to find out in the early 2000s, The Lincoln Electric Company employees were still the highest-paid manufacturing workers in the world!

A little insight into The Lincoln Electric Company philosophy of offering fair pay for a fair day's work has to do with absenteeism. Absenteeism was treated as a disgrace. When someone missed work due to illness, he needed a nurse's excuse and also had to explain the illness to two fellow employees. The thinking behind this seemingly harsh policy was that every person was highly valued and the work he did was important to The Lincoln Electric Company. When someone missed work, the people employed next to him on the assembly line had to do his work as well as their own for the time he was absent. Working at this fine company wasn't for everyone, but for those who did, the financial rewards were hard to beat. Each time I visited the company, I was treated with the utmost respect, whether in the office or in any of the unrestricted parts of the plant.

When I walked down an assembly line with my host, I noticed that everyone was in a no-nonsense mode, busy at their responsibilities. One time I was interested in a particular operation, and after getting permission from my escort, Jim Lincoln Jr., I asked a worker a question. Immediately he stopped what he was doing and answered my question in a very courteous and warm way even though I cost him a few minutes of his work. He then went right back to the industrious job he was doing. Business-like and friendly—what was there not to like?

## Being in Charge

The person in charge of running a company is the one who takes the heat when business isn't going well, and he should be paid accordingly. If the compensation wasn't appropriate for the responsibility, most likely the best man available wouldn't want the job. And having the wrong person in the CEO position could put the business out of business.

In publications I've read and personnel consultants I've talked with, it has been stated that over half of the children of company founders are unhappy working for their fathers or mothers. This is very unfortunate—a lose-lose situation. That scenario can be avoided simply by giving the child the right to make the choice of whether to join the firm. There are numerous instances I personally know about where the son made his own decision, usually in favor of joining the company. When the child does the independent decision-making without any rancor from the family, there is mutual respect and self-esteem for all concerned.

In my situation, I thought my son, a certified quality engineer, would eventually be capable of handling my job. When Tom graduated from college, I interviewed him for a position at Seaberg, much like I interviewed anyone else. He said he wouldn't feel right taking a job until he could get the financial rewards that went with the risks of running Seaberg. I was unable to meet his requirements, and he went to work for a Fortune 500 company, earning the highest starting salary of anyone in his mechanical engineering class at the University of Iowa College of Engineering. I admired him for his maturity and openness in discussing a salary with me.

To help find the right fit for anyone working for a living, there are several aptitude and best kind-of-a-job tests one can take. Several are: www.youruniquedesign.com; www.strengthfinder.com; and www.aimstesting.org. I have not personally taken any of these tests, but they do come highly recommended by persons in the testing business.

# CHAPTER 12

# Discipline Is My Friend

This chapter is going to be about how I feel about discipline and how I used it. In 1991 we completed our first in-house customer survey. This survey was a seven-page list of questions given to each employee for his or her comments on quality, productivity, and other pertinent company subjects. This survey is shown in Appendix C. It was interesting that the biggest problem at our company then, according to the respondents, was management using discipline properly. I wasn't too surprised at this answer because I've noticed in my life that those institutions I consider to be the leaders in their field have a strong emphasis on proper discipline among employees, teammates, or members.

Discipline is many times looked at by people as punishment. To me, that is not what proper discipline is at all. Proper discipline is really all about completing a task or job in the most efficient way possible. Just look at the best college football and basketball teams and how they interact with each other to win the game. Farmers and former military personnel are my first choices to hire because they have been taught the good benefits of proper discipline in carrying out their work.

I look at poor discipline, or a lack of discipline, as punishment for doing a poor job. At our company, I wanted my associates to *have discipline* as part of their work habits, rather than to *have to be punished* (disciplined) for lack of a positive attitude, habits, or work methods.

What does the dictionary say about discipline? Webster's[6]defines it as, "1. Punishment 2. Instruction 3. A subject that is taught: a field of study 4. Training that corrects, molds, or perfects the mental faculties or moral character 5. a: Control gained by enforcing obedience or order b: orderly or prescribed conduct or pattern of behavior c: Self-control 6. A rule or system of rules governing conduct or activity." My definition concentrates on items two, four, five, and six.

What are the word components I used to explain "discipline is my friend"? The nine keys I've used, in order of importance, are: freedom, persistence, training, communication, planning, peace, confidence, habits, and love.

*Freedom* comes from using a set methodology to complete certain tasks in the most proficient manner. At the start of the 1861–1865 American Civil War, the Union Army was poorly trained and lacked discipline. It showed in their high personnel losses compared to the Confederate Army and in the battlefield defeats they suffered. Later when leaders like Generals Grant, Sherman, and Sheridan were given command, they instilled the firm discipline in their troops that ultimately resulted in victory for the Union.

In the most extreme cases, when people won't discipline themselves to follow the rules of their society, they forfeit their freedom and end up behind bars. People convicted of crimes in the United States who have lost their freedom seem unable to control themselves and conform to society's rules that generally have been made for the greatest good for its citizens.

*Persistence* is that wonderful quality that successful leaders use, especially during adversity, to achieve greatness in their fields of endeavor. How was Wilma Rudolph able to overcome a crippling childhood disease to set sports records in track? She persistently, in a day-by-day fashion, worked toward her goals. Or what about Vince Lombardi when he was coach of the Super Bowl Champion I and II Green Bay Packers? He used the same plays over and over again successfully during games because his players practiced those same plays to perfection before the games. On a personal level, how was I able to complete a marathon in 1981, fourteen months

---

6   Webster's New World College Dictionary, fourth edition, Wiley
Publishing,Cleveland, OH, 2002, page 410.

after having a heart attack? It happened because I applied intelligent and purposeful persistence in my day-to-day training.

Proper *training* is: instruction plus theory plus practical supervised practice directed toward a certain goal. The over twelve years of medical school a neurosurgeon needs to complete his training as a doctor are necessary for him to just get started in his profession. I observed one of our employees once at a company Christmas party. His four children ranged in ages from two to about eleven years old. As Santa Claus gave a present to each child at the party, Lee Fong's children patiently waited until all of their brothers and sisters had received their present before opening their gift. Each child slowly and carefully unwrapped his or her present and even folded the paper neatly after lifting his or her gift from the box. And these children were among the happiest with what they got, and they were delighted with what each brother and sister received as well. This was obviously a result of the fine training that Mom and Dad were doing at home.

In the workplace, for the Seaberg machinists, welders, and fabricators to become federally certified took four years of training in quality assurance, statistical process control, and night school in print reading, geometry, and trigonometry. Plus, each apprentice needed eight thousand approved contact hours of instruction and experience in setting up and operating selected machines in the plant. What training gives you is a chance to do real work under someone else's guidance in order to learn the best way to perform a task, operate a machine properly, or ship a finished product.

At Seaberg Industries, I encouraged, "Ready, Fire, Aim," a phrase that Tom Peters, who wrote *Thriving on Chaos*, coined in reaction to customer needs. This was the case only if we practiced how best to do what was needed. If our methodology was sound and well communicated, it was easy to have a strong bias for action even when we didn't have all the facts, since in most cases we probably never would know all we would want to about an opportunity before we needed to act on it. Ray Kroc, founder of McDonald's, was emotionally ready to start a fast food franchise before it was completely thought out when he first met the McDonald brothers and eventually bought the restaurant that started the huge international success of McDonald's.

*Communicating* is something one never seems to get enough of in life. It requires discipline to learn how to communicate best with the people with whom you are dealing. An airline stewardess may use simple hand signals she's developed with a coworker to provide better customer service during a flight. Or look at how Lebron James of the NBA's Miami Heat basketball team knows where Dwayne Wade and Chris Bosh are on the court and if they are looking for a pass just by raising an eyebrow. Morse Code was developed as an advanced means of communicating after operators were taught to follow the code by tapping out their signals, rather than just tapping out whatever dots and dashes they wanted without knowing what the taps meant. As a layman celebrating a fifty-year wedding anniversary in 2011, I believe the chief cause of divorce in America is a lack of good communication between husband and wife, and I feel marriage communication starts with the husband.

*Planning* is simply thinking things through before taking action on a decision. Thorough planning brought about the astounding success of Desert Storm I and II in Iraq. To coordinate various nations' languages and cultures, involving over 500,000 troops, took planning on an immense scale. This before-action work called for the various players to do only what they had planned to do, whether mapping Baghdad's bridges ahead of the bombing, flying a helicopter as part of the first-wave assault, or driving a water truck to a previously designated troop resupply point at a specific time.

*Peace* is a part of discipline because I know that after I'd given a project my best effort, I have a calm and confident feeling about my involvement in the work. What would I have to fear if I used a good plan to work out a problem to the best that I'm capable of giving?

*Confidence* comes from doing a project well through proper repetition. When I was in the army, I was assigned to a unit that had nuclear weapon capability and trained often with our unit in how to arm and use it in field maneuvers. When I was first exposed to and took part in procedures for detonating the weapon, I was intimidated and a little nervous. But after going through repeated drills successfully, I gained confidence that our unit could properly set off the bomb if the need arose. In the same way, anyone who participates in athletics knows how important confidence is to his performance, and he usually can't gain that confidence without many reps of the same pass, jump shot, block, tackle, etc.

A technique we've used at work to build self-confidence involved cleaning. Our vice president at the time, Craig Kinzer, would select an area of the plant that he wanted to have cleaner and more orderly as part of his waste eliminating program. He would have the person responsible for that area come in with him on a Saturday morning for a few hours of overtime work. Craig had a chance to work with his fellow employee on a one-to-one basis to help solve a problem and establish a set of standards for housekeeping. The worker learned more of what was expected of him, how valuable he was to the organization, and that he was essential to the company's long-term success. It was then easy for him to improve his self-esteem and gain confidence from doing a job well. Then he could go on to do more jobs better.

Confidence also pertains to your opinion of your fellow employees. If you have confidence that the QA personnel will inspect your work properly, you feel better about your work, and you will increase your own confidence by having their confidence in you increased as you do your assigned work properly and without any defects.

Habits, both good and bad ones, come about through many repetitions of an act. Publilius Syrus was a first-century Latin philosopher and writer from Syria. He wrote in his book titled *Maximus*, "Speech is the mirror of the soul; as a man speaks, so is he." We can communicate verbally or nonverbally by our habits. And thus, we reveal who we really are. It's our choice to select those habits that show good or poor self-discipline in our lives.

Developing good habits is one of the best things a college education can teach you. In my field of engineering, I was taught to use the same methods to solve assigned problems so I could arrive at the correct solutions in the shortest amount of time. I know what I'll be doing in a certain sequence without thinking of what activity I will be doing next. That way it doesn't require conscious thinking about the repeatable things I do, so I am free to concentrate on special or nonroutine tasks. For example, when I owned the company, I would get up at about the same time each workday, have devotions, do my pushups and stretching, shave, and eat my breakfast. Because I had these steady, everyday routines, I got some of my best work ideas while shaving and thinking about the day ahead of me.

*Love* may be overlooked by many in a definition of discipline. This isn't boy-girl or erotic love but a selfless and caring love like a parent shows to his child—love and sacrifice for him but with set standards of conduct he has to follow. When I think of my best teachers and coaches, I think of the ones who were usually hardest on me because they cared about how well George did and wanted him to be the best he could be.

Bill Bishop was my high school assistant basketball coach and the only assistant coach heading into the 1990s to be elected to the Illinois High School Basketball Hall of Fame. He was instrumental in my earning a full basketball scholarship to the University of Iowa. It was only by his being very demanding of me that I rose to the level where he expected me to be. And any student who played for him feared him because he could humiliate you if you misbehaved or weren't trying as hard as he thought you should. That said, most of the better players cared a lot for Bill after leaving high school and would come back to see him when they were in town. At his funeral, many of his former players returned to speak and pay their last respects to a demanding and loving man.

The opposite of love is indifference. I know if I didn't care about someone's performance, I usually ignored what he or she was doing. If I really cared about someone, I would encourage and gently push him, sometimes like "ugly on an ape," until he performed to the level I knew he could attain. Working with my children when they were young was so much fun for me as I encouraged and taught them how to walk as babies, helped with school work, showed them how to show respect to their mother and adults, or talked to them about dating as teens.

There are times when you must discipline—that is, challenge or encourage your employees to reach for new attainable goals. And this is done sometimes against their wishes. But if you have corporate goals to which they have at least tacitly agreed, they should readily get with the program you've laid out. Along with this goal setting, we should realize it is human nature for employees to resist change to some degree if those persons aren't the initiators of the new idea, even if they realize those ideas are best for them. Of course, the best way to counter that reaction is to involve the persons affected early on in the decision-making process.

An example of following through on discipline is when I wanted to better encourage one of our salesmen to get more sales credited to his account. It finally came down to the fact that he had to at least earn his commission or leave the company. Rather than leave Seaberg, he chose to have me work in a more disciplined manner with him so he could keep his job; I wouldn't lose a valuable employee; and we could achieve more sales and customers. When I let him know where he stood in very clear terms, he responded with a superb effort. I feel my actions let him know I wanted him to succeed at Seaberg.

A goal I set for my managers who weren't directly involved in sales was for each of them to meet with a different client at least once a month. I made the policy without very much of a chance for them to disagree because I felt so strongly about them knowing our customers well. Even though these manufacturing, accounting, and quality managers met with or talked to our clients whenever there was a problem of some sort to discuss, they had never just gone out on a typical sales call to see what needs Seaberg might fill for our valuable clientele. After we tried this approach, these managers saw the value for them to get closer to the customer. As one of the managers did tell me later, "We've got to do a better job of quoting to this customer because the buyer has to get to a base of only five subs." (A sub is a term for a subcontractor like Seaberg Industries.) It was refreshing and enjoyable for me to hear the statement that he wanted us to satisfy that customer's needs and keep the work.

It's the little things one does in one's work that makes the difference between success and failure. By disciplining yourself to do the little details very well time after time, you can have a successful business.

Last, when you discipline yourself to accept only the very best effort in what you do, you create the kind of pride that builds self-esteem. If you can have that honest feeling that not everyone can do the work as well as you, you have experienced a very good byproduct of using discipline to enrich your life and the lives of those around you.

## CHAPTER 13

# We Must Be Twice As Good to Be Good Enough

My life goal is to always try to do my best at whatever I do. I learned this lesson the hard way. At Iowa in the spring of my junior year, my basketball coach, Bucky O'Connor, was killed in a car accident. This had an effect on my outlook in life. In my senior year, just as the basketball season started, I had a girlfriend who hurt me emotionally. I started feeling sorry for myself, and it started a downward spiral that affected my basketball play so much that I hardly played in any games at the end of the season. It negatively affected most everything else I was doing. And the more I felt sorry for George, the worse it got. To not feel sorry for myself, get over it and not *think about me* was probably the most valuable lesson I learned in my college years.

Since graduating from college, I have striven to educate myself through formal schooling and on-the-job training in the army and at any company where I was an employee. Perhaps it is that I always tended to feel inferior because I didn't feel I had a thorough enough knowledge about whatever job I was given. I feel that a little tension on the job helps one to do his job better, but too many times my intensity boiled over into self-defeating, energy-robbing anxiety.

One of the best examples of my attitude that I had to be twice as good to be good enough happened in the late 1950s when I was at college. Bob Commings was a military service veteran playing as a starting guard on several Rose Bowl championship football teams at Iowa. He played offensive and defensive guard, as it was normal in those years for players to play both ways. His teammates told me that he played every down in practices and games like it was going to be his last one. He was even named MVP by his teammates his senior year. Bob knew he had to play hard because he weighed an unbelievable 165 pounds, blocking out and running around 220+ pound opposing linemen. Today linemen are three hundred pounds and only play offense or defense—quite a difference.

I describe Bob's attitude and corresponding effort as trying to *"be twice as good in order to be good enough."* This phrase was given to me by a local manufacturer, Julian Weigle, who became a very good friend to me. Julian was a Jew successfully making it in a non-Jewish manufacturing world, and one day I asked him the biggest reason why he succeeded financially as one of the largest tool and die manufacturers in the Midwest. He said this phrase was taught to him by his father as he was growing up in Davenport, Iowa. Julian shared this with me when he saw how hard I was working to feed my family and grow a business. Consequently, we became good business friends. I was even able to relate to him that I worshipped a Jewish carpenter named Jesus Christ.

The first machine I bought, other than a small welder, an anvil, and that railroad spring compressor, was an old, used Bridgeport vertical mill that Julian Weigle, owner of Swan Engineering, sold to me. He later told me he would have either sold it to me or given it to the local high school for their industrial arts shop. He would not have sold it to someone who would try to take work from him. I can still remember the day in 1974 his fork truck driver loaded the Bridgeport onto a wood pallet and drove it on a fork truck a block down busy Highway 67 to my rented shop at the back end of the auto body shop. I didn't have a fork truck of my own then, so we used the Swan one to set the machine in place.

Julian knew I was going into business anyway, and he wanted to offer me some friendly encouragement and let me know that I had a few friends out there. I later was able to send enough business his way to repay some of his kindnesses. This friendship started in 1974, lasted until he passed away some twenty years later, and is a fond memory of how people have helped me along the way.

The small manufacturing shop president/owner is quite close physically and emotionally to the factory floor where changes are constant and quick—hectic, too! Each day I went to work, my attitude was that I had to earn the respect of our employees that day.

## When Being Too Focused on Your Work Can Be Your Undoing

One incident concerning my son, Tom, sticks vividly in my mind to the present day. It was the middle of summer in the mid-1970s, and we were using the small shop parking lot and entryway to do finishing work on product for a customer. The square thirty-eight-hundred-square-foot, flat-roofed, white-walled, concrete block building just didn't have enough space for doing final assembly, so if it wasn't raining, we would do that work outside.

I was focused on our shop work and needed to have some cleanup done in the shop, so I called home from the office and told Tom that I needed to have him come down to the shop to help out. I went back in the shop to help with the work we were doing and forgot about Tom. Our shop was located in an alley just behind US Highway 67. This was a very busy, four-lane road (now five lanes wide) that went right through the middle of downtown Bettendorf. Large eighteen-wheel semi-trucks traveled this street throughout the day carrying their loads.

For some reason, I happened to glance up from our alley/parking lot/work area at the highway between two buildings that faced the busy roadway. In that instant, I saw my seventh-grade, twelve-year-old son, with his baseball hat pulled down so as not to be blown off by the traffic, pedaling on that very busy roadway. He had ridden his bicycle two miles, hugging the edge of the pavement in circumstances he shouldn't have been in, so he would be at the shop to help me when I needed him.

I was shook up and thought to myself, *What kind of a father am I to demand that my young son make a dangerous journey like this for me?* Needless to say, he went home with me that afternoon after work, with his bike in the back of the truck. I have asked God to forgive me for my thoughtlessness, and He has, but the memory is still burned into my mind.

Letting our management guard down can have catastrophic consequences if we're not aware of our surroundings. An example from our American history of relaxing at the wrong time is the story of Chief Joseph, one of the greatest military strategists in all of history. He led a remnant of the Nez Perce Native Americans toward Canada from Idaho in 1877. The five hundred-member tribe of warriors, women, children, and old people, with some twenty-five hundred head of horses, successfully and ingeniously eluded five thousand United States Calvary troops and scouts. But understandably, the Nez Perces were tired from the exhausting trek. The senior chief overruled Chief Joseph, who wanted to keep moving until the tribe was safely into Canada. But the chief halted the tribe about sixty miles south of the border to rest. Because the tribe relaxed too soon, they were captured just short of safety. If they had only kept moving and remained as vigilant as Joseph wanted, the Nez Perces would have escaped to their Canadian sanctuary.

In business, a complacent attitude by management can be the firm's death knell. Conversely, an alert and enthusiastic attitude in this present day of fast-changing strategies and business climates leads to employee confidence in the CEO or president and helps make the enterprise stronger financially.

I feel I was never able to fully relax with my customers. We became friends, but the clients sometimes had demands put on them by their management that went counter to what I desired. Therefore, I looked at the situation as an opportunity to help solve their challenges. This mindset was crucial because of the occasional rapid schedule changes for the assembly lines at customer plants. For example, in 1991 we were able to receive prints via fax (no Internet then) in the morning, quote the job, receive approval, and deliver small lots of fabricated parts in the afternoon by our company truck, if this kind of response was needed.

Obviously, we couldn't do this every day, but we did just this kind of thing on occasion. No matter how good a friend you can become with a client, he is still the customer, and he deserves the best you can do. Because of these occasional rush orders, things sometimes get so hectic that I felt like a commodities trader on LaSalle Street in downtown Chicago on his busiest day.

As I mentioned, a hectic business pace was both good and bad. The good was that there was no fat in our company, and everyone counted. The bad part was the stress of meeting schedule changes. From this I also realized that I couldn't just half retire when it was time for me to step aside. My work was either persistent service and concentration or getting out because the job required full-time effort to keep our heads above water and stay profitable.

An important facet to this chapter's small business principle of giving your best effort every time is what I learned a few years after starting the company in 1973. I have taken Cleaver Aptitude and Personality tests that showed my basic temperament to be sanguine, with a choleric backup. This means that I enjoy doing many tasks and keeping busy but with goals firmly in sight. This is not a bad profile for management or sales. The short side is that I became restless with handling too many details, causing me sometimes to "not see the forest for the trees." Initially I was so afraid of failing and at the same time having so much fun with creating a new business that it took me three years before I realized I needed to get deeper into selected details, rather than into all of them and driving my fellow workers nuts.

Then the pendulum seemed to swing the other way and I got too much into details. I began losing the survival battle on the management end. I got despondent and down on myself. It was times like these when I felt so low that I had to reach up to touch bottom.

Early in my work career when I was employed in the plant engineering departments at plants of Union Carbide Corporation in Ohio and The Pillsbury Company in Illinois, I found that if necessary, I could drop an assignment for a while for a change of pace or work on something new and more interesting. Not so at the small business! If I dropped a job for a while because we were losing money on it, or a higher-priority job came along, we couldn't just stop what we were doing or we would lose a customer. This could be especially painful if we had given our word we would do the work under a difficult deadline.

Once, during my first year as a manufacturer, I cost ARI Industries $15,000 ($75,000 in 2011) because I took a much-needed week's vacation with my family. I was wearing too many hats and didn't have a well enough trained staff to handle all our customer needs. The loss I refer to was on one job where we were designing and building several machining fixtures, and I ran out of time to work out the details for my crew to follow before I left.

This may seem like a small amount, but out of a first year's sales of $72,000 ($360,000 in 2011), it becomes rather significant. The employees were too new, I wasn't able to train an effective second-in-command yet, and I didn't have time then to effectively delegate the work to be done. So I went off hoping that the men would solve any unforeseen problems. The problems didn't get solved because I had the solutions in my head and didn't effectively pass them on to the men in the shop very well. When our family returned, I got to the job and didn't rest or sleep very much until the problems were addressed, solved, implemented, and completed to the customer's satisfaction. If you have ever had to meet a small business payroll with its inherent cash flow problems, you can appreciate what I was experiencing.

But what this kind of commitment means to a win-win kind of buyer in a client company is that the small contractor working for him is extremely loyal to him. The subcontractor will show a loyalty far above what people in the buyer's own company have in getting many of his projects completed on time, at least at the same quality, and on many occasions at a faster delivery rate. This is one reason why a prominent Fortune 50 company in the Midwest subcontracts as much as 80 percent of the cost of their equipment to others to make. I've read where this is the real secret for the manufacturing success of *Japan, Inc.* It is because the small business worker looks to his/her work not as a job but as food on the family table or the home mortgage payment or a calling.

For a manager or executive in larger firms, he may want to work to the best of his abilities because, "I'm just trying to keep my job." This statement means many things to these persons, and I think it's a valid and very good statement. For the little guy, this often means, "How can I stay solvent?" whether he's operating a body shop, shoe store, consulting service, job shop, or some other business. In the larger enterprise, a person can lose his job, which can be difficult. But as a small business owner, you could lose the farm, your home, and everything you own. The latter circumstance is fairly common when you have had to borrow money from the bank. It is a highly motivating factor in how hard you are willing to work at keeping the business.

When I was about eight years old, I learned a very valuable saying from my dad that has stuck with me since then. Dad supervised the night shift, from 5:00 p.m. to 5:00 a.m., at a local tool and die shop, E. G. Erickson Engineering Company. It was an early afternoon. He was preparing to go to work and was in the family bathroom shaving with his ceramic shaving cream mug, brush, and disposable razor. He was wearing his clean khaki work pants with his white tank top undershirt (also called a "wife beater," from the play, *A Streetcar Named Desire*, by Tennessee Williams). I was standing next to him curiously watching him attack his whiskers under the shaving cream at the bathroom sink. He turned, looked down at me, and said in his casual business voice, "George, a *winner never quits, and a quitter never wins.*" That was a significant emotional experience (SEE) for me.

I remembered that statement many times in my young life through my schooling and sports and flight school. But I had to find out if I believed in this saying several months after I had started my venture and was the only full-time employee.

Rewards of Giving Your Best

One of the sweetest moments with my dad happened at one of the saddest times in my young life. In the 1955–56 season, my high school team was rated as high as number two in the Illinois basketball poll. We had a twenty-five-game winning streak going into the sweet sixteen final tournament in Champaign. We lost our game with Princeton 52–51 in the last few seconds, after being ahead by eleven at the half. In the locker room afterward, I was crying hard because in my youthful thinking I thought that if I gave it my best effort, it would be enough to win the game. Dad came into the room in the blue suit and tie he wore to games, quietly walked over to where I sat in my drenched uniform, and without saying a word, bent over and kissed me on my wet, tear-stained cheek. His whiskered face felt like mild sandpaper against my face. He then stood up and quietly left the locker room. This is the only time he ever did this in my teen years. I'm now seventy-three years old, and I remember it like it happened yesterday. I was a very fortunate person to have such a loving man who was my father.

At the beginning of my owner career, I was doing some welding for a new customer at the Ever Tite Mfg. Co., a small two-person firm in an old brick one-story building in west Davenport, Iowa, along some railroad tracks. I was working out of my home then, and the Ever Tite plant manager let me use any of his 110 (I counted every one of them) old machines as I was considering buying the place. My "office" there was a dirty and oily wood skid with steel legs where I could put my paperwork and tools that I owned.

One day while trying to do a job, I literally sobbed, shaking from my frustration at not being able to satisfactorily weld this little job. I continuously prayed as I kept trying to weld a half-inch round bar that was eight inches long onto a one-inch diameter, one-sixteenth-inch thick wall, by six inches long tube for my construction equipment customer. I needed to finish and ship this work in the morning to put food on the family table. But I couldn't stay alone at my friend's plant, so I went home and called a friendly welding supplier. He came to the plant the next morning and showed me the more proper machine settings to use for the stick weld job. I completed the job successfully and got paid in time for my family to be provided with groceries. Later I was told how hard it was to weld different pieces like these together successfully.

For most people, life offers many interesting and intriguing surprises and turns. In the mid-eighties, the small bank I had been doing business with closed its doors unexpectedly when the top two officers were arrested by federal agents for fraud and theft and went to prison. Security Bank, Bettendorf, Iowa, was in a local market that was attractive to two of the largest nearby Iowa banks. The much larger bank was about to close on purchasing Security, my loan there was up for review, and I was assured that my loan would be assumed by the new bank owner.

For some reason, after two months, the first bank reneged and withdrew its offer. This meant that my loan would not be renewed. I asked one of the loan officers what I could do, and he said he didn't have any idea since his bank was no longer involved. When he told me this, I chuckled to myself and said that *somehow* I would get the loan. I walked out of the building a little shook up and without a clue where I could get another $450,000 loan for my undercapitalized company.

For persons who haven't applied for relatively large loans of this sort, it usually takes months to fill out the application forms; present your case to a bank; have a loan officer look at it with you; have him present the data to his bank's loan committee; and then, if it is approved without a further review, have the loan officer present the loan request to the Small

Business Administration (SBA) local office for their approval. And I still had to find a bank interested enough in the company to consider taking over my loan. You might say that while I had complete confidence my concerns would be met in some way by trusting in the Lord, I was a pretty nervous guy because I was rapidly running out of time.

Within a few days, I contacted the other bank that was now closing on their offer to purchase my formerly prosperous but now defunct bank. Their loan officer agreed to ask his bank to purchase my almost defaulted loan. By this time, I had only two weeks before I would be in irreversible arrears on my debts. The new banker told me he would work on my application, but he had never known of a SBA application being processed and approved in two weeks, much less in two months. If this bank had been a certified lending bank, we could have gotten the job done in a week, but since it wasn't, we had to contend with another delay in the loan process.

But the new banker and I got started anyway. I got whatever data the vice president, Brad Tregloan, wanted. We dotted the Is and crossed all the Ts and completed my application in a few days. To say that the banker did an exceptional detailing job would be an understatement. And he got the SBA Application approved in only one week! This had to be a banking first of some sort.

I know if I had let my discouragements get the best of me that our company would have ceased to exist in 1984, a little over ten years after beginning. This loaning episode confirmed my dad's borrowed saying that, "A winner never quits, and a quitter never wins."

It was also crucial that I spent a lot of time on my knees praying to the Lord for the guidance and blessings He did give me, not only in 1984 but throughout my career at Seaberg Industries.

## CHAPTER 14

# How Have People Become Employed at Seaberg?

When I first started our company, I averaged over seventy hours working each week, just as I expected to do. I just didn't think it could be so terrifying and at the same time so satisfying. Because I couldn't afford the best manufacturing help, and out of necessity to get parts out the door, I had to hire some people with marginal abilities and sometimes unusual personal problems that were often brought with them in the door to work. This led to my wanting to care for their social needs and at times allowing too much permissiveness on my part at work.

The strangest and very best story about my hiring someone occurred in September 1973. In the summer, we moved into the back of a small body shop owned by a friend, Jim Tully, who I met when we moved to the Quad Cities in 1972. Our space didn't have an office, so I asked Jim if I could build one, which he kindly agreed to do if I paid for all the building costs. For several weeks after I started the room construction project, I would work making parts during the day, go home for supper and see the kids, then go back and build my office out of concrete blocks. I covered those blocks on both sides with a plaster-like covering called Block-Bond rather than use cement to hold the blocks together. I also added two windows so I could see into the shop and added an entrance door to complete the basic construction.

One day in September, I drove to Peoria to make a routine sales call on a customer. Just as I crossed the Mississippi River on I80 from Iowa into Illinois, I spotted a young man with a beard standing in Levi's and a blue long-sleeved shirt at the entrance ramp hitchhiking and looking at me with the most forlorn look on his face. In those days, I picked up lots of hitchhikers on the highway because it was safe to do so and I felt young and strong enough to take care of myself.

I was so bothered by that young man's facial expression that I almost got off at the next ramp to return and offer him a ride. I was pressed for time, so I told the Lord that I would stop for the next hiker. Surprisingly, since it was a warm and sunny day, I didn't spot another person to pick up on that hundred-mile trip to Peoria and on my return trip home later. I feel that hitchhiker could have been an angel when I think of the consequences of my actions the next day.

That night I finished installing the ceiling tile around the recessed fluorescent lights as the last thing to do to completely enclose the office. In the morning when I went into our new fifteen-by-twenty-foot office in the newly rented thirty-eight-hundred-square-foot space, I was swarmed by hundreds of flies in that small office. We hadn't had a killing frost yet, and the flies had somehow swarmed in sometime during the night. I stormed out of the office and told someone I was going to K&K Hardware a few blocks away for fly paper.

I made my purchase, and when I was driving one and a half blocks away from the shop, I spotted a young man wearing a dirty white T-shirt and Levi's with a ponytail and scraggly beard with a downcast, I-don't-care look on his face. I told the Lord I would pick up the next hiker, so without thinking, I pulled over to the curb and asked him if I could give him a lift. There was something immediately charming about this polite and engaging twenty-something, so I invited him into our office and then decided to interview him for a job on the spot. This was my introduction to Craig Kinzer, eventually president of Seaberg Industries when I sold the company in 2006. In September of 1974, he was trying to become a house building contractor.

After the interview, I tried to call him several times and couldn't reach him. This was in the days before cell phones and answering machines, so it is understandable that we couldn't connect. I finally reached him after about two weeks and offered him a job as a welder since he told me that he knew how to weld. He accepted the offer, but I didn't know why until much later. Much later, Craig told me that in the morning just before I called him, he was praying to the Lord asking Him for guidance to find a job, and the phone then rang, with me on the line! This is another case of the good that happens when we ask for God's direction in our lives—what I call a God-cident.

His employment was working out so well for me that when I told him I needed another employee in the shop, he asked his high school buddy, Mark "Rocky" Robinson, to apply for a job at our place. Rocky did apply, and I hired him as a fabricator.

One rather amusing episode happened several times with Craig and Rocky of which I was unaware. On Mondays I started at 3:00 a.m. at the shop doing the coming week's employee and machine scheduling, a job I enjoyed doing. Weekday work started at 7:00 a.m. and ended at 3:00 p.m. for the other employees. Craig and Rocky were best buds, bright kids, and were in the talented and gifted program in their high school in Brecksville, Ohio. They would tool to work in Craig's beat-up old truck, and just as they were about to turn off the highway running by our shop in to work, Rocky would ask Craig if he wanted to get a coffee first. But this already was 7:00 a.m.!

They would leisurely drive down to a restaurant for their coffee and then later just as leisurely drive back to the shop. But just as they got to the turnoff, Rocky would ask Craig if he wanted another coffee. Craig said, "Sure," and they would turn around and have another cuppa. They then would show up at around 8:00 a.m. for work. I couldn't let them go because I was short of men (we had some eight shop men then), the job market was tight, and they were so talented and efficient once they got to work. Craig finally told me this 1975 story in 2008, time enough for me to laugh about it. Ah, the joys of starting a small business.

A clear indication of just how gifted these two twenty-three-year-old new hires were was when I needed to build an addition to the shop, with Jim Tully's permission. Craig and Rocky approached me and in their creativity suggested building the addition as a geodesic dome. I decided on half of a dome so it would be flush to the present building. The half dome was to be fifty feet in diameter to house a single-torch flame cutter and steel plate storage for cutting. The only trouble was there was a six-inch rise from the present building corner thirteen feet out into the yard. Using pencil and paper, they figured out the size of all the plywood triangles with the complication of providing for the rise and then sawed them out before putting up the wood frame. When they nailed the different-sized triangles to the frame, every piece fit perfectly. Not very many experienced carpenters or fabricators would have been able to do that. The picture on the cover of this book shows the triangles that formed the shell of the geodesic dome.

**1975. Front entrance to A.R.I. Industries shop in Bettendorf, IA, forerunner of Seaberg Industries. The racks are where Dale Schweinberger's new Mercedes-Benz was parked when our fork truck ran into it.**

1974. Larry Gainer, our first full-time employee, on the first fork truck we owned carrying a blue homemade hoist for carrying steel at shop entrance.

1974. Fork truck with hoist. In background is the view between buildings where the highway is located on other side of car. Once I made my twelve year old son ride his bike down dangerous Highway 67 to help me at the shop.

1975. Herman "The Human Crane" Buchwald with a fabricated fixture ready for shipment to the customer.

1974. Craig Kinzer forming a steel part on the railroad car spring compressor press that was converted to a press brake in the shop. This is where the author taught himself to weld the steel guides to the press cast iron components.

1974. The family Plymouth station wagon serving as the company freight hauler. The car springs were tested, but never broke while hauling parts.

1975. George Seaberg with special fabricated cart for a customer. Note the small A.R.I. logo on the back above the cart handle.

About a year after starting the business, I thought I would hire men on parole from prison to help get them get a start back into society. The first ones I employed worked out fairly well, and I felt I made a few friends among them. But none of them would stay working for me for longer than six months. They were white, Hispanic, and black, but they just seemed to get "itchy feet" and wanted to move on.

I remember the day I changed my thinking on the hiring of parolees. By this time we had relocated across the river, and I was still hiring former prisoners. It was about 1976 when we were a fifteen-employee company located in Moline, Illinois, and I hired two young men who were friends from Davenport, the only ones with past criminal records in our employ at the time. After they began working for us, we started having some petty thievery. We were able to catch one of them in the act of taking someone's personal tools, and I fired him.

I was never able to catch the other one because he was quite intelligent and very careful. Willy was very engaging, with a pleasing personality, and he was popular with his fellow workers. He was so bright in figuring out his shop work, and nobody could ever beat him in chess on the noon breaks. I tried everything to catch his thieving, even calling a school principal friend in Chicago's inner city, Hazel Nelson, and asking her how I could catch him. Even being as street-wise as Hazel was, we couldn't come up with a scheme to nab him in the act of stealing a tool.

It was such a waste to see this charismatic young man, whom I personally liked, not be able to overcome his character flaws. Our theft stopped when Willy quit. Later I learned he got in trouble with the law again and was put back into the Iowa penal system where, at twenty-three years of age, he had already spent half of his life behind bars. I never heard about him again, and I think he probably never survived to his thirtieth birthday.

After this experience, I told the rest of the crew that for a company as small and financially fragile as ours, it was going to be business as usual, and whatever social service help we now gave to others would have to be done after hours and not on company time. It was impossible then to have social ministry and business at Seaberg because it took away from our necessary business focus.

After that experience, I told our employees how much their future pay was affected by what a few bad characters could do to the company. The employees already working for us started taking a closer look at new hires after that. This strictly business stance in hiring eventually evolved to a three-person interview process that screened all job applicants, with me usually being one of the interviewers.

I borrowed this interview idea from The Lincoln Electric Company that I have referred to previously. At this time in the 1980s, every job applicant at the twenty-five-hundred-person main plant of Lincoln was interviewed by the three factory division vice presidents. One interviewer might spot a character flaw or unusual attribute that others might miss. Three viewpoints in an interview are usually better than one. The idea is that there never will be a problem transferring an employee to any one of the three plant divisions because the person in charge of that division had interviewed and approved the applicant. This has apparently saved potential friction within the company.

If I felt that a person's honesty was in question, he never got past the interview stage. Since 1982 we have learned it is better to do without a warm body than have stressful customer work because of an unqualified employee. Inferior (unqualified) workers will eventually cause all kinds of quality and production problems.

When I left Seaberg in 2006, our hiring process went something like this:

1.  Craig or I looked at all job applications. We would look to see if the person met our minimum requirements, such as at least having a high school or GED diploma, using a present employee as a reference (the applicant got an automatic interview if an employee recommended him or her), and what background experience this person had. It was at this point where we usually disqualified 80 percent of the applicants.
2.  We then filed the remaining applications into categories of professional/management; clerical; technician; machine operator; machinist; CNC machinist; and welder/fabricator.
3.  When a specific need arose, we looked at our applicant file. If there were not enough qualified candidates, I placed ads in the

local papers. In the past, using this technique usually satisfied our requirements.

4. We then set up a two- or three-day period where the applicants were asked to come in at agreed-on times to begin interviewing.

It was surprising to me to learn how few small firms would take the time to call the applicant references. Maybe the owner didn't feel he could take the time to do this checking. I know I've felt that way too many times. And you're usually your busiest when you're trying to hire someone. However, calling references was just one more nugget of information that could help in the hiring process.

Things we primarily looked for in prospects were: neatness, positive attitude, desire for the job, mental ability to think, education, habits, his personal tools, work experience, print reading ability, and math ability.

After selling the business, the new owners resorted to using personnel agencies to screen out unfavorable candidates. If the temporary help firms approved of someone, he was then interviewed at the company by at least one owner. This was more efficient, and even if there was a fee charged by the agencies, the owners felt their time saved more than they paid for the service.

*Positive mental attitude.* This was one of the more important personal attributes we tried to determine during the interview process. My thoughts were identical to comments made by Dr. Charles Swindoll, a noted Christian minister and speaker:

> The longer I live, the more I realize the impact of attitude on life. Attitude, to me, is more important than facts. It is more important than the past, than education, than money, than circumstances, than failures, than successes, than what other people think or say or do. It is more important than appearance, giftedness, or skill. It will make or break a company ... a church ... a home. The remarkable thing is we have a choice every day regarding the attitude we will embrace for that day. We cannot change our past ... we cannot change the

fact that people will act in a certain way. We cannot change the inevitable. The only thing we can do is play on the one string we have, and that is our attitude ... I am convinced that life is ten percent what happens to me and ninety percent how I react to it. And so it is with you ... we are in charge of our attitudes.[7]

Abraham Lincoln said, "Most people are about as happy as they make up their minds to be." I agree with the statement. If the going gets a little tough in the workplace due to outside circumstances, the person who constantly chooses to take a positive view of things will help carry, and in some cases will save, the company when there is little hope for survival. When I had my heart arrhythmia and was out of commission for several months, my wife was *not* going to let anything or anyone let the company disappear. She didn't like doing it, but she was a real mother bear about keeping the company on firm footing until I got back. If you met Sue today you would see a quiet, friendly, and private person—unless the chips were down. Craig Kinzer, then my vice president, was a great help and support at that time with his usual positive outlook.

If an applicant was being hired for a position in management, or for a highly technical area like engineering, we would modify our format slightly. We have used such interview techniques as Cleaver Aptitude Tests (I've found these to be 100 percent accurate), handwriting analyses, and/or interviews with plant team leaders.

If the person accepted our conditions of employment, then he was hired. At the time of hiring, the necessary government data and proper insurance forms were filled out. Then his orientation began. First, our accountant explained our brief policies and procedures pamphlet, followed by the personnel review format, made introductions to the office personnel, and then was brought out on a plant tour where he was introduced to every one of his new fellow employees (the only persons he might not meet could be those on the second or third shifts). I particularly felt that it was very important for a new person to be introduced to all our employees to:

1.   Help them feel welcome sooner by showing that little bit of extra attention.

---

7    Dr. Charles Swindoll, *Homemade*, USPS, Vol. 15, No. 11, November 1991.

2. To help that new hire realize how important he was to our organization (more of that "Do you walk the talk?" dialogue later).

Next, he met with our maintenance manager, Dave Paxton, who was also our fire and safety director. Dave would explain the appropriate clothing, such as renting company uniforms, buying safety shoes before working, when it was required to wear safety glasses, and other safety procedures we followed. The new employee was shown how to properly dispose of shop towels, where the fire extinguishers were located, and other similar safety/fire procedures. The new hire would also begin fork truck driver training if he didn't have a fork truck driver's license. No one was allowed to drive a fork truck at Seaberg without a license.

After Dave completed his orientation, he introduced the new person to our quality assurance and training manager. The manager explained QA terms and procedures. He also gave the trainee his *"I care about quality"* card and explained what each statement on the card meant. Depending on what work level the new hire began, the training then continued on a path geared to meet the new person's needs and abilities.

Our vice president of manufacturing next explained the part process sheets and how to properly use them. The new man was then assigned to a team leader for orientation into his specific work assignment. The team leader served as his coach and teacher until he felt comfortable in the new job.

Within a short period of time, the new employee would spend four contact hours in the beginning quality assurance course, ten hours in the statistical process control course, and two hours in the building a chain of customers course, all taught on company time.

From the above description of our new employee orientation, you can see that we spent a fair amount of money before the person, whether in the office or shop, became productive. But we believed that even for a small business, this would save costs in the short run as well as long term.

## Chapter 15

# Personnel Reviews: Know Where You Stand

This chapter is about what I think is the best way to help an employee reach his or her full potential. The best way is to let employees know where they stand relative to other company employees in their job performance. The most productive workers I've been associated with like to have their work measured and recognized.

Even though I used about five company review systems while we developed our system, the bulk of what I did came from The Lincoln Electric Company. I even used part of their published articles of incorporation when I incorporated my company. Lincoln began their merit rating system in 1942, long before others even thought about it. They put numbers to their evaluations rather than just subjective opinions.

In my almost fifty-year professional military, engineer, and owner career, I studied many employee review plans to see which one would be best for helping an individual being evaluated to want to perform better after his review. The first one I had was while on active duty in the army. In my opinion, the army process seemed too political and meaningless. Almost every company commander I knew evidently thought he had to have the top 10 percent of the army's officer corps under his command, which was impossible. At least that's how the ratings I saw turned out. I hope that by now a more objective and honest rating system has been instituted in the military where the officers are rated more objectively and honestly.

After leaving what was an enjoyable military tour of duty flying helicopters, I had my first review in industry. This evaluation was a little better, because a few constructive criticisms were given to me, along with the "atta boys." I believe that personnel evaluation systems have actually improved over the years as companies have paid more attention to their employees and treated them as the valuable assets they are rather just being nice. I think part of it is the boss or manager not wanting to hurt employees' feelings and also wanting to be a nice guy and popular with those working for him or her.

I want the reader to please understand that it is important to find the most objective way for a person to know where he stands in his efforts to work to the best of his abilities. The key is to measure as objectively as possible by putting numbers to the dedication a person shows to the company for whom he chooses to work. A good performance rating system at a small company will include such things as contribution to quality, professional development, cost contributions, sales contributions, and how well one manages the company assets under one's responsibility.

I wanted to use the same format to evaluate employees in all company job classifications. Besides being simpler to use, if someone changed his position from, say, a machinist to a salesman, his overall performance would be easier to track when using the same format.

Every six months, all employees in our company were given a personnel review. I conducted reviews of the four managers who reported to me. They in turn reviewed with me the job I was doing as it related to them. After the manager reviews were completed, the rest of the company employees were given their individual feedback meetings. My goal was for each review to take no longer than fifteen minutes because if there was a relatively high level of communication among employees daily, there would be no surprises that would require a lot of explanation in a review.

For our sales manager, there were no reviews for him to conduct since we had no other full-time salespersons. The controller conducted reviews with the office technicians. The engineering manager had his reviews with the engineers and technicians in his department. Obviously, the biggest review effort fell on the shoulders of the vice president of manufacturing, Craig Kinzer, because he had almost 80 percent of the plant employees under his responsibility and authority.

Craig had seven team leaders (TLs) and two managers who reported to him. After he conducted his personnel reviews and the appropriate people signed off on them, the TLs and managers reviewed each one of their personnel. I approved *all* personnel reviews to keep a control on personnel matters and to be sure that these important employee meetings were properly conducted.

Our goal was to have all employees reviewed with my approval initials (the last step in the process) within one month of when the process began. Ideally, the process started the middle of each May and November.

The following is the format of our *Employee Rating System*.

---

Date _____

*Employee Rating System*

Employee name _____

1. Done twice a year: May and November.

2. Ratings were made by each manager of the employees under his responsibility.
   A. The president rated the VP of mfg., controller, QA mgr., and sales mgr.
   B. The VP of mfg. rated TLs, maint. mgr., and mfg. engrg. mgr.
   C. Controller, QA and trng. mgr., and maint. mgr. rated all the personnel reporting directly to them.
   D. TLs rated the personnel reporting directly to them.

3. President reviews *all* ratings twice each year. I do not feel this is micromanaging but being sure on my part that ratings were done and that they were fair to all.

4. Four areas comprised the *rating system.*

    A.  Output—This rating was done jointly by the TL and the VP of manufacturing or with other TLs in the conference room.           25 points average

    B.  Quality—This rating was done jointly by the TL and the QA manager or with other TLs.       25 points average

    C.  Dependability—This rating was done by the TL.
                                   25 points average

    D.  Ideas and Cooperation—This rating was done by the TL and the engineering manager.      25 points average

5.  One hundred points were all that were allotted per member in a group. For example, five persons in a group meant the team leader had five hundred points total to use at his discretion. If someone rated over 110 points, a letter justifying this had to go with the rating.

6.  This rating helped determine your pay raises; bonuses; promotions; and layoffs. Other factors that determined pay were company financial health and market conditions.

Output—This rates how much productive work you actually turn out and your willingness not to hold back and also recognized your attendance record.

1.  Ability to understand the individual job requirements.
2.  Your skill at doing the work effectively and efficiently.
3.  Days absent _____. Each day is a half point deducted in computing that period's bonus. Lost days due to work accident or work-related illness do not count toward days absent.
4.  Preventive maintenance competence is part of this.
5.  Rating. <u>1</u>     5     10     15     20     25     30     35

Quality—this rates the quality of the work you do. It also reflects your success in eliminating errors and in reducing scrap.

1.  How well does your work contribute to reduced variability around client specification targets?
2.  Frequency of re-inspections due to your work.
3.  Process quality improvements.

4. Inspection competence.

5. How well do you use and maintain proper QA maintenance systems (SPC, gaging, first article inspection, part count, reject report)?

6. Housekeeping is part of your quality rating.

7. Rating.

| 1 | 5 | 10 | 15 | 20 | 25 | 30 | 35 |
|---|---|----|----|----|----|----|----|

Dependability—this rates how well your team leaders have been able to depend on you to do those things that have been expected of you.

1. Days late _____. People are expected to be at work at least five minutes before shift change so as not to inconvenience others, especially those on the preceding shift.

2. Work safety performance.

3. Personal and machine housekeeping.

4. Care of company and personal tools.

5. Time card maintenance (clarity and neatness of your writing).

6. Rating.

| 1 | 5 | 10 | 15 | 20 | 25 | 30 | 35 |
|---|---|----|----|----|----|----|----|

Ideas and Cooperation—This rates your cooperation, ideas, and initiative.

1. New ideas and new methods (poke yoke, kanban, JIT, return on investment, and process improvements) are important to your company in our continuing effort to reduce costs, increase output, and improve quality, work safety, and our relationships with our clients. This part credits you for your ideas and initiative used to help in this direction.

2. It also rates your cooperation (how well you work with others as a team). Such factors as your attitude toward coworkers and the company; your efforts to share your expertise with others; and your cooperation in installing new methods smoothly are considered here.

3. Flexibility in meeting company work requirements.

4.  What kind of schooling/training have you done/had in the last six months to help improve your productivity?

5.  Rating.

| 1 | 5 | 10 | 15 | 20 | 25 | 30 | 35 |
|---|---|----|----|----|----|----|----|

        Totals

        Output               _____

        Quality              _____

        Dependability     _____

        Ideas and Cooperation    _____

                     Total         _____

Team Leader or Manager     _____

           President     _____

               Date     _____

---

Our people, with their excellent talents and attitudes, were the heart of our company's day-to-day successes. Whenever I was invited to speak about Seaberg Industries' accomplishments, I always said something like, "You can replicate our plant anywhere in the world, but you can't replicate the people in it. That is what spells the difference in the successes we've had."

The following is another method that some companies used for rating people in purchasing functions:

1.  Personal character development. This has the highest priority. This includes schooling to help the person's general development with such subjects as Dale Carnegie public speaking courses. Specific development courses could include work toward an MBA, becoming a certified purchasing manager, a professional engineer license, a certified quality engineer license (almost a customer requirement in the later 2000s), or an American Production and Inventory Control Society certification.

2.  Quality contributions to the company. It might be a faster way to process quotations or discovering a uniform method for

evaluating supplier quality. Some companies now subcontract out the inspection function with incentives for how many supplier rejections they discover. I think this is terribly short sighted by the client companies since it tends to destroy cooperation between supplier and client. One item I've observed in my past relations in working for large companies is that many times the costs the clients mention to suppliers that have been internally generated are far off the mark. International Harvester Company went bankrupt, but it was from something other than not knowing their piece part costs.

In 1982 when Seaberg started dealing with IHC in some detail, their purchasing personnel had the best grasp of piece part costs of any company we had been dealing with up to that time. With this company we were able to work together on analyzing their internal costing only after the project manager was able to uncover the true costs of the parts we were seeking to make for the company. From that pioneering work, that particular manager at the East Moline plant, Ron Mason, went on to bigger and better promotions with a company that later bought much of the former IHC.

3. Cost pricing. I thought this would be the top priority, but evidently the company doing this was taking the long view toward the purchasing employees' understanding that "price-only" wasn't necessarily the best value to the company.

4. Cost reductions. It was interesting to see this as fourth on the manager's priority rating system. What cost reductions have you made in the items you buy for the company? Have you come up with a way to negotiate a win-win contract that substantially reduces prices? Some of our client personnel have done outstanding work in this area.

5. Asset management. How well do you manage the assets under your authority? This might include a trend toward fewer suppliers, or it might be a creative new way to sole source families of parts. It could also be how many field trips are taken to visit suppliers or how effectively the buyer used his time, since time is definitely an asset.

For Seaberg Industries, we needed to use a more objective, transferable form for rating our employees than the above rating system. However, the above style has been successfully implemented in larger companies.

**1981. Seaberg employees inside the Moline plant in front of a new Mori Seiki turning center.**

**First row, l. to r.: Mike Parkin, Ken Sparbel, Kevin Baker, Cheryl Wedra, Mary Kay Widen, Thurlow Adams.**

**Second row: Tom Knapper, Tom Seaberg, Greg Foster, John Devinney, Charlie Bicknell, Dean Grandfield, Dennis Flockhart, Rhett Bicknell, Craig Kinzer, Harold Paget.**

**Third row: George Seaberg.**

**1982. New W.A. Whitney Plasma Cutter-Punch, first big financial purchase. One man on this machine was more productive than 10 persons in fabricating. This unit enabled Seaberg Industries to get into production in the oil industry and kept us in business. John Devinney is the operator.**

**1983. Completed oilwell workover rig prepared for shipment at the Moline plant. Seaberg made two prototypes before production was halted because of the cataclysmic drop in oil demand.**

1983. Oilwell workover rig opening an older oil well in Salem, IL. These units were used to reopen capped oil wells to begin new production. At that time these rigs were the only ones in the oil fields using John Deere engines for power. George and Tom Seaberg standing with unidentified customer.

1983. A different view of the same workover rig at the work site showing the pumping jack that will be placed over the oil hole after the well is opened. The pumping jack will extract the crude oil for delivery to a refinery. Tom and George Seaberg standing next to wildcatter who will complete the oil well hookup.

## Chapter 16

# The Team Leader

A few months after my first employee, Larry Gainer, agreed to join our company, I promoted him to supervisor because I couldn't supervise the floor and run the business at the same time. I also thought he could handle the responsibility. Larry also operated equipment while coordinating work the other men did. I still had to travel to see customers, quote work, do all part inspections, work out financing needs, organize the work for the shop, and run machines myself. I was also building our office in the evenings during that time in the summer of 1974.

A few years after that, while still located in the back of the body shop, we kept growing and got to the point where we needed someone besides me who would spend over 90 percent of his time supervising the shop work. About then I felt a need to add a position of vice president of manufacturing. This job was necessary for someone to lead several foremen and handle administrative duties for me when I had to be traveling.

This new layer of administration was in accord with accepted wisdom of the 1970s. "Watching the employees" consisted of specifying what work each department had to do, inspecting work in process, troubleshooting problem areas, and working with people problems.

I still believed that something was missing in our operations. I then did away with the supervisor position and instead formed the team leader (abbreviated to TL) function. As proof of the correctness of this action, our sales per employee per year dramatically increased. We had created a synergy of every employee wanting to work together more as teammates than as individuals. In 1990 we lowered our "direct labor" (I prefer using the term "total labor," so I only used it here for clarity) as a percent of sales by over 30 percent.

The TL functioned much like a squad leader in the army or the marines. It's the management position closest to, and part of, the people making the parts and is the interface between the administration and the hourly work force. In the military squad, the leader is usually a sergeant and answers for his personnel, trains them, and helps take care of social needs when on the job and sometimes off the job. The TL has a machine to operate and can make product on any of the machines and do any of the functions of those under his responsibility.

At Seaberg the TL can have anywhere from none to as many as eight persons he works with/for on his team. When he doesn't have anyone but has a specialized machine profit center to manage, the potential is there for the TL to have others temporarily work for him on short notice. Such was the case for the CNC turning center team leader once, where his work was built around operating two turning centers without anyone reporting to him but assisting him as needed by a fork truck driver supplying parts to him and another trucking away his finished parts.

The team leader worked *for* his team because the other team members were his in-house customers, and he worked to satisfy their production needs much the same way as they reciprocated to him. There were also dotted line relationships on the organizational chart for persons with the same job function on another shift he didn't work directly with but to whom he gave specific instructions.

For example, our first-step processing and shipping team leader was on the first shift and among other duties, did the processing, material ordering, training, and scheduling of work that was done by the CNC plasma cutter-punching machine. He also trained and instructed the third-shift operator on preventive maintenance and routine maintenance to perform on the machine and scheduled the production work of the second-shift operator. The second- and third-shift team leaders did the personnel reviews for the men on those shifts, but the first shift TL had significant input on those reviews.

What did a team leader do that was different from what a foreman or supervisor did? The biggest differences were that he was neither an enforcer of management decisions nor a go-between between management and the worker. This was because he was a worker and a manager like everyone else in the company. Group pressure was the enforcer of standards. This would take longer to implement than more traditional ways, but this method of achieving productivity gains was better simply because it was fairer to all employees (the poor performers were more easily exposed), and it gets support from all the employees involved in a specific problem/opportunity. Quality audits and process time analyses showed where the problems were.

If an employee under his authority had a problem that was identified by the responsible TL, the first step to correct it would be to retrain the individual. If the person with the problem didn't respond affirmatively, then we resorted to our four-step disciplinary procedure:

1.  Verbal warning
2.  Letter of reprimand
3.  One day off without pay
4.  Self-dismissal. By this I mean that an employee wasn't fired. He dismissed himself because he didn't live up to the required standards.

Usually a verbal warning was all that was needed to correct a situation that got beyond the retraining stage. A letter of reprimand did get the attention of the offender many times with good results. One time we put a letter in one of our welder's file and he got so determined to prove how good he was to me that he proceeded to set all-new welding quality records. And he just continued to improve, to everyone's benefit. He got the pay raises he deserved from his new attitude.

Whenever a person was given a day off without pay, he shortly thereafter usually dismissed himself by not performing up to Seaberg and client standards. When a person was fired, he really demonstrated that he chose to not follow our work standards.

In order to become a team leader, the person was either the best at his job or had good lead-by-example qualities, much like a sergeant in the military. Of course, we have made our share of promotion mistakes, but we wanted an employee who we felt had potential to be given the opportunity to see for himself if he could fill a team leader's shoes. The order of qualities we looked for in a TL were:

1. High output. He had to have earned the respect of his fellow employees by his example of a continuously high level of productive work.

2. Quality. Low rejects and good inspection techniques were important.

3. Dependability and diligence in his work. The TL was at work on time, so we could expect the employees for whom he was responsible to be on time. And when the TL was dependable, the rest of his team followed his example.

4. Ideas and cooperation. We needed a constant flow of innovative ideas to remain a strong company. When the team leader helped create this atmosphere and encouraged cooperation among his people, it was much easier and cheaper to get the product to the customer.

5. Personal demeanor and housekeeping. It was a real challenge for me to find a way to make this important to some of our employees. But usually, if a person had positive self-esteem, he had good personal hygiene habits.

6. Integrity. When a person is trusted with his work, the good that results from this trust becomes contagious throughout the company.

7. Ability to instruct. The TL needed to be able to teach skills to those who worked for him. That is, he would be able to do on-the-job training (OJT) of anyone put in his charge. I liked to hire ex-military because they responded well to training and they had probably been taught how to train others.

One other requirement we generally had was that the TL was in the apprenticeship program or was a graduate. We did make an exception for one man. He was very talented, knew more in his job than anyone else in the company, and always shared his knowledge freely with his fellow employees.

The TL rated those reporting to him twice a year, as was previously covered in chapter 15. He also prepared the team work instructions after getting them from the vice president of manufacturing (this position was later changed to manufacturing manager). The TL then had the freedom to look for the best ways to improve on the work assigned to his team.

The benefits of this working relationship to Seaberg were:

1. The person actually working at a process could express his views more freely without fear than under a supervisor method of management.
2. Productive work got done with a minimum of overhead since all hands did direct labor work.
3. Personnel problems were reduced since the team tried to work them out and didn't have to be reported up the ladder for approval in handling whatever the problem was.
4. It was more fun for all employees to work in this kind of atmosphere and thus more and better work got done.

Peter Drucker commented that it is a coming trend for institutions to have flatter organization charts with the lowest management level of people taking more responsibility for the work output. Why? I think that world-class companies chose to be flatter because it got them closer to their customers. Too bad our federal government is going in the opposite direction.

In January of 1990, I told our managers that I was going to start working four hours per week on the second and third shifts. This wasn't a very popular idea with anyone but me. The employees thought I was going to play *I Spy* (which I actually did to find out why we weren't producing better). But I was also able to become better friends with most of the off-first shift people, which only seemed normal to me since I had hired them. A few below-average workers didn't like my presence, and they eventually left, mostly because they couldn't keep up with the good work the other employees were doing. Plus, I was able to look more closely at the implementation of many of the ideas our technicians, machine operators, machinists, and welders had shared with me.

As they learned to trust me more again, the Poke Yoke (mistake proofing) ideas from everyone began to rise. During 1990, my estimate is that we implemented fifteen to twenty Poke Yoke ideas per employee, almost all costing less than $500. In fact, about 90 percent of these money-saving ideas cost well below $100.

We continued to increase the number of good things we did for the company. The proof is that we lowered prices, increased profits, and increased wages. In 1991, I estimate that we implemented about fifty Poke Yoke ideas per employee per year, and this figure continued to improve each year.

At the same time in 1990, our newly promoted quality assurance manager, Rhett Bicknell, who was then a ten-year employee, said he wanted to work out of his position and didn't want to have *any* inspectors. Because of his superb attitude and work ethic, he *did* work out of his position ... right into a promotion to our newly created position as quality assurance and training manager. He just walked as he talked by doing away with a need for a full-time QA manager. He could then "hire" one of the better shop employees to work in the QA lab on a three-month training program as an inspection technician. There the technician worked full time inspecting all kinds of parts under the teaching and guidance of Rhett. After a year, we had four more shop people who were better versed in inspection methods and techniques and statistical process control (SPC) who returned to the shop floor as a machine operator, welder, or machinist. There the newly trained employee could do an even better job making production parts and serve as his own inspector.

Whereas the quality lab used to be a beehive of activity, the office was now empty most of the time on the second and third shifts, and all the shop personnel were now out on the floor running machines and making good parts. All the while our quality was improving. In the mid-1990s, our reject rate was at 0.5 percent and continued to fall. Our clients also noticed this improvement because they kept detailed performance stats on quality, price, and delivery on their suppliers.

I put in the budget low-cost items that our TLs could use to purchase miscellaneous equipment for their departments based on our financial performance the previous month. This was a small way for the TLs to feel they were making a more significant contribution to company profitability and growth. They had to spend that $200 within the next month or they lost it. I monitored it closely to be sure they were sound purchases. These relatively inexpensive items proved to be outstanding productivity improvers. I kept the dollar amount per team leader low so no one lost his perspective on the idea that the best productivity improvement ideas were in the little things we did. These little things became significant productivity improvers over a fairly short period of time.

CHAPTER 17

# The Customer Is Always Right

In the early days of Seaberg Industries' operations, it was easy for me to feel looked down on by the people to whom I was trying to sell our services. It was probably pity on their part and an inferiority complex on mine. Being in the place where I needed work in order to feed my family made me quite sensitive to others' remarks and jokes. But no matter how I felt, I knew that *the customer is always right* even when my position on an issue differed from the customer's. This is much like the "no questions asked" policy of most leading retail companies handling returned goods from the customer, such as Craftsman or True Value hardware tools.

Our company mission statement was to "Create A Customer and Satisfy His Needs." What did this mean? We certainly weren't trying to create another company but rather to take an existing concern and turn it into a client of ours by satisfying the client's needs through manufacturing and furnishing products in our market niche. And during this beginning-of-a-relationship stage, the small supplier felt like he was walking on eggshells when dealing with the new customer. He didn't want to inadvertently hurt any sales progress that had already been made.

Each customer we dealt with had similar needs of wanting a quality product, delivered in a timely way, at the best price, with an ability to meet changing production needs. But one of these four customer needs (quality, delivery, price, flexibility) would be dominant at any given time. One customer might say they wanted all four but only let their work out to the lowest bidder (strictly an anti-W. Edwards

Deming thing). Another might only want the delivery because *their* customers would only buy when the product was in the back room. If you supplied oil field products during the late 1970s oil boom, and if you could deliver the product on short notice, you had a sale without regard for the price. But several years later, it seemed that you couldn't give away your oil patch products. A severe oil shortage occurred when the Gulf of Mexico oil spill happened in 2010, putting over eighty thousand people out of work in the Gulf area. The people repairing the spill couldn't get the critical equipment no matter what the cost. The moral of this story is that sometimes the customer knows what needs to be done (cap the oil well hole) but can't get the right solution (how to cap the oil well hole).

The human body exhibits some seventeen thousand different kinds of nonverbal communication. It's easy to understand that I was always alert when visiting with our clients because I wanted to pick up on anything, especially nonverbal kinds of indications, that would give me clues on how to have them want to choose Seaberg when they needed to have services of our kind done.

A classic case in my business was the way part drawings were interpreted when the specifications on the drawings were not complete. If we had problems understanding what to do, who should we contact? Some buyers wanted to be involved in *all* the details while other buyers wanted different personnel in their company to be contacted who were more competent in drawing interpretations. If we were awarded the bid with a new buyer, we had to be careful that we accommodated this new person satisfactorily. And sometimes because these buyers were kept very busy, they could become irritated at even small comments from us that might prevent us from having any follow-on orders.

This brings up another point I wanted to make about supplier-client relationships: We tried never to assume anything about the customer because by common understanding, *assume* means "to make an *ass* of *u* and *me*." We wanted to *know* the facts when trying to please those who indirectly provided for our families, not *think* we know what they wanted. I've found in my experiences that the better clients let us know in no uncertain terms when we screwed up in our business dealings, but along with those kicks in the behind, we also got lots of "Atta boys!"

A significant breakthrough came about in 1990 when one of our clients let us voice our opinions on mutual business problems. Up until that time, this company had never tolerated any of this kind of feedback from any suppliers. But when the buyers realized that they would save money by these kinds of negotiations, they quickly changed their attitudes to a more cooperative we're-on-the-same-team policy.

That same client's 1989 official corporate statement to their certified suppliers was, "Be the best, through a winning partnership." And they continued to work at it, to our thankfulness. The process seemed slow at times, and then there would be a spurt where we would be pushed rapidly along in this working relationship.

Professional salesmen and business psychologists state that it is human nature for it to take at least three visits by a salesman, including phone calls or emails, to a customer before an order is written or a sale is made.[8] It doesn't make a difference whether you are selling cars, encyclopedias, or mutual funds. The reason why is that people need exposure to what is being sold and time to mull the idea or proposal over in their minds. Of course, if it's an incidental item, like a candy bar, or an emergency, like a burst appendix, the rule doesn't apply. But for my first several years, if it looked like a buyer was interested in what we offered after my first visit, I tried to make the other two visits within two weeks but was careful to not appear pushy for a sale.

In those early days, it seemed the more desperate I was to get an order, the more often I got the work by this fast-track selling. A word of caution about trying to go too fast is that sometimes when the first order comes quickly, follow-up orders stop repeating themselves quickly because the buyer can feel he is being pressured into making out a purchase order.

The Pareto Principle of 20-80 also pertains to customer dealings. This means that 20 percent of our clients give us 80 percent of our sales. I've tracked this phenomenon since 1973 when my company was started. Each year I listed the top 20 percent of our customers based on sales figures, and I found that their orders totaled 80 percent of total sales every year within a few percentage points. And it made no difference if the 20 percent were mostly new or old customers. My brother-in-law

---

8    Chief among data available are: Brian Tracy, *The Psychology of Selling* CDs; and Denis Waitley, *Psychology of Winning* CDs

was a successful insurance salesman, with his own agency. He told me that each year he lost 20 percent of his customers for any number of reasons, so in five years he could be out of business if he didn't look for new customers. I felt somewhat the same way. That is why we were constantly on the lookout for new opportunities while keeping close to our present customers. For me, serving the customer properly was a lot of fun, especially when I won a "package of gum" with them by wagering on Hawkeye football and basketball games. Sales follow-up was a lot of work and took up a lot of valuable time. And that follow-up principle definitely was worth the effort.

CHAPTER 18

# It's Great to Have Competition (but Don't Let It Get Too Good!)

Without competition, the human race would still be pounding rocks by hand instead of planning a manned space mission to Mars or going to the local Starbucks for a latte.

An example of the evolving of good competition is grain harvesting. For thousands of years, grain was harvested with a hand sickle. Then during the American Revolution, the scythe was invented to allow a man to cut grain in a standing position versus stooping. Production went from two up to three acres of harvesting per day, a 50 percent gain in production. In about 1831, the horse-drawn reaper was invented and eventually increased grain production to seventeen acres per day. And the grain equipment competition was on! Many of these kinds of companies were started, and before long the harvester was patented, which in turn led to the invention of the combine to make it possible for the farmer to multiply his efforts many more times.

I won't get into the evolution of the computer too much. I used a slide rule and pencil to make engineering drawings in college in the 1950s. Recently I helped start a robotics club at a local high school. I'm seeing young people write their own programs from the Internet and developing outstanding 3D exploded view drawings of their robots. This is evidence of free-market competition at its best.

In Western European countries and in the former Eastern bloc, we know that a certain amount of competition helped people work better. The clearest illustration I can think of has been the differences between the eastern and western parts of Berlin, Germany, in early 1995. Without competition and free-market incentives, I saw in East Berlin that only one block-long street of apartments were improved during the forty-five-year "Great Leap Forward" for Communism. The East Germans were all given the same wages whether or not they worked at a job, and they only paid about $3 per month for their apartments. There hadn't been any construction of note, and all the buildings were an ugly gray color.

Contrast that condition with the many thousands of kilometers of streets of new or rebuilt apartments in the western part of the city because of a free-enterprise society. West Berlin at night was brightly lit up like Tokyo, London, and New York City, while East Berlin at night was completely dark, with very few essentials like street lights. Thank heavens all that has changed since that time. It is true there was some competition in East Berlin for the better, higher-cost apartments. But the Berliners who were used to a free-market system earned much more and could afford the much nicer and safer dwellings.

At Seaberg Industries, who the competition might be was neither a key nor a dominant factor in our strategic planning. And it didn't necessarily determine whether we should get into a new market. It's really a case of deciding if a potential new market fit our strategic plan, if we could meet potential customers' needs, and if we could generate a profit from the move. Chapter 8, "Success Isn't an Accident," covered strategic planning, so this part of analyzing our competitors won't be discussed further here.

In the early years of the company, whenever work slowed down, I used to drive around town looking into my peer companies' parking lots to see how busy they were. It was a pointless gesture. It would have been a better use of my time to continue concentrating on training our people or visiting with clients to see what other opportunities the company might have for work. And if our competitors were also not busy, I would get some comfort from that. Talk about misdirection of effort on my part!

Thankfully I eventually grew out of this silly, nonproductive habit. On my part, another good dose of, "Seeing what I can do for my customer today" was what I should have been doing, such as better telemarketing, seeing new customers, or looking for ways to give better service to present customers. In this case, it's good to have a bias to take positive action, or as Tom Peters has written, "It's Ready, Fire, Aim" many times to overcome lack of inertia on a problem or project. If I didn't take this positive action, I know it would be easy to get into an "analyze and paralyze" kind of attitude. That was neither efficient nor effective, no matter how you looked at the problem. It only took about ten years to grow out of that time-wasting habit, but I did grow out of it.

I would be remiss not to mention how competitive Japan became in the US markets. In 1989, for the first time the number-one-selling car in America, the Honda Accord, was not from the Big Three—it was from Japan, Inc. For the first time in American history, we lost an unheard-of lead in the domestic car market. This new development was a big reason why I started a company: to prove that a little guy could beat Japan, Inc., in the American marketplace. You could say that I had an "I'll show you!" attitude about Japan's growth in the United States. Throughout my career in manufacturing, I was able to profitably under-bid work that a Japanese firm also bid on. In fact, the only time I lost out to a foreigner bidding on American soil was when the reverse auction craze was in full bloom in industry.[9]

These auto companies—Ford, Chrysler, and General Motors—seemed to be defensive rather than taking the competitive fight to the Japanese. To think that the Japanese were invincible was not only a mistake; it was also grossly incorrect. When one of the first Japanese manufacturers, Toyota, sold their cars in the United States, it seemed to be a comedy of errors. They had very little money to spend promoting and testing their vehicles; the autos broke down; and they rusted out faster than the American-made cars. But they never quit, and look what happened to our respective economies as a result of their tough-mindedness in the marketplace. I salute and thank the competitive Japanese for their spirit, spunk, and work ethics. They re-taught us something we seemed to have forgotten: it's a competitive world out there. Proof of this was a series

---

9   A reverse auction is when a company puts out a group of documents on the Internet for anyone to bid on making. On the bidding date and time, companies start bidding their lowest price for that work. Inevitably, a Chinese company would get the bid with the lowest price. Within a year, this practice was stopped because the low-bid firm in almost every case couldn't deliver and the company who took the bid got burned.

of pictures circulating on the Internet showing World War II bombed-out Hiroshima today with its sparkling and prosperous city and then cutting to pictures of inner city Detroit in 2010 with a question asking who really won World War II.

What the people of Japan accomplished as world-class manufacturers is very admirable when one thinks about how they got to that enviable position. For several centuries it was basically a feudalistic society ruled by the Meiji dynasty. At the end of the nineteenth century, the system of government became imperialistic-capitalistic. These people then began to learn the value of working together for the country's common economic good. This form of government existed until World War II ended in August of 1945.

At a seminar I attended on manufacturing excellence, one of the speakers was discussing marketing and showed a slide depicting why customers *quit* buying, whether the purchase was a car, videotape, camera, tractor, or prescription:

| | |
|---|---|
| 1 percent | Die |
| 3 percent | Move away or other reasons |
| 5 percent | Develop other friendships |
| 9 percent | Competitive reasons |
| 14 percent | Dissatisfied with quality |
| 68 percent | Attitude of indifference toward the customer by employees, managers, owner, or president |

When I saw the figures, I immediately thought of my own sales failures. They seemed to fit with the above statistics.

I believe the Japanese became dominant in the industry because they had several key ideas they constantly kept before them. Japan, Inc., had a national strategic plan. They had long-term goals kept constantly before them. As a small country, they had nowhere to go (they had a "backs-to-the-wall" mentality, the same as Israel today), and they listened hard to what the US consumer wanted in their cars. The Japanese showed a strong concern toward what the customer thought of their products, which the American consumer picked up, versus the perception of indifference by the American auto companies toward their customers. The Americans just had seemed to quit trying to compete.

My small company competed against other Japanese firms, so I felt the sting of their expertise in manufacturing. Most of our more-expensive machines came from Japan or were made in America by a Japanese company. In the 2000s, virtually all machine tools were made in Japan, now considered the machine tool capital of the world. Their products were just more valuable because they cost up to 40 percent less and were readily available for purchase. The only problems with the Japanese products happened early on. For instance, if we had an electronic problem, we couldn't understand their English translations of the Japanese. By now all those challenges have been resolved.

For a while, late in the 1990s, the American machine tool builders came to the party to compete at least on a par with the Japanese products. But it didn't last. It just seemed that the Americans weren't as determined as the Japanese. Our government also didn't seem to offer any incentives to the Americans with tax or tariff issues.

But along with this thinking, I feel that the second Gulf War did much toward US manufacturing businesses regaining some lost confidence. I am strongly opposed to war and arms sales, but I am also for taking a stand on some issues like those caused by the 9/11 attacks on our shores by terrorists. The United States demonstrated to the world our technological superiority and determination to follow an issue to its conclusion. This just showed that, overall, the United States still has a competitive edge.

It seems that most small businesses in our country have been comparing favorably against foreign competition chiefly for one reason. These firms have a trench warfare attitude where they realize that a few mistakes or careless market maneuvers will put them out of business. To counter the out-of-business threat, the little guy had to concentrate hard on what he was doing and be fast on his feet in being alert to his customers' needs and his own profit picture. And it's an ever-changing arena: what looks like a good situation can turn into a disaster if the owner/president doesn't keep a close watch on his company's affairs and competitive position.

In our kind of parts business, you get work only by competing either with other shops, against customer in-house people (we compete within our own company for work), or with the large company against the world market. The latter is becoming the case more and more as large companies continue to downsize their supplier bases. And we compete by offering the Big Four: Quality, Price, Delivery, and Flexibility. In the 1980s it was only the first three, but competition proved the value of also being flexible to client demands in order to be closer to the customer and do a better job of building a chain of customers.

There is a good side to the adversity caused to American manufacturers by Japanese and German imports. It helped us get out of our complacent attitudes that had been happening since World War II. To show how great the inroads Japanese manufacturing had made, US consumers thought the new Mitsubishi cars were of a higher quality than the Chrysler cars that were made on the same assembly line in the Diamond Star plant in Bloomington, Illinois. Even people living in that city accused the Diamond Star workers of putting more effort into making the Mitsubishi versus making the Chrysler cars. The only difference between the cars is the nameplate and a few cosmetic features—and the price tag. The Mitsubishi autos sold for more because of consumer perceptions that they were superior to the Chrysler ones.

In Japan large companies make up only 1 percent of the work force. The bigger firms use many small companies to make their products and enjoy a good markup, at least in the 30–40 percent range. In America it used to usually be a smaller markup because the products otherwise wouldn't sell. At Seaberg we were willing to help other ethical competitors just as we had been helped by others in past years. It's the price-only competitors who I didn't have time for because they got business we wanted and then they went bankrupt when their pricing structure proved they didn't know their costs. One time we bid on a large amount of work for a long-time client but lost it to a firm that bid the cost of the material only, thinking there would be little or no cost for their labor. They were bankrupt less than a year later because of their lack of costing knowledge.

The better the US suppliers get:

1. The bigger the pie gets for the Americans (I really enjoy bidding and winning work done on Japanese and German prints). Instead of a $1 billion market, it can be a $5 billion market in the United States from competing worldwide.

2. The more value-added work we do. Value = Price + Quality + Delivery + Service.

CHAPTER 19

# Profits: Ever Important, Sometimes Elusive

Corporate profits have been difficult for me to accomplish. If I didn't thoroughly enjoy the work I did and the people I associate with so much, I probably would have gone into another line of work long ago. But I did like the challenges this work brought to me most of the time, so I chose to be right where I was, operating a machining and fabricating firm.

Many times people in other businesses or working for large corporations have the misperception that the small owner is financially well off. When my father was living, he used to say about a local small company, "Deere sure made that guy wealthy." This just wasn't the whole truth. With few exceptions, these little businesses existed because the owner worked seventy- and eighty-plus-hour weeks for years. This was also the same for many executives who also worked long hours at large client companies. I had a dear friend, Tom Kataras, who owned a family restaurant, apartment complex, and later a farm to live on, all just south of Chicago in Homewood, Illinois. Tom was at work at 5:00 a.m. every morning to get things ready for the day and left only when he was comfortable with his help being able to close up late. And he put in some very long hours, especially in his early years. Would you be willing to risk everything you own plus work those kinds of hours?

# Security Bank Failure

On December 9, 1983, besides living in a poor economy, I was in dire straits because Security Bank, where I had my company loan, was closed because the vice president, Harold Abdo, was arrested for embezzling $520,000, and another employee had stolen $55,000 over a twelve-year period.

My CPA friend and Deere retiree, Don Martin, was helpful in putting together proposals for me to take around to several banks to get another loan to meet current expenses and move to another site. Our business needed more space, as I was observing from my business forecast. I was looking at a place in an outlying town through that town's bank when it was announced in the news that a Davenport bank had bought Security Bank's assets. We then made a proposal to the new owners to consolidate all our loans into one Small Business Association (SBA) loan.

Our company was located in Moline, Illinois, then. That required the Davenport, Iowa, bank to work with the SBA Regional Office in Illinois rather than the one in Iowa. This required more time to work through the paperwork of transferring SBA coverage from one state to another. I told the bank vice president that we needed $30,000 to make payroll that week, and he said that nothing could be done in such a short time.

He called me back a short time later and made a special effort to get us the necessary money. In order to get this cash, I had to sign our home mortgage over to a bank again. The Lord blessed us on this effort mightily by allowing this unusual banking move to happen to keep the company going.

At the same time, another company with about two hundred employees went into Chapter 11 bankruptcy. Pearson American Machine Company, located nearby in Galva, Illinois, was closed because their bank apparently wouldn't extend credit and called in the loans. That company owed $185,000 and had $181,000 in cash reserves in the bank. The bank seized the cash, thereby forcing the bankruptcy. We had just recently started doing business with Pearson, and the future with them looked very promising. Maybe the Lord was just helping me avoid a worse situation down the road.

We all know that if a company doesn't make any profits, sooner or later it will close its doors. Now how do we know how well we're doing? Most executives have their own set of favorite ratios or data that tell them how well the company is doing. A somewhat extreme example of simplicity in having a good feel for the business is about a steel mill CEO in Sterling, Illinois, who had his desk in the main office building waiting room and operated his company (large enough to have many miles of railroad track on the plant property) successfully by the book he kept in his back pocket. I am sure he had a good idea how his company was operating.

I couldn't pretend to run our much, much smaller firm like that steel mill CEO at all. But what I did use to judge operations were a few simple data points and ratios. One of the first was a weekly cash flow statement, as shown below. We developed this over years of experimenting with different data. I used this rather than a monthly source and applications of funds statement.

## Weekly Cash Flow Statement
### Revenue

| Customer | Month and Week | | | | | | | |
| --- | --- | --- | --- | --- | --- | --- | --- | --- |
| | Jan | | | | | Feb | | |
| | 1 | 2 | 3 | 4 | 5 | 1 | 2 | 3 |
| ABC Co. | 5000 | | | 7000 | | | 6000 | |
| JKL Ind. | | 25000 | 7000 | | | 15000 | 75000 | |
| SQR Co. | 50000 | | 65000 | | | 75000 | 70000 | |
| XYZ Ent. | | 90000 | | 90000 | | | 90000 | |
| Total Rec. | 55000 | 115000 | 72000 | 97000 | 0 | 90000 | 96000 | 145000 |
| Beg. Bal. | 40000 | 25000 | 75000 | 47000 | 64000 | 34000 | 54000 | 65000 |
| Payroll | 30000 | 30000 | 30000 | 30000 | 30000 | 30000 | 30000 | 30000 |
| Accts Pay | 40000 | 35000 | 70000 | 50000 | 0 | 40000 | 55000 | 95000 |
| Savings | | | | | | | | |
| Other | | | | | | | | |
| Total Disb. | 70000 | 65000 | 100000 | 80000 | 30000 | 70000 | 85000 | 125000 |
| End Bal. | 25000 | 75000 | 47000 | 64000 | 34000 | 54000 | 65000 | 85000 |

The weekly cash flow statement served the same purpose of helping the company watch where the money's going but on a weekly basis, rather than on a monthly basis as the source and application of funds statement.

To give me a monthly history of what we did as recently as last month, I used a figure called $ sales/employee/year ($ sales per employee per year). This figure rapidly gained acceptance among manufacturing firms in the United States. Maybe it's because the Japanese have been using it for years, but for me it instantly summed up our sales, profits, and other financial ratios. In the late 1980s, Japan, Inc., used a figure of $120,000 sales/employee/year for their largest manufacturing companies as an appropriate figure. One large Midwest company used a figure of $52,000 sales/employee/year as a red flag for watching a supplier closely. You can be assured that if a machine shop is below that figure for very long, he probably won't be around much longer. In my business, I included *all* employees in computing this number, especially since the direct/indirect labor line continued to get fuzzier and fuzzier and thus, less significant. I feel that $55,000 was substandard, and that $110,000 was exceptional for job shop kinds of businesses.

A rather unusual figure I used was one that a banker friend gave to me. He felt that this condenses all the financial data he needed to get a quick snapshot of a firm. He used what was called the *Z Score*[10] to rate all of his loan accounts monthly.

## Z Score Formula

$$Z = 6.56 * X1 + 3.26 * X2 + 6.72 * X3 + 1.05 * X4$$

X1 = Working Capital/Total Assets
X2 = Retained Earnings/Total Assets
X3 = Earnings before Interest and Taxes/Total Assets
X4 = Book Value of Equity/Total Liabilities

10  "Spreadsheets, the Z Score: Detecting Financial Distress Early," by Jason O'Neal, *CFO Magazine*, December 1988. "How Much Growth Can a Firm Afford?" by Robert C. Higgins, *Financial Management Magazine*, Fall 1977.

Z Score Ratings

| Healthy | (above 2.60) |
| Gray Zone | (Between 1.10 and 2.60) |
| Unhealthy | (below 1.10) |

Additional data I liked to use were as follows:

- Quick Ratio. A ratio of 1.2 is a realistic number that shows cash assets strength.

- Current Ratio. A ratio of 2.0 is a historically acceptable figure that shows current assets strength.

- Debt/Equity. A ratio of 1.5 shows how much equity you have to cover costs.

- Average Days Collection. Twenty to thirty days was acceptable. This number showed how many days it takes to get paid for services rendered.

- Cost of Sales/Inventory. A ratio of 2.0 showed how fast inventory was turned monthly.

- Inventory Turns. A good number of twenty or higher told how fast you turned over the inventory annually, based on the selected month's numbers.

- Accounts Receivable/Accounts Payable. A ratio of 2.0 was acceptable and indicated how well the company managed its cash.

- Book Value. This is an objective number showing the company's value without goodwill being added.

In our business category, the net profit before taxes averaged 4.1 percent in 1990. (Several years before that, the figure was 5.3 percent in the industry.) Also, in the early 1990s the quick ratio averaged 1.2; days receivable forty; days inventory eighteen; and debt/equity 1.6, so you can plainly see from these figures that this was not a business for the faint-hearted or for someone who wanted to get rich quick.

At Seaberg's, we wanted to be a higher wage payer, but it was crucial to have objectives of a current positive cash flow and profits in the longer term, according to Drucker.[11] Obviously, if we didn't have a positive

---

11   Peter Drucker, *The Essential Drucker*, Harper Collins Publisher, NY, pages

flow and profits, we couldn't stay around as a business. During several of our dark times when our financials showed a distinct red color, we remained solvent because our suppliers were so understanding of our plight and extended special terms like letting us pay our bills later than we or they wanted.

A short aside to this happened recently to me on a visit to my former company. One of our steady tooling supplier salesmen over the years was also getting ready to retire and told me that working with Seaberg was one of his most enjoyable career jobs, especially during the tough times when character showed in who one dealt with. Jim Ziel was very upfront with us and also compassionate in his dealings.

There were several customers who made some of their payments to us early after we asked them. It was a hard thing for me to ask the hand that fed us to also do it earlier than normal. Right in the middle of one of these times, International Harvester Company, at that time our fifth-largest customer, extended their pay terms from 45 to 120 days! This was definitely a bummer. When you add that ingredient to an already sad situation and throw in the fact that at about that time our bank refused to grant me any more credit because of our financial condition, you might understand why I felt like I needed to wear knee pads because of my earnest praying.

What made matters worse was that my time was mostly taken up with worrying about how to get cash to keep operations continuing rather than going after sales. And our in-house accountant had to shift his concerns from cost accounting and strong financial control to who to pay when and how to meet our weekly payroll. As a result, I found it easier to make the necessary but unpopular decisions like which personnel to discharge, suppliers who we would pay later, and which customers to keep. I would like to recommend an experience of this sort to everyone running a business, no matter what size. We survived. And we became a stronger, more disciplined, and better competitor because of those trying times.

Often I used our company bank officers as financial advisors in various customer or supplier transactions. A banker deals in financial matters all the time, and he looks at your situation from a different perspective

28-30, 2001. (CITY, STATE: PUBLISHINCO., 2001), PAGE NUMBER(S).

even though he usually has your company's best interests at heart. And there were times when he wasn't emotionally caught up in an apparently "good opportunity" for the manufacturer and he could be more objective. A competent lending officer can also be an indicator of your company business barometer. There were times when the banker said no to me, and it was hard for him to say that. But it was usually in our own best interests too. As in almost all life situations, it has to be a win-win situation for the bank as well as for the business. The bank just looks at your business and the way you conduct it from a different angle.

Generally profits are lower at a company that doesn't have their own product. This is why I spent so much time investigating opportunities where Seaberg Industries might have an exclusive product to furnish to customers. A business friend who manufactured a product line said that you can get used to making something for a dollar and selling it for five. As a subcontractor, we seem to make it for a dollar and hope to sell it for a dollar and a nickel.

I was once at a supplier cost accounting conference hosted by one of our clients. One of the subcontractors there had a proprietary product line. He told me that with his own product line he could charge $90/hour for using one of his CNC machines to make his products, but when he subcontracted as a job shop, he could only charge $50/hour for the same machine doing identical kinds of work. End of subject.

# CHAPTER 20

# Now You've Got Your Product: Is It the Right One?

"Are you going to make fence posts or build Caterpillar parts?" This was asked of me by one of our client buyers on his first field visit to our young company, still named ARI Industries, when it was located in the back of the body shop from where we were renting space. Jon Bateman was concerned that we didn't have enough quality tools and gages to fulfill our production commitments to Cat. But he could see that I was determined to succeed with my business. As one can well imagine, I was quite surprised at his statement, especially since we were already doing a good job of furnishing them quality parts for the past year. But he was just thinking down the road that we could get to a higher level of work for his company.

Shortly after his visit, Jon sent me to one of his best fabricating suppliers near Chicago to learn how to become a better job shop. We both knew I was as new to this business as wet green paint. The recommended supplier opened his doors to let me see how he operated his company. At the time, I was little more than a one-man shop, and this gentleman employed about one hundred people. Ron Lubick told me that he was made a better supplier when his company was competing with a quality house, no matter what size the competition was. What he strongly disliked were price-only companies that were incompetent but temporarily took market share from him, only to disappear in a short time because they would price themselves out of business. He said, "I've got a lot of time for guys who are good at what they do. This only makes our customer stronger if they use good suppliers. This, in turn gives me more business over a longer period of time." Ron was a friendly and class guy who was very successful in his business.

Even though cash flow was still very tight then, I immediately began purchasing more quality assurance equipment. It turned out to be the right decision since we *did improve rapidly* in our ability to deliver parts on time with better quality at a competitive price. I can still chuckle and quote Jon's question at the beginning of this chapter over thirty-five years after it was because of how correct he was and how effectively he got my attention. We have been good friends ever since the first time I was shown into his office in the Caterpillar Morton Parts Depot.

Once a potential customer was identified, we kept asking the buyers questions about what was needed from a small business like ours. Each company has their similar but different policies and procedures, and the plants within a company act quite different in how they want to be treated. *Marketing needs constantly change because consumer needs constantly change.* The factors we used in-house to help us decide which products to market were the following: people, equipment, timing, funds available, and training. We also tried to take advantage of the peculiarities of our Midwest geography, like concentrating on producing parts for farm equipment versus oceangoing ship parts, even though we made parts for firms on each coast that were not in the ag or construction fields.

One of the earliest lessons I learned about marketing is that the customer isn't a company but rather the specific person in a company that might want to use our services. It's true that each business has a specific personality based on its executives' personal traits, but it still comes down to performing to the standards of the individual who signs those purchase orders. And it's interesting how different the personalities are among different plants of a large corporation.

For instance, in the Quad Cities where I live, Deere and Company at one time had about six purchasing groups for machine shops to contract with for work. A small firm like ours had to know the differences in temperament between each department even though they were guided by the same basic company policies and procedures. Operating this way was characteristic of large, decentralized companies operating competently. The company culture seemed to be made up of many unique personality traits like past personal history, specific customer groups, traditions (we've always done it that way), and the like. Company personalities today are more diverse than ever because of expansion of businesses overseas and easy international travel.

I've found individual expressions to be fairly typical of large companies and a strength in business because what the individual does for his employer provides good diversity of viewpoints and contributes to bottom-line profits. In the past, some of these persons may not have felt that their contributions were significant. This doesn't seem to be true any longer, at least to the degree it was in the last century.

Probably the biggest revelation I had in marketing for a job shop–type company was that if I couldn't adapt my personality to be compatible with my customer, there was almost no likelihood we would be able to do work for that customer. This is because if either during negotiating for work or when a small problem arose during manufacturing because of my not understanding the buyer properly, it could quickly become a huge problem and a lost business opportunity. However, if the buyer and I were conducting business on agreeable terms where we could respect and trust each other, even the large problems would be amiably worked out to an advantage for both parties.

CHAPTER 21

# Off to Market We Go!
# (What Have You Done for Me Lately?)

A small company has neither the cash nor the staff to do extensive market surveys using consultants that are typically hired by bigger companies. What I relied on since first going out to look for business was being able to call friends and acquaintances throughout the country for their feedback on various market conditions. For example, I would call the vice president of a welding equipment company to see what his opinion was on what kind of work seemed strong in the metal-working trade outside the Midwest area. In the early 1980s when the agricultural and construction equipment business was getting very slow, work in the oil fields was booming. I used this information to be able to find work for the company that was a big help in coming through a dark economic period for Midwest manufacturers. It's ironic that my first contact for oil work was in Iowa, the *only* state in America that hadn't ever had a producing oil well. It pays to follow every lead one gets, regardless of how unlikely it may seem.

Supplier networking, rather than being viewed as a target for collusion, in reality will multiply suppliers' abilities to meet their customers' purchasing needs. It fit well with the continuing trend to outsource work that the customer companies did for reduced costs of manufacturing. At Caterpillar several years ago, it was common knowledge that 80 percent of the cost of an engine then was parts purchased from subcontract suppliers.

In the large aircraft contracts in the late 1980s, a vast majority of the work was done by subcontractors, however large they were (like Boeing subcontracting work to Alcoa, Northrup, and General Dynamics). This is a trend that's becoming more common in large construction projects where the general contractor manages the overall project and coordinates the work of the subcontractors where these relatively smaller firms are specialists in the work they are under contract to do. It is like the sheet metal company doing the building ductwork, the electrical contractor installing all the electrical, etc., for the general contractor.

Whereas you used to see security guards on a company's payroll, now you see that work handled by subcontractors, such as Per Mar or ADT because it's more cost effective. Many times the Fortune 500 firm gets a quicker response to company's needs than when using their own company personnel. Plus the security people can be let go without the fuss of company paperwork.

In our business, *anyone* in the company could help on a project being done if he or she could do it better. This was encouraged, which kept costs low. An engineer who was part of the purchasing team might call one of our machinists to find out the best-machined finish we can normally make on hot-rolled 1045 grade steel without having to make two finish passes or perform a grinding operation. This act helps keep unnecessary costs out of the product. It was just a matter for us of getting as close to the customer as possible with our best "resident expert" without caring who it was.

I recall being at the Chicago Machine Tool Show at McCormick Place years ago when one machine tool manufacturer displaying there said that it took *seventeen different union crafts* to unload and install his company's display. That was such a waste of good talent by the unions, but the union chiefs wanted to have everyone employed regardless of the costs to the displayers. Stunts like this are what drove businesses to move elsewhere to right-to-work states or foreign countries.

Caterpillar knows that for their suppliers to be better at what they do, they need to be able to talk to their competition for some of their ideas. In fact, Caterpillar's Engine Division has gone so far, like many other fine companies doing similar activities, as to host an occasional business meeting for their top suppliers from around the world. Cat reveals future strategies and tells these suppliers how they can help the company be even more competitive.

This is one of the finest marketing arrangements I've seen where a small business is involved with one of its client companies. This sense of client trust creates commitment from the supplier to ensure he furnishes a superior product. This is another case of a win for the subcontractor and a win for the customer.

Being Caterpillar certified was important to our marketing efforts with other companies we sought to work for. It pre-qualified us as being competent and capable of providing services in the area for which we were certified. This was a good time saver for both parties and prevented "re-inventing the wheel." Or if we were to go through a certifying process for another company in our market, much of the administrative work was already complete or at least started. Personally, I preferred being visited and examined by a certifying team for a firm interested in seeing if we would be a good fit for doing work for them.

Small subcontractor businesses tend to mirror their clients' behavior and business habits. A large company finds out what the consumer wants and then delivers. For instance, Toyota and Honda do this very well, and the small guy becomes an extension of his customer/client.

In business it takes visualization, confidence, and concentration to succeed. This is similar to what most college basketball players do. In 1957 Iowa played the University of Minnesota at Williams Arena on the Minneapolis campus, where as a sophomore I had to guard their All-Big Ten forward named Cline. In that game, he seemed unstoppable and scored forty-two points off me. It was so bad for us that during a timeout late in the game, I asked if someone else wanted to guard him. I didn't have any volunteers.

That summer I was a counselor at a boys' camp, ironically in northern Minnesota. I put the name *Cline* in large, black block letters on a two-foot by three-foot piece from a roll of white paper and tacked it to the ceiling over my bed in the log cabin where I slept near the boys for whom I was responsible. Then I saw that name when I went to sleep at night and first thing in the morning when I woke up. All summer I visualized how I would guard him the next time Iowa played Minnesota.

The next season when I got in the game at Williams Arena and guarded him, I held him scoreless, just as I had imagined I would do. I felt so strong about guarding him well that I never let him even touch the ball. Visualization certainly worked for me that time.

**2011. Present Seaberg Industries, Inc. main plant, Rock Island, IL. The company moved here in 1984, and have made three building additions since that time.**

1984. Employees in the machining area of the new plant in the Rock Island Industrial Park.

Seventh row: unknown; Dick Vogel; George Seaberg; unknown; Harold Paget; Larry Schol.

Sixth row: Mike Bousson; Mike Parkin; Greg Foster; Steve Baker; unknown; Lee Fong Heu

Fifth row: Bill Diehl; Tom Knapper; Harold Raaen; Mike Carpenter.

Fourth row: Craig Kinzer; Charlie Bicknell.

Third row: Dean Grandfield; unknown; Steve Evans; Jobhn Devinney.

Second row: Jo Spurgeon; Rolland Wiedenhoft; Cheryl Wedra.

First row: Ed, Lee Fong Heu's cousin, who worked for the CIA in Viet Nam.

1986 technology. Dean Grandfield, Welding Supervisor, is shown standing at the magnetic strip schedule board in the shop office, keeping track of jobs under his responsibility. Job #s are in left hand column in white. Status of work for each job is on yellow magnetic tags. The yellow tags were moved daily as the jobs progressed through the plant.

1995. Caterpillar certification ceremony.

January 1, 1995. George, President, and Thomas Seaberg,
Asst. to the President, in their new office arrangement.

2011. Tom & George Seaberg, good friends.

**2011. George & Sue Seaberg at home.**

The author when he played for the University of
Iowa. In the 1957-58 season the team was second to
Michigan State midway through the season.

# CHAPTER 22

# Where's the Business?

Jack Nicklaus, who I still consider to be the greatest golfer of all time, once said that if you do one thing very well, the world will beat a path to your door. In his case it was chasing a little white ball over a grassy field with a few sandy places thrown into the mix. But doing this very well led him into designing golf courses, endorsing clothes, and other enterprises. As most people know, it made him a millionaire many times over, with the golf-related businesses furnishing the biggest part of his income.

In the late 1980s, Ted Turner, founder of the TCM classic film TV channel, sensed that people would like to see old black-and-white films in color, so he risked all of his holdings to purchase the rights to colorize old Hollywood films. This was against the wishes of most of the people in the film industry. As we now know, Turner succeeded in this high-risk, high-reward venture quite well. He succeeded so well that in 1990 he paid $21,000,000 to start a buffalo ranch near Big Sky, Montana.

We all have Significant Emotional Events (SEE) in our lives. After all, this is what helps to make us the unique individuals we are. Morris Massey[12] explains that the Significant Emotional Events we have influence our decisions when we travel through life every day. When I first started our business, I had to do all the work to earn the pay to put food on the family table. I very quickly learned where to put my efforts to obtain the best return on my time and not to waste the time of others.

---

12   The People Puzzle, by Dr. Morris Massey, 1979, Reston Publishing Company, Inc., Reston, VA, page 18.

One of the first things I learned at that time, as far as sales are concerned, was to qualify the customer. How do we go about doing this? When I was the company owner, I did this so often that I eventually only used a mental checklist, as shown below, to see if I should pursue a further course of action with a potential client.

Checklist

1.  Is this the right kind of business for the company to be in? I appreciate and like to drive cars, but Seaberg wouldn't be able to make high production run automotive parts even though the company is a machining and fabricating house. It's just not our market niche. On the other hand, we got into the oil business in the early 1980s because the work was similar to what we had already been doing.

2.  Is the timing right for us? If we had so much work that our people worked six days at week, ten hours per day serving our present customers, we would then need to put off making contacts for more new work. In 1987 I let our company become committed to too much work at once. This was because for several years our manufacturing people rightly kept after me to bring in more sales so the shop would have a good backlog of work for the foreseeable future. Then we got so much work that the year turned into one of the most stressful in my entire work career.

3.  Is this the right company for us to work for? Is the "social chemistry" between the parties right to pursue any business opportunities further? Would we be able to satisfy their needs? For instance, if a client required my personal time twenty-four hours a day, I would have to decline because I know I wouldn't be strong enough to hold up for very long. We wouldn't be the right fit for that firm.

    On the other hand, if that client needed Seaberg *employees* on call for twenty-four hours a day, we could accommodate that company because we operated our business around the clock, five days a week, plus part of Saturdays. In fact, part of the reason we went to a three-shift operation was so we could handle emergencies that required manufacturing during the night.

    There was a company I wanted to do work for shortly after we opened the doors because the kinds of work they subcontracted were ideal for our fledgling firm. I kept showing the buyers samples of our products for seven years before we had the opportunity to quote and subsequently do work for their buyers.

Walt Disney summed up that kind of perseverance very well in a job interview he had with Victor Animatograph Co., which was located in Davenport, Iowa. His animation idea was rejected as being lousy, but they said he could become a salesman for their movie projectors instead. He didn't accept the job and instead moved to California to follow his dream of creating Mickey Mouse, Bambi, the Lion King, etc. In his interview with a Davenport newspaper many years later, he said, "I didn't give up. Be determined. Never be discouraged. Believe in yourself."[13]

In 1987 one of our clients told me that we were successfully competing directly against small companies in at least eleven countries: Brazil, Belgium, Canada, England, France, Korea, Japan, Mexico, the Netherlands, Sweden, and West Germany. When those in the United States were added to the list, I realized I had to know our business pricing very well to remain competitive and profitable.

4. Am I talking to the right person? Sometimes I've had great conversations with the entirely wrong person. I learned to try early on to find out if the person I was talking with had the authority to make purchase orders or contracts. Many times it's been difficult to remain tactful and qualify the person. Also, how do you draw information out of the buyer to better find out his needs? This is what the art and science of selling is all about—matching needs to capabilities.

One thing I realized after being in business several years was that we couldn't be all things to all people. Some of my long-time customers jokingly questioned if years later I still believed that statement of trying to be "Mr. Everything" to our clientele.

Before that it seemed we used to bid on making anything you could make from metal. Some of the bids we won we made no profits on because we couldn't be competitive. While we had a good working

13 From a column written by Bill Wundrum for the Quad City Times, Davenport, Iowa, March 4, 2011.

knowledge of how to process the work, we didn't know enough about it to know the shortcuts necessary to make a profit. For instance, when the University of Iowa's Carver-Hawkeye basketball arena was being built in 1980, we won the bid to furnish the catwalk that is suspended from the ceiling over the basketball court. We lost money doing this job because we spent too much time and effort making the catwalk to more exacting specifications than was necessary. Our work fit together so well at the construction site that the erection company had bid $70,000 to put it up in about a week and they had it installed in one day. This job, more than any other, proved to me that we couldn't competitively make columns and beams for buildings while making engine components at the same time with the same employees.

What service is your company best at furnishing? Put another way, "What do you do best?" When you closely examine business failures, frequently this question never seems to be asked by the bankrupt owners. Another question to add on to this one is, "Is there a need for the work my company does?" Cast iron toys were great to own in the 1930s, but there's no market for them today, other than in collectors' homes. The same thing is true for car tire inner tubes and IBM typewriters.

We've always built our business around the major equipment in the plant that made us a little bit different from our competitors. When we purchased our first Whitney fabricating center, we were the smallest company to own one, according to Whitney. That set us a little apart from other job shops. In fact, having that equipment kept us from going under during the economic depression in the Midwest in the early 1980s when the area was dubbed the *Rust Belt* instead of its traditional name of the Corn Belt.

The most important thing I looked for when seeking new business was how well my client knew his work. If he was very competent, then he would know how best to match his company needs with subcontractor abilities. It has saved us much time, money, and frustration over the years when we dealt with buyers who knew their business in detail. My personal opinion is that many times these purchasing personnel are more valuable to their companies than they have been given credit for by their executives.

CHAPTER 23

# Thirty Minutes or Your Parts Free!

This chapter title reflects what people might have seen on TV. At Seaberg Industries, with Kanban, JIT (just-in-time), and "a plan for every part," etc., it seemed that our turnaround time for shipping product was approaching that thirty-minute figure from the time the ship order arrived in the plant. At the Mitsubishi-Chrysler assembly plant in Bloomington, Illinois, plant personnel would place their individual supplier order for any kind of car seat in their Mitsubishi or Chrysler car lines the plant called for in any random order with the seat subcontractor. Forty-five minutes later, that particular car seat was received at the assembly line! I think that auto inventor Henry Ford would appreciate some of the strides American industry has made the past several years in manufacturing productivity, like at this Mitsubishi plant.

Seaberg Industries didn't approach that Mitsubishi-Chrysler high production figure, but we have reduced our delivery substantially since our inception. What used to take one month to bid, two weeks to get a decision on whether we were awarded the work, and twelve weeks to order material, produce, and then ship the work, we've been able to do considerably faster. For certain kinds of parts, we were able to quote in the morning, make the parts during the day, and then ship the finished parts that afternoon.

Since 10 percent of our normal sales required fast-changing, short-interval scheduling, Seaberg personnel paid a lot of attention to lean manufacturing practices. We stressed the following ideas to realize our JIT objectives.

1.  What are the customer's needs? Many times a new client will say that he needs quotes and parts ASAP. What does that mean? Today? The next day? The next month? If he truly does need for our company to stop other work in process, is he willing to pay for it? Almost three-fourths of the time when we called back with a quote for doing emergency work, the buyer would defer to a more normal delivery schedule rather than pay extra for the hurry-up time costs.

2.  Administrative accuracy. We stressed looking over the print or e-file and the purchase order very carefully to be sure we knew *exactly* what was wanted. The print/file gave all the part data needed to make the product. The purchase order would furnish such data as quantity required, due date, destination, payment terms, and any special instructions, such as painting, unusual packaging, etc.

3.  Quality. It took over twice as long to remake a part if it wasn't made to client specifications the first time. So we practiced a "slow, but fast" method of processing work. An example of this is how older, more-experienced operators performed their work. Their motions are smoother and not as jerky as a younger, less-experienced person's movements. When the older ones appear to be going slow, they are actually performing at a peak efficiency because they have no wasted motion. I have performed time studies on workers at different times during my career, and I still was occasionally pleasantly surprised when a good operator got more parts per shift, or per hour, than I thought he could do.

4.  Flexibility. If a company was going to achieve a JIT operations format, the employee must be willing to be mentally flexible in performing his tasks. When he continually kept his customers' needs (both in-company and the paying customer) in mind, he found it much easier to efficiently carry out these important duties.

5.  Adaptability. This is similar to flexibility but with a few differences. Adaptability begs such questions like, "Can I change my processes (i.e., machines or methods) (adapt), to the changing needs (flexibility) of my customer without sacrificing quality?"

6.  Speed. When we employed true just-in-time techniques and methods to furnishing goods to customers, we achieved a

relatively fast factory throughput. If everything was done with good discipline, the speed with which a part was manufactured to customer needs was optimum.

What happens most of the time in our JIT mode of operation is that we gave higher value in-house for the product we sold to the paying customer because of the saved production time. These were most of the benefits of this way of manufacturing:

1. Our paying customer. For example, Deere & Company gets the latest data on what the farmer wants in a new combine in Montana because Deere can delay their order to us because of any last-minute changes the farmer may want to make.

2. The cost of purchasing raw material used to make a part is delayed because we don't need to stockpile the raw materials. Our suppliers are also required to be on a JIT method of operation for the whole plan to succeed.

3. Time to put the work in process was considerably shortened (which also helped the manufacturer to get the combine order in the first place).

4. Because we were a small company, the network needed to rapidly fabricate and machine, as well as inspect, the work was much faster than at a larger company.

5. Billings were usually made the same day that the work was shipped to our customer. Faster billings meant faster cash flow for us.

And for that added value to our customer, we generally got paid for our services more rapidly than in past years without having to offer a price discount to getting paid sooner.

CHAPTER 24

# Waste Is Anything That Does Not Help the Client

Japanese business literature has listed seven kinds of waste or things to strive to eliminate in a manufacturing environment: Waiting; Correction; Overproduction; Processing; Materials Handling; Inventory; and Motion. From everything I've read, it's been a mania or obsession with these productive and efficient people.

If this topic is so important to the people in one of the leading industrial countries in the world, maybe we need to take a closer look as to why we might also adopt their definition of waste, as related to manufacturing.

## Waiting

For several years, there seemed to always be at least three people waiting in our manufacturing manager's office for decisions on what to do next! This was one of my pet peeves because of the tremendous amounts of otherwise productive time lost by personnel needing to know what their next job was to be. In fact, it was nearing the point where my manufacturing manager was going to lose his job. Eventually we worked out a procedure where he learned to empower the employees in his charge to better think out their work needs and priorities without his constant input. In all fairness to him, he was being too conscientious and wanted to be sure that work under his responsibility was done correctly. What he needed to realize was that while more mistakes might be made in the near term, in the long run, he would be able to accomplish many times more work through this delegating action and also prevent useless mistakes.

Another instance of eliminating waiting as a waste causer came through the efforts of quality assurance inspectors. The quality lab used to always be the most crowded part of the plant, especially at the beginning of a shift. In December of 1989, the QA manager told the production personnel that one of his goals was to eventually eliminate the need for his position. What he was going to do was put almost all inspections out at the machines where the parts were being made. He succeeded very well.

## Correction

A better-known word to define this kind of waste is called scrap. Like the other definitions of waste, it has many hidden costs that can't be found but can only be guessed at. A Japanese economist has postulated what is known as the four-in-one rule of thumb when trying to identify scrap costs. For every dollar of proven scrap or rejected product, there is $4 in hidden costs associated with the $1 of identified scrap.

There are the obvious costs like new material and labor needed to replace scrapped-out parts. This is strictly an accounting procedure and therefore easy to note. The hidden but known costs are there as well. The first thing is the cost of a too-cautious attitude by those involved in the scrap problem. I knew from my own experience running machines that if I made a bad part, I slowed down to be sure I identified the reject problem correctly. I didn't want to make another bad part. Of course, some of the other employees might want to spend time talking about it too.

What about the subcontractor to Seaberg Industries who has to hurry up to reprocess parts we made wrong? His charges may or may not be higher the second time around. If a customer has enough of these kinds of emergencies, the sub will have to start charging more to make sure he builds his profit from this work.

If someone forgets to do a part of the process, like not dipping parts in rust preservative, and lets the parts get rusted, it has to be corrected immediately. The rest of the processing is halted, and production costs start escalating until the correction is completed.

One of the worst things to happen to a small firm is to have parts rejected at the client's facility. In the 1990s, there were few, if any, receiving inspectors and inventory surge areas. So when the parts were delivered to the client assembly line and were wrong, the whole line stopped. All the client employees in that part of the plant knew *who* the sub was that caused the stoppage.

In the 2000s, companies started to subcontract the receiving inspection jobs in customer plants. Some companies paid an incentive based on how many parts were rejected. To see how ridiculous this has gotten, one supplier had met the print specs on drilled holes in a plate that was painted. The parts were rejected because the hole size was smaller because of the paint coating on the inside of the hole. After the customer tied up the shipment, it was decided that the parts could be shipped only if the holes were free of paint. That in itself wasn't a problem, except that the supplier had to reprocess the parts at their own cost even though they had completely met the specifications as written. The part was requited, and the supplier eventually recovered some costs. To be fair, the customer should have owned up to their mistake and compensated that supplier.

Parts that are rejected at the customer go through at least eleven costly steps the subcontractor incurs when the parts are returned to him:

1. The shipment goes back to the supplier direct-collect.
2. Receiving costs at the dock and in the office
3. Debit to the subcontractor, a cash flow transaction
4. Rescheduling (disruption and replacement costs)
5. Remanufacturing
   A. Probable material replacement
   B. Added setups and re-runs
6. Subcontracting (at SI it was possible that at least one of the below steps would have to be done)
   A. Heat treating
   B. Grinding

C. Plating

D. Cleaning

E. Painting (stripping away the old paint may or may not have to be done)

F. Freighting to these different places by SI

7. Reinspection

8. Reshipping

9. Reinvoicing (office labor)

10. Lost confidence and more cautious productivity by employees

11. Goodwill (lost confidence by client, possibly the biggest cost of these listed here)

Overproduction

Another word for this to a manufacturing manager is insurance. The manager knows he has to meet customer needs of on-time delivery and is tempted to overproduce for that "just in case I need it" time. There are times in a job shop when you have to start out making extras to be sure of getting one correct part, though that has substantially diminished in the 2000s. One special part we made for a client was the most difficult part we made. It was a part machined to difficult tolerances and then heat treated. During the heat treat (we had been making this particular part for over ten years in one to five pieces per run), it wasn't known *exactly* how the treated part would react because its chemical characteristics were somewhat different for each run. The parts even occasionally cracked during heat treatment. But we were improving; what used to take up to six months to make we could do in three months. We only needed to make two extra parts in a run. Even though we made a few extra parts as our insurance, this was the exception to the rule of making parts to the customer quantity in each run.

In previous years, it was normal for our clients to accept overproduced parts, but it didn't happen after 2000 because most orders at the client factories are for products already ordered by their customers and not for dealer inventory. One help we have occasionally had was for our clients let us ship fewer quantities than was called for and make it up on the next short run.

This topic is closely related to *inventory* because what you overproduce usually goes into *inventory*. But there are several other costly items to consider. For instance, the cost of cash to overproduce parts versus the cost of avoiding extra setups was a constant battle. In a job shop many times you didn't have any extra space to house machines with permanent setups or you didn't have enough specialized work to build work cells for only one particular part.

One of my first salesmen used to work for a large agricultural equipment company. He told me that before the 1980s, conventional shop wisdom in many large corporations required the production departments to make many extra parts because it was "known that some parts are going to be bad so that these extra parts can be thrown aside in assembly." *Ouch!* Inventory auditors would then see these tubs of extra parts and think that they were good quality pieces when they were actually rejected parts that hadn't been identified as such. Then the counts would be wrong and the assembly lines would have to shut down periodically because there weren't any good parts to assemble to the final products. You can imagine the kind of chaos this created throughout the plants where this practice was the accepted norm. Sometimes the good ol' days weren't so good after all, and it took foreign competition with better-quality practices to wake up American manufacturing.

## Processing

In chapter 36, I discuss in detail a better way we found to process our production. This project did only one thing: improve the flow of paperwork. But it was the biggest cost saver we had ever installed at the company. It was truly gold in our own backyard to spend time improving and streamlining our processing. For many years we were "too busy" to do proper processing. To some degree, we were receiving too many new jobs to spend the proper amount of time figuring out the best process before the work was sent to the operations department.

When we went through new work surges, we took some calculated risks by shortcutting the pre-production process if we recognized parts that were similar to what we did in the past. After we completed the run, we got the opinions of the machine operators to see where we could improve the process for subsequent runs. Then we completed the process loop by having manufacturing, engineering, and other personnel involved in producing the part refine the written process.

Then all the parties in the part team would "brainstorm" the process to make the job more efficient and profitable. This was the biggest difference between large and small companies in my experience. In a small company, the degree of speed in improving a process is much faster because all involved employees were located next to each other. If a fabricator didn't like his new fixture, he would just walk over to the die builder and engineer within a few minutes to get the issue settled. Or if a CNC machinist wanted to try a new milling cutter, he would walk to the tool crib tech who usually did the tooling ordering and maybe also call the designer of the fixture to explain why he might have a better method. Many of our best ideas for improving processes came from the people doing the producing of the shop floor. After witnessing this kind of interaction, it was easy to see that listening to the operators was one of the biggest assets we used in meeting client needs.

Material Handling

For many years, there was industry documentation proving that the most expensive production employee in a plant was the fork truck driver. He was adding nothing to the value of the product while he *was adding overhead cost,* and too much driving created opportunities for damaging product en route to manufacturing sites. I recall walking through a construction equipment plant and having a supervisor show me a building structural column with a one inch by six inch slotted hole two feet off the floor in it from when a fork truck driver ran one of the truck forks right through the steel. It was surprising to me that the column hadn't ever collapsed.

Many studies of large companies also showed miles of overhead conveyors that did nothing but add excess inventory to the plant since parts were being inadvertently stored on those conveyors.

In our Rock Island plant, I studied and documented the unnecessary costs of material handling. Because of that observation, we put some of our machines on wheels and installed electrical quick disconnects on them so they could be wheeled anywhere in the manufacturing area to form a flexible work cell for a short run of parts.

Early in the 2000s, I bought several hundred open-topped four-by-six-by-twelve-inch green sheet metal boxes to temporarily store parts while in process. Because of our intensive work in improving and reducing part processing time, the plant personnel were shortly able to do away with 80 percent of these tote boxes as a further improvement. The boxes did save us money, but the men improved the work even better. To me, that was teamwork at its best.

What much of material handling improvements came down to was letting the people making the parts feel they could call their own shots to find the best ways to eliminate waste. After I set the tone by explaining what waste was and giving a few examples, it seemed that everyone was trying to come up with as many ideas for improving profits as I was. Most of the time my manufacturing vice president and I were the last ones to find out about another neat idea the men implemented to cut down on material handling. These were some of the times when I've felt the most satisfaction about running a manufacturing business.

## Inventory

There are high costs involved in just keeping track of what inventory a company has, in the office and within the plant. The accounting department has to be sure an accurate count is maintained. The production personnel have to keep moving product around as needs for material change. They have to clean it or otherwise prepare it for production. The buyers have to keep up-to-date on how much excess inventory is at the plant, and the company has to pay one way or another for the space needed for excess goods.

A friend of mine was promoted to plant manager of a Fiat-Allis large construction equipment facility in the 1970s. As soon as he was in his new position, he reduced the plant raw material inventory in the yard by $11,000,000 ($54,000,000 in 2011) in just six months, a large savings by anyone in manufacturing from just looking for hidden costs. It was hardly noticeable in the outside yard but very obvious on the company balance sheet.

A plant needs space to contain any occasional extra material, but it shouldn't become a habit to always be building more warehouse space without a good reason. In the early 1980s, two years before the Farmall

Works of International Harvester Company, located in Rock Island, Illinois, went out of business, the company spent about $26,000,000 ($55,000,000 in 2011) to build a high-rise warehouse for storing excess inventory. Because they put up a costly *automated* building like this, it was no wonder the doors were closed at the place that was once the largest US producer of farm tractors.

And what about the costs associated with scrapping out out-of-date parts? We sometimes had to make extra parts and store them as inventory for when the customer would need them later. Several times the parts had revisions to them that made our stocked parts obsolete and we had to take a loss on the parts. We kept trying to calculate the most profitable lot size for making parts, but it was usually an educated guess. According to the contract we signed, the customer had the right to change the lot sizes within an agreed-upon number of days before shipment by us. Sometimes parts took longer to make than the allotted time allowed and we took a hit, but that was how business was conducted, and we couldn't face the possibility of shutting a production assembly line down. Fortunately, this former practice was mostly eliminated by the time I sold the company.

We still carried several client parts that were stored at no cost to us. Some have been at our site without a need to further process them before returning them to the customer. At the time the customer wanted to make a lifetime supply. If this was done for several thousand different parts, it would be easy to see how expensive this kind of operation could become to the client.

## Motion

When I first went to work on a railroad section gang as a summer job while in college, one of the old timers, who was one of the better workers, showed me how to look like I was working hard shoveling track ballast when I was hardly doing any work at all. As a young college kid, I thought you were supposed to work hard all the time to the best of your ability. Welcome to a different kind of work than what I was used to doing.

My reason for stating this incident is that almost anyone can be fooled by an operator doing a job if someone wanted to do that. The way I tried to reduce the wasted motion syndrome was for the employee to feel secure in being able to keep his job. I found out long ago that the insecure employees are the ones who try to fake working hard because they feel they might run out of work and be laid off. That would be the worst case possible for them. What I tried to do was let these fellow employees realize that I needed them to get the work done because I couldn't do it alone. I also told them that if we didn't make a profit on the parts we produced that I would have to re-quote the work to reflect our processing costs and possibly lose that work. And if we couldn't make profits on enough of our work, the company would go out of business and we'd all be looking for another job. I guess I tried to make the point with them that we were all in this together.

If cleanliness is next to godliness, then dirtiness must be next to what? Aside from making a place more pleasing to the eye, what is the value of it being clean and orderly? If you can't see something because of untidiness or dirt, you are experiencing lost motion. One of my pet peeves was seeing people walking around when their chief job was operating a cost center, and *everyone, including the cleaning techs,* was operating a cost center.

In early 1991, we put up a sign inside the plant that said: "*Waste* is anything that does not help the customer/client. I am committed to helping reduce or eliminate this waste." We left room for any employee who wanted to sign his name below this statement, and all the employees who wanted to sign their names were invited to do so. We left the sign available for a week for signing and then plasticized it and put it on the wall of our shipping department where every part shipped to a customer passed through. Almost all of the employees made a commitment by signing their names.

We weren't trying to be cute with another possible with-it cliché, but we wanted to have the person signing the two-foot by three-foot sign to become more committed to making sure *he or she* would see that his or her job included eliminating more waste from it.

If it didn't help the next person in the customer chain, it was probably a waste of time and/or money. The exceptions to this were ideas and projects that were longer-term investments.

# CHAPTER 25

# Guerilla Warfare

---

Guerilla warfare is a very good and necessary item of business to take care of so you don't lose market share to others interested in the same kind of work as you're doing. This doesn't mean subterfuge or deceit; it means integrity. It also means filling a need that no one else has done or isn't doing very well.

The term "guerilla warfare" was first used in relation to business to describe the Harvester Wars that took place in America in the period from 1880 to 1900. There was so much competition for the farmers' dollars that the reaper and grain harvester salesmen became extremely creative to make a sale in an oversold market. And to make matters worse, the manufacturers were so concerned about keeping market share that plant production was never reduced or adjusted to keep abreast of the ups and downs of product demand.

On a large scale in the twentieth century, Japan changed from a feudal society to a one-government society with a strong emphasis on industrial production in the 1930s. And South Korea switched from an agrarian to an industrial society after the Korean War ended in 1952. The leaders of these countries showed shrewdness and farsightedness in bringing about these economically beneficial changes for their countrymen.

Much of my feelings on this topic were based on others' (customers') perceptions of Seaberg Industries. If clients believed we were weak in a certain segment of our services that was important to them, we wouldn't get a chance to prove ourselves even if this perception was erroneous. Or

169

if customers believed we were capable of difficult work others couldn't do, we usually worked the problems out satisfactorily if we thought we were capable of meeting the challenge. This meant that we *had to* spend a lot of time with our clientele to make sure we communicated properly to them how we could best serve them and meet their requirements.

We have been looking at making a proprietary, patentable, or patented product ever since we started in business. A little over a year after beginning, I applied for a patent for a cable tensioning device used to hold combines on rail cars that were being shipped to their dealers. But the idea wasn't unique enough to justify being patentable. Our range of interest in manufacturing ideas has included making oil well workover rigs during the oil boom of 1981, a Franklin-style wood-burning stove, components for the biomedical field with the University of Iowa, products for the chiropractic business, and ergonomic products in the material handling industry. I kept thinking, Maybe one of these days ...

One American industry that was very strong one hundred years ago and is almost nonexistent in our country today is the dress shoe manufacturer. When New England shoe companies were at their strongest, at the beginning of the twentieth century, there didn't seem to be anything these companies couldn't do in making footwear. In Bedford, Massachusetts, they had companies housed in specially constructed four- and five-story brick buildings about a quarter-mile long and only forty feet wide. Within these structures, the companies designed and built shoe manufacturing equipment, their own milling cutters and drills, and their own brand of shoes and boots. They were totally self-sufficient and financially strong. Now there is only one manufacturer left in New England, Alden Shoe Company, which is located in Middleborough, Massachusetts.

What happened? From my view, they seemed to fail to cover their market flanks and be alert to ever-changing market conditions. And when the imports started coming into the United States, the companies couldn't adapt fast enough to new marketing strategies. Fortunately for Americans, a few companies like New Balance and Capps Shoe Company did adapt and are still making shoes in America.

A Samurai Lesson from History

*A Book of Five Rings* was written by Miyamoto Musashi, a fifteenth-century Samurai warrior who was never defeated in individual combat and who described his strategies in this book. Musashi didn't meet his adversaries head-on unless he saw that he had a distinct advantage. He would bluff, use innovative techniques, wait for a better time to confront, etc., to ensure a victory in his battles. And by using his brains, he always won and was one of the few who ever retired as a Samurai since they usually died "while serving in office." In business we also can rarely meet our competition head-on and survive in our competitive situations. We want to maximize our strengths and minimize our competitors' strengths. I first learned about this book when it was recommended by Xerox Corporation as a marketing tool.

Compared to other industrialized nations, the US workforce is still the melding pot of the world. We basically have maintained our independence mind-set, have an outstanding work ethic when faced with the proper challenge, and still have the best overall university educational system in the world. But the Asian countries, namely South Korea and China, are rapidly catching up. Other nations are mostly mono-racial. However, Europe is coming closer to achieving a cosmopolitan status, which might benefit them if the countries can halt their socialist bent.

How can we take the best advantage of our cultural mix?

The answer seems quite simple to me, but implementing the answers is another matter. Management needs to get out of the way and let those most familiar with the processes do the work they're trained to do. This is covered in detail in Chapter 35, "The New Professionals." We need to educate *all* of our employees, not just the management. This is covered more in Chapter 31, "Education: This Is Where It's At."

One thing Japan's large businesses have done is make excellent use of their subcontractors for making subassemblies and complete products for them with only the large company logo on the product. When American companies first went to Japan, they contracted with these large companies rather than the ones that made the products, so they had to pay an uncompetitive surcharge on their US products. When the Japanese came to our country, they dealt directly with the smaller businesses and upgraded their competitive edge.

# Crisis = Danger + Opportunity

The main reason for practicing what I call guerilla warfare is that a company seems to be either in a crisis, trying to avoid a crisis, or coming out of a crisis—and it is not necessarily a bad thing. John F. Kennedy, in 1959 just before he was elected president, referred to the Chinese symbol for crisis as being danger plus opportunity. This same definition was also used by Richard M. Nixon and business consultants and motivational speakers and has gained great popularity in colleges and the popular media. The definition has been disputed by scholars, but it is still thought of as comprised of two separate words, danger and opportunity.

So, if we are alert to the good side of the word crisis, there will be a good opportunity for profitable growth. In my former company's case, during the late 1970s and early 1980s there was a world oil boom going on. Because so many people wanted to drill for oil, we took advantage of the opportunity to manufacture equipment for companies long dedicated to work in the "oil patch," as the oil people referred to their work. We sought this kind of work on both borders and the West coast. Our Midwest crisis at the time was union strikes at our major customers, and we had to innovate to keep the doors open.

Many times, after doing a market survey to the best of my ability, I felt I had to take a serious risk by buying an innovative and more-efficient new machine to stay in business and be awarded somewhat nontraditional kinds of work for us. One of my decisions at the time involved whether to purchase a new plasma cutter punching machine for $600,000 ($1,500,000 in 2011) to keep up with the present market plus gain some new market share. This machine with one operator replaced the work of ten workers and with higher quality for the customer. It was a hard decision for me to make when annual sales were less than $5,000,000 ($12,000,000 in 2011) then.

When purchasing most equipment for the company, we used a return on investment (ROI) of one year to be paid back for the machine cost. For example, if a drill grinder cost $20,000 to buy, we expected to recover that cost in increased efficiency and/or quality within one year.

For any major equipment purchases, it was almost always based on a marketing decision—that is, to either keep a customer or exploit an opportunity with potential customers. I am convinced that buying that plasma cutter was a divine inspiration to me, as our Midwest customers went on strike just after the machine was delivered. But fortunately for us, this equipment attracted new customers in Texas and Oklahoma who probably wouldn't have looked at us if we hadn't had that machine on the plant floor. Anyway, I drummed up new work by emphasizing the capabilities of our new Whitney Plasma-Punch Cutting Machine.

Betting the company happens in Fortune 500 companies more often than one would think. Mr. Douglas of McDonnell-Douglas bet the company by investing in the new DC 8 airplane; Ted Turner bet his company on colorizing old classic films; and Walt Disney bet the company on producing *Snow White and the Seven Dwarfs* in the 1940s when his company was just getting established. As most people know, it grew to be an entertainment giant. Mr. Hewitt, a past CEO of Deere and Company, bet the company by creating a construction equipment division when he could have played it safe and not made any waves on his watch. Risk-taking is critical to an economy's health and survival. A risk-taker from South Korea, the chairman of Daewoo, at one time risked the entire company by going into new markets that helped ensure that firm's economic survival.

In guerilla warfare, you find out as much as you can *ethically, morally, and legally* before acting on a risky project. It may not be anything more than a patent search, but knowledge (also known as business intelligence gathering) is almost always crucial to being able to make competent decisions on risk-taking.

Large companies that are leaders in their fields have to be very vigilant to stay in business. They can be put out of existence if they become complacent like General Motors, which lost its leadership to foreign car companies. The man I've also called my economist guru, Peter Drucker, once said, "Managers should be uncomfortable. If they are comfortable, then they are not doing their job." The Hershey Chocolate Company has to constantly be aware of what Nestle is doing in the food business to make sure Nestle doesn't get too much of a niche advantage in their common products.

The chairman of the men's grooming giant Gillette said in the annual report several years ago that the company has to remain vigilant and cannot relax even though they are the biggest company in men's shaving products. Alcoa is the recognized world leader in aluminum production. The company executives talk all the time about the consequences of losing their leadership position among other aluminum producers. Alcoa runs the company like they are about to lose that position. As long as any company has determined and uncomfortable leadership, it will probably remain a leader in its industry.

At Seaberg whenever we received any business honors, we advertised them to let others know that we were still in business. We were proud of our employees and the manufacturing expertise they continually demonstrated. If we didn't tell others about these accomplishments, who would? I guarantee you it wouldn't be the XYZ Machine and Fabricating Company who would tell our customers that Seaberg was the best machining and fabricating company in the Midwest.

# CHAPTER 26

# A Word about Reciprocity

The Bible's New Testament in Galatians 6:7 says that a man reaps, or gets, what he sows or does. Second Corinthians 9:6, also in the New Testament, says, "Whoever sows sparingly will also reap sparingly, and whoever sows generously will also reap generously." In a takeoff on those words, I've observed that whatever you do in life, positively or negatively, usually seems to return to you in one way or another. In Matthew 19:19 Jesus urges us to "love your neighbor as you love yourself," which means we are to treat others as we wish to be treated. I've summed it up by saying that, "Life is reciprocity."

Des Moines, Iowa, at one time had some twelve business clubs where reciprocity in business was practiced. One of them was called the Breakfast Club and was comprised of approximately sixty persons who were presidents, partners, CEOs, or owners of local businesses. The idea was to refer business to each other and help solve common problems. They met once each week with members taking turns hosting the program, usually about something they had done or were doing in their respective firms. Another was a group of about sixty businesspeople in Des Moines who met once a month to exchange ideas. It was called the Des Moines Reciprocal Club. The idea behind starting the group was to find like-minded persons who would reciprocate with their business success ideas to help each other improve their own businesses.

Everyone likes to be treated with respect and courtesy by others. To have this happen, we should be the instigators of good manners. How nice it is to start the work day with a cheerful hello and a smile? Usually when that happens, the person addressed returns the same kind of greeting. Have you ever noticed that if you are walking somewhere and are preoccupied or have a frown on your face, like I have had too many times, that what is reciprocated to you is the same grumble and frown by people you pass?

One of my uncles, Charles Crowe, was a luxury car salesman who at the age of sixteen in 1920 bought his first car for $450 cash ($5,100 in 2011)—not the easiest thing to do. He was in the car business from 1920 into the late 1950s and personally financed many of the car loans his customers made. Being his own banker earned him even more money in the sale of a car. He told me more than once that no matter how bad or ill he felt inside, when he stepped inside his workplace at Lytle Motors in Davenport, Iowa, he always acted cheerful and was ready to make a sale. The congratulatory letters he received from Chrysler executives in Detroit attested to his professional salesmanship and success.

Uncle Charley was born in 1904 and learned to become a fiscal conservative from having grown up in a poor section of Davenport. His parents' home was near Sacred Heart Cathedral on the east side of town where many European immigrant families lived in the latter part of the nineteenth century. He scratched for honest work and made the most of his slim opportunities as a young boy. After he started selling cars in those Roarin' Twenties, by 1928 he had wisely invested in the stock market and planned to be fully retired by the time he was thirty-five. But in the Wall Street Crash of 1929, he lost all of his small fortune because his broker didn't take care of Uncle Charley's and others' stock market assets. The broker ultimately fled to Switzerland to escape prosecution for his underhanded deeds.

As an aside, Uncle Charley told me the week after he was wiped out that he begged and borrowed any money he could come up with and went right back into the market. He told me that was the smartest thing he ever did with his money. In 2000 I saw some of the Canadian Railroad stock certificates he bought in 1929. These stocks had split about eight times by that time.

He could have felt sorry for himself in his financial ruin and quit trying to go on, but that wasn't his nature. He never felt sorry for the circumstances someone he trusted had put him in. Because he remained cheerful, his customers remained cheerful too and kept buying their Plymouths, DeSotos, and Chryslers from him. In 1945 after the end of World War II, he was financially back on top after paying back all his creditors.

One of the older prominent bank presidents by the name of George Thompson of Moline, Illinois, told me many years later in the 1970s that he reciprocated Charley's friendliness and friendship and always had time for him. This was because Uncle Charley kept his promise to pay off his debts when he could have ducked the issue like others did at the time. But those kinds of people don't walk with self-esteem and with their heads held high like Uncle Charley did. And you would never know Charley had any wealth by the humble and friendly way he conducted his life.

I noticed that as I positively projected my expectations of an employee to him, he usually responded in a willing way. If I carefully laid out my requirements to someone and they matched his abilities and then walked away, that person would, in turn, accomplish what I thought he could do. I have practiced this with people with relatively few capabilities and with ones with high IQs and observed that they all responded about the same: they normally reciprocated my verbal and body language by performing to a much higher level of performance than if left to themselves without that positive encouragement.

## Life Is Reciprocity

Some time ago a mixed martial arts world champion and I started a weekly Bible study for men at a gym in Bettendorf named Champions Bible Study. After a few years, every week all of those in attendance who cared to would sign and send a greeting in a card to a young man who had made a bad choice when he went to celebrate his twenty-first birthday with friends. That night this young man, Curtis Fry, got so drunk he didn't know where he was or what he was doing and accidentally walked into a seventy-six-year-old man's apartment and fell asleep in what he thought was his bed for the night. He accidentally killed the man and ended up serving time in prison for first-degree manslaughter.

I was in a local store buying about $50 worth of encouragement cards to send to Curtis after each of our weekly sessions. I asked a store clerk if I could have a discount after I explained to him the reason for buying the cards.

The man asked me to come back a week later when the woman in authority was back in town. When I did go back to the store, I saw that the discount was about 50 percent. I wanted to thank the person who was so gracious to me. The woman who authorized the discount actually made the donation herself on her own credit card! I had to talk to her for a bit before she reluctantly told me that she just wanted to help someone who cared and was compassionate to another human being. She was an angel for her kindnesses to me. I couldn't think of a better example of what reciprocity is all about.

Have you noticed that as humans we tend to live up or down to our own expectations? Many studies have been made on salesmen to see how they were performing after they did far better than their expectations. The salesmen usually unconsciously slowed down to bring their earnings closer to their perceived goals. Or take most college and high school basketball teams when they get an unexpectedly huge lead over an opponent. The players get quite uncomfortable with the lead because they don't know how to handle the point advantage and tend to slow down their play and become more cautious. Then when the other team starts to close the gap, the winning team sometimes can't pick up the pace again and often loses the contest.

As part of encouraging our employees to not only be efficient in making parts but to be effective at part-making as well, we encouraged effectiveness by having them sometimes reflect on a work problem while waiting for a part to be inspected. Then when they solved the problem they were thinking about, it gave them that little bit of confidence to more easily address the next machining or welding challenge at work.

When I still owned the company, one small way I chose to thank my employees for their productivity efforts was through handing out Golden Rule Awards at our Friday semimonthly company meetings held at the end of the first shift on company time. I started out by recognizing special efforts for Poke Yoke (Japanese for mistake-proofing ideas costing less than $500) with candy. But being health conscious and handing out candy didn't compute, so I switched to giving out fruit as the award. Later as I expanded the reciprocity awards to include special help ideas or actions, I ended up passing out bags of uncooked microwave popcorn. It was later that I expanded the awards to include team efforts at improving productivity and began giving Hardee's gift certificates to the employees involved whenever a specific production record was set, whether it was in machining, welding defects per thousand inches of weld, or fabricating.

CHAPTER 27

# Integrity: Where Do You Stand Outside the Company?

When I was a junior playing basketball for the University of Iowa, I had an unusual experience concerning integrity. At the beginning of the season, I was starting ahead of a sophomore who had been a high school All-American. This was Larry's first season of varsity competition because in the 1950s in most conferences, freshmen weren't eligible to play. The purpose of this rule was to help the young men to adjust to life away from home. This man wasn't used to sitting on the bench, and my playing ahead of him caused him to quit playing to the best of his ability. Part of it might have been that I wasn't a star player at Moline High School. The coach, Bucky O'Connor, thought I could handle not starting better than the other man since I didn't have the same high school credentials, so he had his assistant, Sharm Scheuerman, who he felt had a good relationship with me, ask if I would mind if the sophomore started instead of me. It hurt, but I said it was OK. However, I appreciated the coaches' integrity in dealing with me by being up front this way. Even though I was hurt while I was being complimented for the character my parents had instilled in me, the coaches had my complete loyalty. Incidentally, after the season was over, this highly recruited player left school.

What is integrity? According to *Webster's Dictionary*, it is, "1: the quality or state of being complete; unbroken condition; wholeness; entirety 2: the quality or state of being unimpaired; perfect condition; soundness

180

3: the quality or state of being of sound moral principle; uprightness, honesty, and sincerity."[14]

If a company or society loses this mark of good character, it is the start of a decline in trust and respect among each other. If it continues unchecked, it many times signals the end of the firm or society. History is replete with cases citing the start of the decline of societies like Rome and Greece when the leadership became selfish and greedy for power and wealth. A case in the first decade of the twenty-first century involved a billionaire, Bernard Madoff, who led many investors to lose much. Some even lost their hard-earned pensions because he had no integrity in running his business. Now he is in prison until he dies because of his Ponzi scheme that hurt thousands of trusting individuals by robbing them of their retirement income.

One case that affected Americans living when Richard Nixon was president in the late '60s and early '70s affected how we felt about our national leader whose lack of integrity caused the Watergate Scandal and led to Mr. Nixon's impeachment and removal from office in disgrace.

A recent case of lost integrity occurred in the Ohio State football program where successful coach Jim Tressel was forced to resign as coach for the misdeeds of several of his players, including the formerly most sought-after high school quarterback in the country. This quarterback was forced to forgo his senior season because of pending allegations. The errors in these men's integrity will haunt them for the rest of their lives. Was it worth gaining a few dollars at the expense of their and their families' reputations? You be the judge.

## Japanese Integrity

In 1985 our oldest daughter was on a Campus Crusade for Christ summer mission to Tokyo. She observed that the Japanese were so honorable and trustworthy that if any money was accidentally dropped on a sidewalk, it wouldn't be touched by anyone. People would stop and wait for the person who lost the money to discover the accident and return to retrieve his or her lost money. And in the tragic earthquake and tsunami of March 2011, where over ten thousand people perished,

---

14 Webster's New World College Dictionary, fourth edition, Wiley Publishing, Inc., Cleveland, OH, 2002.

it was reported that there was no evidence of any looting of damaged property. I'm sorry to say that would not be the case in much of America today.

## Integrity at Seaberg Industries

If I had known that I would have had to delay paying our bills beyond thirty days before starting Seaberg Industries, I never would have begun operations. Delaying the payment of bills was about the most painful thing I had to do since opening the doors. I had never ducked my bill-paying responsibilities and would never do so. Whenever we've had unusually severe cash flow problems, I would call my suppliers and personally explain the situation to them. Or I would send out letters to them explaining what I was doing and when we planned to restore our normal bill paying. Or we would work out written repayment schedules. The main thing I've striven to do was keep my word and meet my financial obligations when I said I would.

# CHAPTER 28

# Trust: Where Do You Stand?

Trust is earned. There is no easy shortcut to achieving this quality. Trust is what is called the character of the person or institution. Put another way, it is one's experience over time in dealing with someone else.

In the Klondike Gold Rush of 1897, part of the route to the Canadian Yukon was to go up fifteen hundred ice and snow steps to cross over the high mountain pass on foot in the winter. The trail was too steep for horses or mules. The Royal Canadian Mounted Police required each person to have two thousand pounds of food to take over this pass, and it could only be done on foot. The prospective miners would carry their food in fifty-pound increments and start a pile of supplies on the other side of the pass. That called for each man to make forty difficult round trip treks up fifteen hundred slippery steps and down fifteen hundred slippery steps to move his individual supplies. As the men reduced the starting pile, the ending pile would grow. If someone stole any of someone else's pile on the mountain, justice was swiftly administered by Judge Colt, and the thief's body was dumped over the side of the mountain because it was in the wilderness and there wasn't time to litigate in the miserable weather. Being as tired and cold as they were, they didn't have time to discuss any mistrust issues among themselves or bury the thief.

We live in a world of earned trust—phone-in orders to stock brokers, purchasing agents to contractors, etc. On the Chicago Board of Trade, if a broker is thought to be dishonest, he is ostracized by his peers, won't be able to conduct any sales, and goes out of business.

In medicine, people trust surgeons with their lives. A cardiologist inserting stents into a patient or a surgeon opening your skull on a procedure literally has the patient's life in his hands. And if the surgeon uses robotics to do the corrective surgery, he has to trust that the manufacturer of the robot has made a 100 percent reliable machine.

What about the boy who takes your daughter out on her first date? When my daughters went out with a young man for the first time, in a firm and certain way, I let him know how precious that daughter was and to show her proper respect. Years later one thing I've noticed some caring fathers do is have a young man who wants to date his daughter come to her home for a short visit before taking her out. One man told a boy who was going to take his daughter out on a first date, "One of the most valuable persons in my life is going to go out with you." This dad made the comparison of asking the boy if he'd let a stranger drive his new BMW without at least talking to the prospective driver first.

A good example of trust for me happened a few years ago. It concerned one of the salesmen-partners (at the time there were about twenty of them) at a local True Value franchise store in Bettendorf, Iowa, named K&K Hardware. I overlooked a small bottle of glue I was buying as part of some supplies I needed for a home project, and it made it home without me paying for it. The cost was $2.69, and when I called the store to tell him what happened, he just asked me to pay for it the next time I was in the store. It was just a small thing, but the trust he showed in my honesty bought my loyalty for life for that store. Maybe this kind of incident is why this had been the largest True Value store in the United States at one time.

A few years ago a close friend, Harold Paget, who retired as our maintenance manager, passed away. Shortly after the funeral, his wife, Johnette, told me of an incident I had forgotten about. Harold was trying to extract a damaged drill from a CNC vertical mill in our Moline plant and couldn't get it out. Now Harold had more common sense than anyone I have ever known, so this had to be a very difficult job to do without damaging an expensive machine. To back up this statement, he told me when he was a boy the only way his dad would let him drive a car was to figure out how to put a junked Ford in the back yard together. Harold was one of thirteen kids, and his dad didn't have time to show him what to do. The car was in pieces outside on the ground, and Harold figured out how to put it all together and then get it running. At Seaberg's he amazed me when he even learned how to repair electronic circuitry without ever having taken any courses in the subject.

Back to the situation we were in at the plant. I was busy, and as I walked by, I asked Harold how the extraction was going. He said he didn't know what more he could do, so I told him we needed to pray about it. He agreed, but I told him I wanted to do it right now. He was surprised at my sudden willingness to ask him to stop what he was doing right then. He and I asked God to help us solve the problem. When he went back to the job, he just lightly tapped the damaged drill, and it just fell out of the tool holder onto the machine bed! When he got home, he exclaimed in a somewhat awed expression to Johnette what had happened. Harold was already a devout Christian believer, but I think his beliefs went up another notch that day.

One time I was driving from our Illinois plant over to visit a Caterpillar factory customer in Lafayette, Indiana. I usually made this trip after working all day at the office to save productive time. I was just over the border traveling on Indiana State Route 26 East about 10:30 at night and could hardly keep my eyes open on this little-used country road. I earnestly asked the Lord to help me stay awake and trusted in Him to help me. Immediately, the largest buck deer I had ever seen, which was also an *albino*, bounded swiftly across the road in my headlights right in front of me! The stag had a full rack and passed from left to right about fifty feet away and vanished over a small hill. This incident happened in the 1980s and I haven't forgotten that experience or gotten sleepy while driving since that time. Good things come from trusting God in our lives.

At one time I conducted a seven-page survey of our employees to find out how I could better serve them. I realized it would be hardest for the older persons to voluntarily fill it out because of bad experiences some of them had at previous employers, but I went ahead with the questionnaire anyway. I was a little nervous too since I wasn't looking forward to having others tell me what I was doing wrong and how badly I was doing my job. However, the criticisms weren't as bad as I feared they might have been.

Forty percent of our people trusted me by filling out the form and signing their name so I could contact the responders for more details if I needed to do so. And what a wealth of data I got! It took me about a year to implement all the good ideas they gave me. The interesting thing I've found from tapping this knowledge reservoir was that the reservoir never goes dry. The other things I found out was that I was not as good at what I did as I thought and that I shouldn't be so hard on myself. You can see a copy of the survey in Appendix D.

We have done other employee surveys that were shorter and dealt with single issues like smoking on plant property, maintenance, education, etc. These were usually done on short notice and were just another means to find out how the employees stood on different issues that I felt were pertinent to company operations. By design the questions were short, concise, single-issue topics reaching all personnel and another way to get ideas from our most important asset—our employees.

It has been said that up to 80 percent of American workers do not like their jobs or what they do for a living. If this is so, how can you trust someone to do his best if he doesn't like what he's doing? That is why I encouraged anyone who didn't like his job at Seaberg to go get a job somewhere else. But my first suggestion was that he look inside our company to see what would satisfy his desires. If he couldn't be fulfilled at Seaberg, I would even help him find a job elsewhere if he was a good employee. I knew I couldn't give my best effort if I didn't like where I was working, so how could I expect any more from a person who was dissatisfied?

Buyers at many large companies said that the small suppliers should do work for many larger companies as a hedge against economic downturns of a segment of the national economy. This sounds good, but the thing they *all* knew but didn't bother to say was, *"But you better take care of me first!"* This part of their integrity could have used some refinement.

When I was recovering from a heart problem, I found out what trust was all about from the Old Testament in Isaiah 40:31: "But those who [trust] in the Lord will find their strength renewed. They will soar on wings like eagles; they will run and not grow weary, they will walk and not be faint." In the first months of my recovery, whenever I would go walking, and then running a little bit later, I would recite this verse over and over.

Concerning trust, if I asked one of our technicians to take a part into inspection because we weren't sure of the quality, I trusted him to do it. He trusted my judgment in raising the question, and I trusted him to do what I asked. In our small firm, this tech was at the fourth level of management while I was at the first. So what? He knew that I would pass along my request to his supervisor so the supervisor would know what business the tech and I were doing in his area of responsibility and authority.

I have been told in the past by friends in large companies that what I was trying to do was live in a kind of Utopia. That might very well be the case, but it was the best way I knew to survive in the business world. Why shouldn't I be able to treat my fellow worker with esteem and respect for the contributions he was making to my own economic survival? I would be a fool not to trust my fellow worker. And if I couldn't trust him, he disqualified himself from working at our company.

CHAPTER 29

# Intimacy: Essential to
# a Successful Business

In 1956, the University of Iowa's Fabulous Five basketball team lost in the
NCAA finals to Bill Russell's University of San Francisco team because
the USF team had such an exceptionally talented team. However, the
Iowa team got there with lesser talent because each player knew what his
teammates were doing at all times on the court. This intimacy and team
togetherness the men had was the key ingredient to their successes. In
fact, the media in Iowa ended up calling them the Fabulous Five. I knew
about this because I was a freshman (frosh were not eligible to play on the
varsity then) who practiced running coming opponents' plays against
them daily. My brother, Bill, was a captain on that team and a great
leader who helped me sharpen whatever basketball skills I had during
the summers when I was in high school. The university later retired
the Fabulous Five's jersey numbers, with only two other players in the
school's history having been given that same honor. Undoubtedly their
closeness as a team extended to what they did off the court together.

When I was a senior in high school in 1954–1955 in Moline, Illinois,
our basketball team had a 26–3 won-lost record. All of our ten junior
and senior tournament players went on to play college ball after their
graduation. Most of us were quite close off the court, which contributed
to our doing so well as a team. When I went on a full athletic scholarship
to the University of Iowa, we had fifteen scholarship players on the
freshman team who included two high school All-Americans. This
freshman team had more media-recognized talent than the team ahead

of us that made it to the 1956 NCAA finals game. But we never came close to producing a great winning tradition because of what I thought was an apparent lack of intimacy and trust among my teammates.

In a small company, the owner can become intimate with his employees and the manufacturing processes by respecting and working alongside them without interfering with his work to learn how to do his leadership job better. This is a distinct advantage over large companies where the CEO many times has come from another firm and knows few of the employees. Put another way for the small firm, it's a case of, "Work together or lose the business."

It is just as important in business for company leaders to foster intimacy among their people in the company. William G. Ouchi, in *Theory Z, How American Business Can Meet the Japanese Challenge,* explains this as well as any author I have read on the subject. Mr. Ouchi's basic premise suggests that involved workers are the key to increased productivity.

How do employees get involved? By management creating trust, listening to all employees, and many times just getting out of the way and "let the men do their work." I have heard that statement made to me many times by hourly wage earners at large companies.

Harrison Steel Castings Company was one of those kinds of businesses that displayed teamwork and business intimacy among the employees that has turned the firm into what I call a World Class Manufacturer. It is a foundry located in Attica, Indiana, a small community of some thirty-eight hundred people in the late 1990s. The company made large steel castings ranging in sizes up to six thousand pounds each. Their normal market was casting in the thousand-pound range.

Two of the founder's grandchildren, Wade "Rusty" Harrison and Suzanne Curtis Harrison, bought the company in 1985. After the purchase, they called in the company senior managers and told them that if the managers would continue to operate the company, the new owners would continue to provide the necessary finances and financial expertise. This generation of Harrisons could have taken their money and put it in the stock market or other kinds of investments when the economy was going south. Instead they demonstrated their faith in all the employees by just asking them to be willing to work harder and better to keep the company going. The employees responded affirmatively. During the steel foundries' economic downturn that really started in 1982, the company went from a high of 1,300 to about 650 employees. Beside the quality improvements the company has made, they have gotten into furnishing completely machined castings as a way to keep improving their profits.

International Harvester Company was founded in 1831 by Cyrus McCormick, inventor of the reaper and after whom McCormick Place on Chicago's lakefront is named. A fine book titled *A Corporate Tragedy* by Barbara Marsh tells of the rise and fall of the International Harvester Company. Several excerpts describe what happened to IHC:

> By 1909, Harvester ranked as the fourth-largest corporation in America and the largest farm equipment monopoly in the world ... Following World War II, however, the company's arrogant pride in its heritage blinded executives to the challenges of the modern world ... At the same time (from 1945 to 1976) it was losing market share and financial strength. Harvester's high labor costs—a vestige of the company's long, stormy history of relations with organized labor—exacerbated its competitive disadvantages.[15]

In other words, corporate executives probably felt that they could do no wrong, a sure sign of a lack of people concern by the top management. And their attitudes filtered down throughout the organization.

Before the now-defunct Farmall Works of International Harvester in Rock Island, Illinois, closed, I saw IHC employees in the scheduling and purchasing departments literally shout hatefully at each other across the thirty-foot by sixty-foot room as the norm for conducting day-to-day business. Or I would be told that my company was one of eight bidders on work and that if we got the work, we had better perform—"or else." While these seemingly aloof buyers thought they were doing a good job for the company, there were many subcontractors taking advantage of their purchasing system because of the callous attitudes of the company. An example of this is that one local subcontractor told me he made low-

---

15   Barbara Marsh, *A Corporate Tragedy* , Doubleday, 1985, NY, NY(City, State: Publishing Company, Year), pages 4–5.

quantity prototype numbers of parts for a new tractor. When that part became a production model requiring thousands of each part, he was able to charge the same price he had used for the prototype parts for years in making long production runs without being reviewed by the purchasing department. There were big profits for the subcontractor and careless or thoughtless management by IHC.

One of our supervisors used to be a union officer at the Farmall Works. He told me that for years he was known by uncaring foremen only by his time clock number rather than being addressed by his name. Being known only by a number is demeaning and is also how convicts have been called in our federal prisons. This was also true in German concentration camps in WWII. This sort of treatment doesn't make you want to get up in the morning and give your all to the company that day.

With true stories like these, you can understand why this company had severe union-management problems and ultimately failed even though IHC made very good products. It was rumored that the surviving company was bought for about $.05 on the dollar by J. I. Case of Racine, Wisconsin. I think that Case management learned from the people mistakes IHC made in dealing with the talented people who were a part of the transaction.

Another example of lack of cooperation within a large company happened in one Midwest corporation where payroll went from forty thousand down to seventeen thousand union and hourly members in little over a ten-year period in their corporate hometown. It seems that lack of trust between the union and the company was one of the causes of this unfortunate occurrence.

A good example of how top management of a large company works intimately with their hourly associates comes from the aerospace electronics industry. An industrial engineering manager of an electronics products, multi-plant company with about six thousand employees had an idea of how to improve that firm's parts distribution system. After he got the chief executives' approval to go ahead with the project, he went onto the warehouse floor, and in cooperation with the hourly workers, he met with them during all three shifts for their input and to intimately follow through with his own ideas. His belief in what he was doing, the cooperativeness and friendliness he showed to the hourly operators, and the cooperation of his management associates made the project succeed. The hourly employees had never had an executive show this much interest in them before. A nice footnote to this story is that the success of this project led to his becoming a vice president of operations for the company a short time later. This case is just the kind of thing successful management can do, as William Ouchi mentions in *Theory Z*.

Part of intimacy is getting to know better what you do at your company and learning how well your coworkers know their jobs. It seems that when one starts a business, "He knows not, and knows not that he knows not." In a few years, "He knows not, but he knows that he knows not." In a few more years, "He knows, but he knows not that he knows." Ultimately, "He knows and he knows that he knows." (This came from the eighty-three-year-old cook, Bridget Kelleher, at my fraternity house when I lived there; she had a profound influence on my life.) Noted motivational speaker Leon Danco called this the Wonder, Blunder, Thunder stages of a small businessman's career.[16]

It is readily apparent that most of life's stresses have nothing to do with what happens at work. It has been generally accepted that a happy home life is the most important factor in a person's sense of well being. This is followed by the other priorities to feeling good about life being, in order of importance: living in a clean environment, having close friends, a successful career, a satisfying sex life, and a good income being the sixth most important priority to an imdividual.. By caring about your fellow employees, you can help them to enjoy their lives more and help them to be more productive and self-fulfilled persons as well.

If someone is showing an unfavorable reaction to too much stress, you might be able to help by talking to him or her about the problems and keep an otherwise productive person on the payroll.

---

16   Leon Danco, *Beyond Survival*, Reston Publishing Company, Inc., Reston, VA, 1975, page 25.

## Stress Survey

In trying to foster intimate business relationships I looked for ways to handle or eliminate stress. One way we built employee self-esteem was by focusing on the problem and not the person. This reduces harmful stress that hurts a person's self-confidence, and thus their productivity. The following chart shows the relative severity of stress as related to changes in life situations:

Holmes-Rahe Stress Test[17]

| Event | Scale of Impact |
|---|---|
| Death of a spouse | 100 |
| Divorce | 73[18] |
| Marital separation | 65 |
| Jail term | 63 |
| Death of close family member | 63 |
| | |
| Personal injury or illness | 53 |
| Marriage | 50 |
| Fired at work | 47 |
| Marital reconciliation | 45 |
| | |
| Retirement | 45 |
| Change in health of family member | 44 |
| Pregnancy | 40 |
| Sexual difficulties | 39 |
| | |
| Gain of new family member | 39 |
| Business readjustment | 39 |
| Change in financial state | 38 |
| Death of close friend | 37 |
| | |
| Change to different line of work | 36 |
| Change in # of arguments with spouse | 35 |
| Mortgage over $66,000 in 2011 | 31 |

---

17   "The Social Adjustment Rating Scale," by T. H. Holmes and R. H. Rahe, *Journal of Psychosomatic Research*, II: 213. Copyright 1967, Pergaman Press.

18   In my own personal experience and observations, if a man and woman willingly enter into marriage, all divorces can be prevented if the couple is willing to work the problems together and seek Christian counseling.

| Foreclosure of mortgage or loan | 30 |
|---|---|

| Change in responsibilities at work | 29 |
|---|---|
| Son or daughter leaving home | 29 |
| Trouble with in-laws | 29 |
| Outstanding personal achievement | 28 |

| Wife begins or stops work | 26 |
|---|---|
| Begin or end of school | 26 |
| Change in living conditions | 25 |
| Revision of personal habits | 24 |

| Trouble with boss | 23 |
|---|---|
| Change in work hours or conditions | 20 |
| Change in residence | 20 |
| Change in schools | 19 |

| Change in recreation | 19 |
|---|---|
| Change in church activities | 19 |
| Change in social activities | 18 |
| Mortgage or loan less than $66,000 | 17 |

| Change in sleeping habits | 16 |
|---|---|
| Change in number of family get-togethers | 15 |
| Change in eating habits | 15 |
| Vacation | 13 |

| Christmas | 12 |
|---|---|
| Minor violations of the law | 11 |

Whatever the individual topics were that described a stressor, the corresponding value was tabulated, and when the individual scores were added together, the total would be the test takers' score. For instance, if the individual noted her stressors to be trouble with boss (twenty-three), change in schools (nineteen), and change in sleeping habits (sixteen), her test score would be fifty-eight.

A total of two hundred or more stress points can indicate the presence of or a likelihood of burnout. One of our better employees was having some personal problems to the tune of about 290 on the stress test! If I hadn't had the above chart to refer to with him, he would probably have disqualified himself as an employee, and Seaberg Industries would have lost an important asset who had several temporary setbacks. As it turned out, he got his life back together with professional help and concern shown by his fellow workers.

Another employee was going to declare personal bankruptcy because he saw no way out of his financial problems. After talking his finances over with him in depth, he agreed to give an honest effort to pay back his huge debts. A year and a half after he started his renewed stewardship, he was able to make a cash down payment on his first home purchase. It was at times like this that I got the most satisfaction out of my job.

## Japan, Inc.

The Japanese have been masters at knowing and being intimate with automotive customer wants and desires. They have done a better job of merchandizing in America as Toyota and Nissan have outstripped sales by the former Big Three of Detroit.

Can anyone remember what venerable *Business Week* magazine said in 1958? "With over fifty foreign cars already on sale here, the Japanese auto industry isn't likely to carve out a big slice of the US market for itself." Toyota brought their first car here in about 1960. With four engineers driving and testing it up and down the California coast on very little money, the car rusted out and literally fell apart. However, they were determined and persisted in the project until they had a good product. Their outstanding performance up until the end of the twentieth century is the stuff legends are made of.

An example of the snowball effect, or tipping point, that can happen when people feel intimately involved with the company came about at Seaberg because I did something very stupid. One morning shortly after the first shift started, I was making my usual rounds in the plant to see how the third-shift work had gone. I came to our plasma-punch machine located in a back room and saw our maintenance manager standing up on the rear of one of our fork trucks, acting as a counterweight so the driver could pick up an extra-heavy load without tipping over. He wasn't quite heavy enough, so I jumped on top to help as added weight. In our early years, we used to do this many times, so I felt it was OK to do. After we got our "Keystone Kops" act done, one of the older welders came up to me and politely told me that my head wasn't screwed on right because of the unsafe act I had just done. The fork truck hydraulic system could have blown seals or worse and severely hurt one of us.

Of course he was right to correct me. After I got over my embarrassment, I apologized to the men on the fork truck and the welder. Further, at the next Friday meeting, I gave the older welder, Chuck, a Golden Rule Award for his thoughtfulness. He jokingly then said that he was afraid he was going to lose his job by speaking out when he did. Actually, he was more likely to get a raise. By the way, the counterweight man on the fork truck with me was also the safety director! Some of the outfall of this episode was that fork truck driver standards have been tightened again, driver licenses have been issued to employees who have taken our driving safety course, and new driver safety standards have been posted. As a result, there haven't been any driving accidents since we rethought our safety program, and safety in the rest of the plant also improved.

I've occasionally used my wife as a sounding board for important company decisions I've had to make. In fact, I feel that the kitchen table at home was where some of my better management decisions have been made. I have read where several small businesses even have a kitchen table in the company headquarters that is used instead of a board room for conducting company business. Having your spouse involved not only gives you a chance to have an advisor at hand, but she also can give you future emotional support when you may really need it. It may be in a decision about whether to declare bankruptcy, stay in business, decide if one of your children should be invited to join the firm, or in a worst-case scenario, if one of the children should be asked to leave the company.

CHAPTER 30

# What's This about Health?

Friends and acquaintances know that I usually try hard to maintain good physical health. I know that when I'm feeling healthy, I have fewer mental and emotional distractions to deal with. And if I got a sudden and unfortunate business shock at work, I was much more able to handle the circumstance successfully when I was physically fit. Other benefits I've experienced from good health are a positive mental attitude (physical activity limits depression, negative attitudes), lower health care costs, good work attendance, etc. In fact, my total productivity is much better when I'm healthy, and I can only assume it works for others as well. My wife knows this and always encourages me to "work it out" of my system.

I started running at the Bettendorf Community Center at noon when we were still in the back of Tully's Auto Body shop and I was thirty-six years old. One of our employees, Rocky Robinson, was particularly bright and a good worker. However, he knew how to push my hot buttons, and if he happened to rile me in the morning, I would run it out at noon and come back fully refreshed for that afternoon's business. One particular day Rocky really got under my skin, and I took out my stress by running as hard as I could on the flat indoor linoleum floor. This imaginary track I ran was the size of a small basketball court. That day I remember running two and a half miles in fifteen minutes. That was a lot of laps, but worth the relief from every step I ran. And I went back afterward looking forward to what the afternoon would bring.

I made an error later in my career as far as employee health is concerned. In the late 1970s, we moved into a new location in Moline. We had plenty of space, so I put up a basketball backboard on a wall in a large room we didn't need at that time to encourage the employees in their physical fitness. The young men were so enthusiastic that it also became the most dangerous place in our new home. Guys were spraining their ankles and getting badly bruised, so I had to take the hoop down to have enough able-bodied men to make customer parts.

Two examples to emphasize the consequences of poor health come from my own life. At one time I was afflicted with an unknown viral infection over two years that kept me from feeling well for as long as four months at a time. Sometimes I lost most of my voice for various periods and felt like I was walking through quicksand the rest of the time. To compensate for my only being able to whisper, I bought a portable microphone and speaker to use when I was in the plant and office. When in this condition, I didn't have the energy to concentrate and work hard, I couldn't come up with new energy readily, and the ideas I did think of, I couldn't pursue because I didn't have the stamina to follow through. I was severely limited: I couldn't send out thank you cards; I was not able to prepare short necessary reports; I couldn't make that extra sales call; I couldn't talk to the men in the shop; etc.

The other time that business stress bothered me was when I developed polymyalgia rheumatica, commonly referred to as PMR. I woke up one morning with such severe joint pain that I could only huddle bent over on the edge of the bed and cry. Sue drove me to the doctor's office as soon as it was open in the morning. The doctors made a quick and accurate diagnosis and gave me immediate treatment with prednisone. PMR is a condition that once I had it, it could happen again if I came under a high-stress situation—and it has returned several times, but not as severely as the first time.

This caused me to feel grief about my health because I couldn't function as well as I thought I should. I went through the five commonly accepted stages associated with grief:

1. Denial (I'm not sick. This will go away shortly.)
2. Anger turned outward (Why has this happened to me just as I'm about to make it big?)

3.  Anger turned inward (guilt from being mad at others)
4.  Genuine grief (feeling weepy, remorse over loss of vitality)
5.  Resolution (adapting to what happened that slowed me down)[19]

As I learned from my illnesses, I started a volunteer stretching program each weekday before the first shift began. Since it was done on the employees' own time, there were never more than eight men present. However, one of the employees who participated told me that he had been bothered since his high school wrestling days some twelve years before with a chronic shoulder injury. Several months after participating in the stretching program, his aggravation disappeared! It was easy to see results, but it was still hard for others to want to take the time to stretch.

A Midwest automotive company initiated a five-minute stretching and light aerobics program at its assembly plant at the start of each shift. This workout took place at the employee's workstation, whether it was the plant floor, engineering offices, or the executive offices. It was coordinated by a plant loudspeaker system so that everyone started and finished at the same time. One of the employees told me that it worked very well. That five-minute paid time was more than made up by higher morale, more energy on the job, and a general sense of well-being among the employees.

On a related issue, for more than four years I worked to encourage our employees to quit smoking. I talked about it, passed out articles, and even offered counseling for anyone who wanted to quit the habit. Because one of our employees working in the office was allergic to cigarette smoke, I banned it in the office. Several years after that, I disallowed smoking in our classroom.

I even offered $100 to anyone who would be able to quit for six months. Two out of over twenty smokers quit. Then I announced in December 1990 that I was going to ban all smoking in the plant as of June 30, 1991. I paid only one more person $50 for quitting for three months. After the ban was started, I saw some unpleasant results of my actions: rage,

19  Frank B. Minirth and Paul D. Meier, *Happiness Is a Choice* Revell Publishing, Grand Rapids, MI, 2002, pages 36-39. (City, State: Publishing Company, Year) 36–39.

hate between smokers and nonsmokers, depression, poor work effort, and eventually poor morale.

I expected we would lose a few persons after a few weeks. No one left, but after two months, the animosity among shop employees was increasing rather than decreasing. I obviously had to do something to change the company mental atmosphere. My four choices were: 1. Do nothing; 2. Fire the worst smokers (they were among my most productive employees); 3. Go back to the way things were before the ban; 4. Have a modified ban more suitable to both smokers and nonsmokers. I felt I had to come up with a modified plan to work out of my banning decision.

The way I arrived at what to do was something I had almost always done for major company decisions in the past but had forgotten in my zeal to help improve others' health. I examined my actions in light of several principles used in a service club I used to belong to:

1. Is it the truth?
2. Is it fair to all concerned?
3. Will it build goodwill and better friendships?
4. Will it be beneficial to all concerned?

I analyzed these questions as follows:

1. It is true that smoking is harmful not only to the smoker but even more so to the nonsmoker who inhales secondary smoke.
2. It was not fair to all concerned that I put on this ban.
3. The ban did everything but build goodwill and better friendships.
4. I seriously now doubted that the ban was beneficial to all concerned in the long run. If anything, people quitting smoking would have to be voluntary, perhaps through further education.

While thinking through what my decision would be, a fortunate thought came to me: I might have crossed that thin line between caring for a person and dictating what *I* thought was best for him. These smokers, with their families, were hired at Seaberg Industries while they were smoking. And in the plant shop there was enough open space that there was no apparent danger of secondary smoke affecting a nonsmoker.

Besides, the smokers had been polite about not smoking around nonsmokers in the past.

My decision then became fairly easy to return to the way things were previously to my in-plant ban: no smoking in any classrooms or offices. It was the simplest way to deal with the issue. If I had enforced a smoking ban at that time in our country's history at the end of the twentieth century, it could have been the start of arrogance on either party's side. And that would surely be the beginning of the end of Seaberg Industries. I'm sure this entire issue seems absurd to young people in their early twenties today, but at that time it showed how addictive and contentious the smoking habit was.

In a typical smoker issue, my dad was a serious smoker who consumed three packs of Chesterfields' a day. I thought he started the habit when he was twelve or thirteen years old as part of his rebellion against a father who wasn't around very much because of business concerns. In December of 1973, I was with him when I saw him come down with a flu that wouldn't go away. Then I saw him last only six months after that before he died from throat and lung cancer at the age of sixty-four. A few days before he passed away, he told my mom and me in the hospital that he had made his peace with God and was ready to go to heaven. Shortly after that, he had to have a tracheotomy to breathe and couldn't speak anymore. He was lying in the ICU in diapers and was weakly motioning to me with his hands that he wanted a cigarette. Hours later, he quietly passed into Jesus's arms. I still take great comfort knowing that he is waiting for me to be with him in heaven.

In 2009 I had a high tibial osteotomy, which is a surgery where a cadaver bone wedge was inserted in my shin (tibia) bone. This gave me a lot of pain for several months of my recovery. Rather than continue with potentially addictive pain killers, I was introduced to a stretching regimen called P90X, X Stretch, a high-energy stretching program by Beachbody.com, which is located in San Diego, California. I only mention this as a wonderful way to reduce body pain, and I have told physical therapists, chiropractors, and orthopaedic surgeons about this as a good means to recover faster from operations.

CHAPTER 31

# Education: This Is Where It's At

---

This is the age of the knowledge worker. The day of getting high production with muscle has thankfully been replaced. Now those who achieve the highest production rates are generally those with the most training and education. The self-concept of factory workers has greatly improved from being thought of as little more than a drone in the early twentieth century to one who is higher educated and knows that what he does is vital to that organization's survival. Not just anyone can come in off the street and start running a machine successfully.

In the earliest part of the twentieth century, for white people in the United States the only ways to improve their economic status were sports or education, and sports paid very little. Many immigrants sacrificed much so their children could get a good education or excel in sports to be better off financially than they were. I believe social freedom along with the above two were key reasons why our country became the most powerful on this globe.

The best part of our present system of education is that getting a better education is equally shared by all races who legally come to our shores.

## Severin Seaberg

I own a short note that my grandpa wrote in 1929 and recently had it analyzed by a local handwriting expert, Giles Weigandt. Severin had a dominant melancholic-choleric temperament that showed a man who was humorous, compassionate, and creative. But he was also hard-driven to succeed in whatever he chose to do in his life. I was only thirteen when he died, but what Giles wrote made perfect sense to better understand how my wonderful Grandpa treated me and others I saw him with.

I remember stories about my Grandpa Severin Seaberg being a fifteen-year-old Swedish immigrant alone and fresh off the boat at Ellis Island in 1893. He came from a small inland town called Sjotofta (pronounced shurTOFta), near Goteborg, where he went to school through fourth grade and worked on local farms. He couldn't speak English and arrived via railroad in Galesburg, Illinois, to be with a brother who lived there and worked in the jewelry business. It was interesting to me that he never spoke about his brother or visited him after moving to Moline, to the best of my knowledge.

Since Severin couldn't speak English when he first arrived and had no money, he was taken advantage of and treated like a poor, dumb immigrant. He carried water for $0.16 per day on a railroad section gang. When that first winter came, there was no work and no pay since there was no unemployment compensation if you were out of work. To pass the winter away and not think about always being hungry, he learned to play checkers and develop his English better. I remember that Grandpa never let any of his grandkids beat him at checkers, I think from his younger days of being hungry when there was no work for him. Going through those hard times instilled a determination and drive to never be poor and have to endure a situation like that again. Maybe starving and being poor is why he never spoke about his brother who lived in the same community, but I feel the brother could have helped him more.

Grandpa chose to apply his mind to educate himself by learning to read English and by talking with people to improve his language skills. He once said, "People sometimes ask me what's my college. I tell them the janitor at Augustana (a college in Rock Island, Illinois) was a good friend of mine and he took me through Augustana."

Besides trying to improve his rudimentary English, he would work during his lunch hour and make his own excellent toolmaker tools (they were stamped with his Swedish name, Sjoberg, pronounced SHURbay, on them). He made his own tools because he couldn't afford to buy any. His fellow workers used to good naturedly kid him while they played baseball during their lunch time. I now treasure those tools, which my siblings let me have when we settled our parents' small estate in 1974. Grandpa also used to repair bicycles in the basement of his home when he was younger and helping raise his young children to supplement his income.

A few years after arriving in Galesburg, he found work as a laborer in a Kewanee machine shop at eight cents an hour. In 1898 he moved to Moline, Illinois, to learn how to speak better English and go to work at Moline Plow Co., forerunner to John Deere & Co., for eleven cents an hour. He then went to work for a short time at the Rock Island Arsenal in 1909.

In 1899 he married another Swedish immigrant, Hanna Frieberg (later spelled Freeberg), who was three years older than him. By 1900 Severin and Hanna had their first child, Carl. In 1902 Ruth was born, and in 1910 my father, Reuben, was born.

From there, later in 1909, he went to work as Professor Samuel A. Parr's first employee at Standard Calorimeter Company (later renamed Parr Instrument Company in 1932), on Fifty-Third Street and Second Avenue in Moline. He helped build the company to a fifty-three-person firm before he left in 1920. Because of his achievements in manufacturing, Grandpa later served as an advisor to Professor Parr when he was teaching in the chemical engineering department at the University of Illinois. I don't know if Severin ever taught at the university because his English always had a strong Swedish accent that I loved but was hard to understand at times. He enjoyed his working with Professor Parr as much as any work experience he ever had.

It was while he was at Standard Calorimeter from 1917 to 1919, during and shortly after WW I, that the firm employed women to work in the manufacturing area because of the manpower shortage, much like was later done in our country during World War II. During this time Severin invented an upscale artillery gun sight for the army, even though he disliked war so much.

Fred Harrington, a Moline fireman and electrician, had developed a new fire alarm box and took his work to Severin to see if he could manufacture the piece. They then formed a partnership named Harrington-Seaberg Machine and Electric Company in Moline. In 1923 the firm was renamed Harrington-Seaberg Traffic Light Corporation, with very little capital and one employee, besides the two owners. By 1928 the two men built a new twenty-four-thousand-square-foot, four-story brick factory at Twentieth Street and River Drive in Moline, which is still standing because of Grandpa's exacting construction standards. I say this because I grew up in the structurally sound brick home he built in 1917, which also looks quite similar in 2011 to its appearance in 1917.

As I mentioned in the background in the front of this book, Severin Seaberg was a self-taught inventor and businessman. It was at Harrington-Seaberg that he developed the vehicle traffic light that was sold across the United States. He also invented the first leak-proof valve for bottled gas in the welding industry. The most notable traffic light locations were in downtown Philadelphia; Wilshire Boulevard in Los Angeles; and the Loop in downtown Chicago. He bid on installing the entire traffic light system in the Loop for the grand sum of $64,000 (about $900,000 in 2011). It is interesting to note that parts of the Loop system he developed, manufactured, and sold were still operating in the 1990s. In late 1928 or early 1929, the company was bought by a then-conglomerate corporation named The Gamewell Company, located in Philadelphia. This company was later named Eagle Signal Corp., and headquartered in Davenport, Iowa, before eventually moving to Austin, Texas.

Grandpa was retired at the relatively young age of fifty-two before becoming a housing addition developer and director of a bank in Moline. In World War II, he "enlisted" as a machinist at the Rock Island Arsenal for patriotic reasons and "to be a little closer to Reuben," my father, who was a machinist there.

My sister, JoAnne Lund, is six years older than me. She recently told me one of her favorite childhood memories was taking her doll and talking and joking with Grandpa in his car while he drove to collect rent from properties he owned. She would patiently wait in his car while he went to each house to receive his payments. My brother, Bill, also went rent collecting with him when he was old enough. Grandpa once told him,

"Don't ever go to collect rent in a new car." By the time it was my turn to make those trips, Severin had contracted cancer and was forced to quit personally making the rent collections.

The Seaberg siblings, June 1943. Dick, 13 years old;
JoAnne 11; Bill 9; George 5.

Grandpa had a melancholic temperament and was *always* sweet and gentle to me, which is mainly why I loved him so much. That temperament gave him the creativity to make his inventions as well as develop the vehicle traffic light. He also had to have a strong choleric backup temperament to be able to endure the financial hardships that came his way. My parents told me about three little incidents that testified to his never-give-up attitude.

On one of his two-week trips to the West Coast, he called Grandma long distance from California. This was no small thing to do since long-distance calls were prohibitively expensive at that time. From a Los Angeles location, he first had to talk to the local operator at a switchboard. She then had to route the call by hand through many other switchboard operators to eventually be connected in Moline. When he was finally connected, Grandpa asked if the bank had taken their house that was pledged as business collateral yet. It hadn't, and he could concentrate on making his sale before returning to Moline.

Whenever he traveled to either coast by train, he could only afford to sleep in the coach section. To help him sleep, Grandma would make up a small cough syrup bottle filled with whiskey to help him get to sleep sitting up. Drinking liquor was difficult for him to do because he was a teetotaler. He knew from childhood, growing up near Goteborg, Sweden, what strong drink did because it caused his father to be so abusive to the family.

For several years during the early 1930s, Grandpa and Grandma still lived in the two-story, three-bedroom, and one-bathroom brick home on the corner of Eleventh Avenue A in Moline that he helped design and build in 1917. It was this home I later enjoyed growing up in. Along with my grandparents lived Uncle Carl and Aunt Gertrude Seaberg; Aunt Ruth and Uncle Charley Crowe; and my mom and dad, as well as my oldest brother, Dick. They lived there until Dick was two years old. Mom always told me how very quiet and extra polite everyone had to be with eight adults and one baby living in such tight quarters with only one bathroom.

But everyone survived and went to separate local dwellings after 1932 in the Quad Cities, formerly known as the Tri Cities.

Because of his business survival worries over the years, Grandpa died from stomach cancer in 1951 at the age of seventy-three. Other than feeling sad, the only thing I remember from his funeral is riding in the limousine for family members and counting about one hundred cars in the procession to Moline Memorial Cemetery.

Severin was an excellent role model for me when I think of what an education, self-taught or otherwise, can do for you if you just apply yourself.

1909. Severin Seaberg outside Standard Calorimeter Company headquarters, Moline. Severin was first employee of Samuel Parr, Professor of Mechanical Engineering, Univ. of Illinois, Champaign.

1922. Severin Seaberg in office of Harrington-Seaberg Fire Alarm & Telegraph Company, 1702 Third Avenue (now River Drive), Moline IL. Pictured are Severin Seaberg, President, 42 years old; Agnes Schlofski, secretary; Carl Seaberg, son, at drafting table; Harold Nelson, accountant.

1940. Author, 2 ½ , with Severin and Hanna Seaberg
on curb in front of home on 6ᵗʰ Street and 23ʳᵈ Avenue,
Moline, across the street from Karstens Park.
George was always running over to the park so Mom had to put
a light chain on him and attach him to a front yard tree to keep
him from continuing to get hurt at the playground. He doesn't
remember it, but his eight year older brother, Dick, and sister,
JoAnne, who was six years older and his babysitter, remember it.

# Army Helicopter Flight School

When I graduated from the University of Iowa in 1960, my first job was
going into the army as an officer as a result of being in ROTC while in
college. At that time, if you were healthy, you were either drafted into
military service after graduation or went in as an officer through ROTC.
From the corps of engineers officers' school in Ft. Belvoir, Virginia, I
went to helicopter flight school in Camp Wolters, Texas, for primary
flight school.

Almost all of my classmates were college graduates, but once in flight
training, it didn't make any difference how much education you had.
Three students were assigned to an instructor pilot before the flying
portion of school started.

The school was difficult, with a 50 percent washout rate. I remember
in the first few weeks sitting on my bachelor's officer quarters (BOQ)
bunk after supper, imagining I was in a chopper and practicing my
flying so I could be better prepared for flying the next day. I would put

my feet on the imaginary rudder pedals and then grab the imaginary collective in my left hand that controlled the engine speed and blade pitch. I would then gently and slowly move the imaginary cyclic lever in my right hand that controlled the direction of flight and go on my imaginary flight.

All during flight school, the classroom and in-the-cockpit instruction was intense and required a high degree of self-discipline to make it through. One time, several of us students were sitting at lunch and one student who had just received his master's degree said that helicopter school was, by far, the hardest he had ever studied for a course.

One situation happened at the formal graduation party from primary school we had that showed how difficult the training was. We were in dress tans, and the married men were there with their wives. As we sat there, one of my classmates from a national guard unit had been drinking to get up his nerve and gave a bottle of whiskey to our instructor, former Marine Elmo Walker. He then told all of us that this was for "the meanest SOB I know." The party got real quiet for a bit after that.

This was before the Vietnam conflict officially became a war in 1963. As the war heated up, the flight school requirements were loosened because so many pilots were needed for the military effort.

When I graduated and went to advanced rotary wing training at Ft. Rucker, Alabama, in 1961, we had an episode in the class just ahead of us that brought the tough-mindedness of this training to the fore. One morning a Sikorsky H-34 helicopter had a transmission, which was located right behind the cockpit, explode in flight, blowing through a student's helmet and head, instantly killing him. The class was immediately grounded for the rest of the morning. That afternoon the students and instructors were loaded up and sent back in the air to prevent any student from dwelling on the tragedy and becoming afraid to fly. There was counseling for the students, but the *correct* and difficult thing to do was to start flying right away to overcome any fear they might have developed. This was the difficult but right thing for the army to require of those students.

## More about Education

As I just mentioned, one's education doesn't have to be an accredited, formal one either. Several years after leaving the army, before I became a consulting engineer, I read *Benjamin Franklin's Autobiography*. Mr. Franklin felt his greatest achievement was his starting his own self-help learning program. Briefly, he divided the fifty-two-week year by four to get the number thirteen. Then he thought up thirteen words and/or phrases to concentrate on one at a time for one week each. When the first thirteen weeks were up, he would repeat the process three more times in a year.

I tried his system for myself. Words that I put on my first thirteen three-by-five-inch cards were: *enthusiasm, order, Christianity, think of others' interests, knowledge of business, simplicity, questions, integrity, sincerity, tranquility, silence, moderation,* and *remember names and faces.* They were listed in the order of the importance I put on each thought. Then I wrote phrases, slogans, or other reminders to help me concentrate on the card for the week. For instance, on my *order* card I wrote "organize self" and listed:

1. Plan ahead.
2. Know what you are going to do in a meeting.
3. Make appointments when you can.
4. Set an example.
5. *Resolve to do what you say you will do!*
6. Lose no time; cut off all unnecessary actions.

I was twenty-eight when I made these cards. Years later I changed the priorities and phrases I needed for my self-help to: *creativity, discipline, honesty, patience, quality, goals, enthusiasm, diligence, positive mental attitude, confidence, teamwork, thrift,* and *physical fitness.* I excluded *Christianity* because my Christian beliefs were in each of the newer cards.

In 1990, the then recently resigned chairman of Xerox stated that of the training funds spent by large companies, "80 percent is spent on executives and senior management while the remaining 20 percent is for the rest of the troops." He thought the percentages should be reversed and that this vital resource (machine operators, clerks, technicians, etc.) needed to get most of the education. I agreed with his views.

If you worked in manufacturing and visited our plant in Rock Island, you would see that the facilities could easily be replicated anywhere in the industrialized world by a larger company, but you wouldn't have our Midwestern employees to operate that plant. This was where most of our investment cash was spent—on training employees to the best we could afford. It was ironic to see this most valuable asset walk out of the plant doors each work day.

Since I came to my senses in late 1989 about the true value of educating our employees, we budgeted 2 percent of our sales for training and education until I sold the firm in 2006. Of this amount of cash available, our ratios were roughly 30 percent for management and 70 percent to be spent on the remaining employees. After all, most executives in world-class manufacturing companies were already highly trained and motivated. What I wanted to do was get *everyone* more highly motivated, and I thought further education was the best way to do it.

I thought we were doing a lot toward training by the 2 percent of sales investment we made. The students did their classroom work and studies on their own time. But in 1991, Xerox was spending 3.7 percent of sales on training and education. I had to rethink what I thought was a very high figure.

We started a beginning quality assurance course before it was done at any other small company I knew about. We stressed employee attitudes toward their careers and to not treat their work as just a job. I constantly talked about how important they were to the company's success, and if we didn't have a need for them to be a part of the firm, then they wouldn't be sitting in any classes paid for by their company. The classes were conducted on company time.

To put our money where our mouth was, we gave pay raises based on the training and education the employees got, from bookkeeping to the apprenticeship course. (We also paid for part or all of the courses that pertained to our manufacturing business.) For instance, in the 1990s, for each of the four academic years a person completed in the apprenticeship course, he earned an automatic $.50/hour pay raise.

Without the automatic pay raises for education, we would not have had the success the program enjoyed.[20]

In addition, the apprentice had to complete on-the-job training (OJT) and gain experience in operating various machines in the plant. After completing the eight thousand hours of operating the various kinds of equipment, he received his department of labor certificate and card plus a special journeyman patch on his work uniform. The first three graduates voted to use the journeyman term rather than the certified term since they were older and the journeyman term meant more to them. Our graduated apprentices were officially called certified machinists or certified fabricators. Our certified personnel then became part of our curriculum review committee that oversaw the training the apprentices received.

Over half of our shop employees were either graduated from or in the program when I left Seaberg at the end of 2006. One of the neatest parts of this course for us was that the students' ages ranged from twenty-one to their early fifties. When I talked with any of them, they all felt that they were almost daily applying their night schooling during their work shift.

When I first proposed the pay for education idea to my managers, they thought it wouldn't be rewarding the most productive people. But after looking at the program's success with our people, they agreed that the pay for education idea was working.

The department of labor apprenticeship course in the Quad City area was started in the 1980s as a tool and die apprenticeship course by several manufacturing shops with retired tool and die makers as instructors. As of 2006, there were some thirty local companies sponsoring the course in partnership with the United States department of labor (DOL). Seaberg usually had more students than any other shop receiving this excellent mathematics and tooling instruction.

---

20  The Lincoln Electric Company did not do this. The management thought that if their highly paid employees paid for their own training, they would start earning higher wages through their increased productivity in the office and on the floor. But this company was about the only exception I knew of concerning paying for the training and education of employees.

When the DOL representative agreed to our request for a program, we formed an in-house curriculum committee to decide if this academic work was appropriate and if so, what machines the potential apprentices needed to have experience in operating. The apprentices had to agree to the federal guidelines of eight thousand contact hours for certification. Our committee decided, in conjunction with the DOL, to award certification as a machinist, CNC machinist, CNC plasma-punch machinist, or fabricator. When one of our employees requested admission to the course, he signed our apprenticeship agreement before he began classes. This was a standard form furnished by the DOL to help the labor department and Seaberg keep track of who the students were, how many of them were enrolled, and the previous work contact hours the student had for contributing to his graduation requirements.

The academic course outline is shown in the Appendix E.

We revised the OJT hours to better fit our kind of work and added work projects to the curriculum. These projects were done on the student's own time under the direction of one of our certified machinists who volunteered his time. The apprentices had to complete the projects by the end of each year as proof of student competency.

For those employees who went to night school, the idea of applying their knowledge to work situations became contagious, and people became more excited about what they were doing at work and even thought in terms of having a career instead of having "just a job." And it kept getting to be more fun and enjoyable for the students at their jobs. During work and on breaks they were discussing their school problems and soon they were seeing the value to their work and began to make excellent productivity improvement suggestions. Most of these students were the ones who didn't like studying in high school and told me they could hardly wait to "get out of high school."

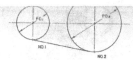

Fig. 7-25. A simple belt drive.

the flat belt or the pulley circumference. In a V-belt system, speed ratios are generally approximations from charts listing the various available V-belt sheaves. Normally the effective outside diameter of the V-sheave is used. This is not necessarily accurate, as true speed ratios of V-belt systems must use the effective pitch diameter of the sheave. (This can be calculated by subtracting twice the distance $X$ between the pitch circle and the O.D. of the sheave.)*

The formula for a simple belt drive ratio is:

$$M_B = \frac{\omega_2}{\omega_1} \quad \text{or:} \quad M_B = \frac{D_1}{D_2}$$

$$\text{or:} \quad \omega_2 = \omega_1 \cdot \frac{D_1}{D_2}$$

where: $M_B$ = Pulley speed ratio or belt drive ratio
$\omega_1$ = Speed of pulley no. 1, rpm
$\omega_2$ = Speed of pulley no. 2, rpm
$D_1$ = Dia. of pulley no. 1, in.
$D_2$ = Dia. of pulley no. 2, in.

Study Example.

1. A V-belt drive, Fig. 7-25, has a driving pulley with a pitch diameter (P.D. = O.D. − 2X) of 5 in. and a driven pulley of 8 in. P.D. If the driving pulley rotates at 1144 rpm, what is the speed of the driven pulley?

*See *Machinery's Handbook, 19th Ed.*, Table 9, page 1057.

$$\omega_2 = \omega_1 \cdot \frac{D_1}{D_2}$$

Step 2. Substitute known values:

$$\omega_2 = 1144 \cdot \frac{5}{8}$$

$$\omega_2 = \frac{5720}{8} = 715 \text{ rpm}$$

**Compound Belt Drive**

A compound belt drive is shown in Fig. 7-26. The formula for solving these speed ratios is a proportion consisting of the ratio of the speed of the ultimate driven pulley to the speed of the initial driving pulley equated to the ratio of the product of the pitch diameters of the driving pulleys to the product of the pitch diameters of the driven pulleys:

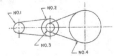

Fig. 7-26. A compound belt drive showing four pulleys.

$$M_B = \frac{\omega_4}{\omega_1} = \frac{D_1 D_3}{D_2 D_4}$$

where: $M_B$ = Pulley speed ratio or belt drive ratio
$\omega_1$ = Speed of pulley no. 1, rpm
$\omega_4$ = Speed of pulley no. 4, rpm
$D_1$ = Diameter of pulley no. 1, in.
$D_2$ = Diameter of pulley no. 2, in.
$D_3$ = Diameter of pulley no. 3, in.
$D_4$ = Diameter of pulley no. 4, in.

**1987, typical textbook math problems from first Apprenticeship course. Textbook was <u>Technical Shop Mathematics</u>, by John G. Anderson and updated in 1989. The problems shown above were replaced four years after the program was started with revised textbooks by the same author.**

**An Army H-34 helicopter that the author was qualified to fly. In the class immediately ahead of the author's class a student pilot died when the transmission, located behind the cockpit, exploded in flight instantly killing the student.**

Because of these positive attitudes toward scholarship and professionalism in manufacturing, a few employees studied for their CPA, considered applying for their professional engineering license, and started engineering school. This schooling would only help Seaberg become better at serving their clients.

All this led to our plant floor attitude toward work as follows:

1.  Operating in a safer manner.
2.  Making a quality part every time.
3.  Making parts as efficiently as possible.
4.  Last, seeing what one could do to improve the part process.

Overall, our employees realized, "The parts you make are what pay your wages."

# CHAPTER 32

# World-Class Manufacturing

The Lincoln Electric Company of Cleveland, Ohio, was founded in 1897 by John C. Lincoln. In 1907 his brother, James F., who played fullback at Ohio State, joined him after his graduation. They were sons of an itinerant Methodist preacher and carried the Christian principles they were taught as youngsters into how a company should be run.

In a four-year period in the late 1980s and early 1990s, in a major expansion, the corporation purchased eighteen foreign companies and incurred debt for the first time since the early twentieth century. After being virtually a single-site manufacturer in Cleveland, and Mentor, Ohio, for almost one hundred years, buying companies outside the United States was only done three other times, in Canada, France, and Australia, by the founder's brother, Jim Lincoln, before World War II started in 1941.

Purchasing that many companies within a few years would be a most unusual move for the corporation, but I don't believe the corporation would have succeeded except for firm, outstanding management leadership and commitment to be the best world-class manufacturer in their field. How many other executives would take that kind of risk in a billion-dollar enterprise? But these persons took the long view and realized that most of their future sales would eventually have to come from outside the United States.

Several other incidents I knew about bear out the company's executive attitude toward being the best they could be. I used Jim Lincoln's articles of incorporation as the basis for my own articles of incorporation and wanted to visit the company. So in 1974, I made the first of three visits to the company headquarters on Euclid Avenue in suburban Cleveland.

Jimmy Lincoln Jr. personally took me on my first tour of the unrestricted parts of the plant. Most of the hourly workers were on a piece-rate system of pay and were very businesslike in their work. But when I asked and was given permission to speak to an assembly line worker, he immediately stopped what he was doing and in a most cordial and friendly way told me about his job, which was a pleasant surprise.

The next surprise came when we went to the cafeteria for lunch. Jimmy pointed to a man running one of the cash registers and told me he was the highest-paid hourly worker in the plant. He explained that he had a free half hour available between his normal work on an assembly line and was given the cafeteria job to do. I can still remember seeing that man smiling and joking with his fellow workers as he rang up their meal costs.

Most hourly workers were on a piece-rate system, even the ones who replaced the light bulbs throughout the company. The hourly costing was fairly administered, except for one time when an industrial engineering manager made a piece-rate mistake. A meeting was held in the cafeteria with the manager on one side of the room and *six hundred men* who had been slighted in pay on the other side. The mistake was corrected in a democratic way, the pay was restored, and the manager stayed employed. But I do think he was demoted to another position.

One other unique issue about the Lincoln culture is the employee advisory board, first started in 1923. This consists of about thirty people from the Cleveland and Mentor plants who are elected to one- or two-year terms by their fellow employees. The board meets once a month with the CEO or president to freely express any concerns the employees have and to discuss company issues that may come before the board.

Since that time in 1974, the headquarters let the foreign companies manage their own businesses in a decentralized manner. But not all the companies were very profitable, and several have been sold over the years. However, The Lincoln Electric Company still looked for other foreign opportunities, and now there are forty manufacturing locations, most overseas, proudly displaying the Lincoln logo. By 1995 the company was debt free. Today the company is traded on the NASDAQ Exchange and is extremely profitable, according to an old friend, Richard Sabo, who retired from his post as assistant to the CEO and president.

I will discuss this more later, but I think the key to Lincoln employee success is that each employee is recognized, appreciated, and respected for their outstanding work. This small item alone separates the good companies from the outstanding ones.

## Guidelines

The guidelines I've used to determine what world-class manufacturing means comes from the Management Chapter of the Bible, Romans 12. There are twenty-two guides condensed into this chapter that give us clues on how we can be better at managing what you do, whether it is running a business or operating a saw in a lumber mill. A book could be written about this style of management, but I have summarized them below.

1. Offer yourself as a living sacrifice that is holy and pleasing to God (v. 1). In other words, do what you say you will do and "walk the talk."
2. Be enthusiastic in whatever good you do, or be transformed into what the Lord has for you to do (vv. 2, 11).
3. Constantly renew your mind (v. 3). Be eager to continuously and constantly learn all you can about the business where you work.
4. Show integrity in your dealings, whether it is mopping floors or writing a business plan. Fight against any form of arrogance in your relationships (v. 3).
5. Teamwork (vv. 4–5). Even Alexander Graham Bell and Thomas Edison needed assistants to help them achieve their stunning accomplishments in the telephone and electrical industries. But my best example of teamwork was shown in the 2011 Academy Award movie, *The King's Speech*, a true story of how England's King George VI overcame his severe stammering by hiring an unorthodox Australian speech therapist, Lionel Logue, to assist him in making critical speeches from 1926 until after 1946. It

was during World War II, when that country needed strong and encouraging words from their monarch, that Lionel was the most help. You may be able to lead, but if you can't communicate to get anyone to follow you, you will come up very short in any significant tasks you take on.

6. Maximize your abilities (vv. 6–7). Don't hold back, but give your all in your projects. Who has ever felt any satisfaction in only giving a half effort?

7. Love others (vv. 9–10). This form of love comes from the Greek word *agape*, which is a feeling of brotherly love and good will toward others you work with.

8. Be righteous (v. 9). How you judge others is how you will be judged by God.

9. Patience (v. 12). This is one of the hardest things a manager has to do. The emergency room is too busy, the phone is ringing, orders need to be processed, and jobs have to be shipped *today!* I believe that only the Lord can give the kind of patience that passes all human understanding.

10. Be faithful in asking Jesus to guide you (v. 12). I know I may have missed a day or two, but I otherwise pray with trust daily to do what He wants me to do.

11. Help others in need (v. 13). Several times in my life I have been on crutches, and I appreciatively remember those who have opened doors and carried my packages when I needed help then.

12. Practice hospitality (v. 13). A hallmark we discovered on trips to Ireland is the hospitality and warmth of the people of Ireland. Who else says to strangers, "A hundred thousand welcomes"?

13. Bless those who wrong you (v. 14). This doesn't mean you are to be a doormat, but be willing to forgive any who wrong you, intentionally or otherwise. And especially because of a leader's pride, it is hard to do. You will live much longer and have a reduced risk of ulcers if you keep this in mind.

14. Work to get along with others (v. 16). It is interesting to me that when I pray for someone I have disagreements with, how friendly he or she starts to become to me. It is not what I do but

what God does to me to learn to love that person in a Christ-like way.

15. Be happy in your work (v. 16). Happiness is a choice you can make or not. Statistics have shown that about 80 percent of Americans are dissatisfied in their work. Work to be part of the happy 20 percent.

16. Be humble (v. 16). What is the point of thinking how wonderful you are and driving others away from you? Do you consider yourself wise? Let others be the ones to tell you instead of beating your own drum. Christ could have come as a king, but He chose to be born of humble parents in a cattle-feeding trough.

17. Be honest (v. 17). If you are always deceitful in what you do, others will know about it, and you will eventually suffer for it.

18. Do not be argumentative (v. 17). You can get people to be more agreeable by using honey instead of vinegar.

19. Be at peace with yourself (v. 18). Be satisfied with yourself while still striving to be the best you can be.

20. Do not take revenge (v. 19). Someone once said to me about being in business, "Don't get mad; get even." That kind of thinking does not bring peace to your soul in the long run. And God says in this verse that He will take the revenge.

21. Follow God's law in loving others (v. 20). We should be charitable with the financial resources given to us. It's amazing how much further my money has gone because my wife and I have tithed on our gross earnings. We did this even when once we couldn't afford to buy a $2.50 roll of film for a vacation when we lived in Springfield.

22. Do good to others (v. 21). This is very similar to point twenty-one, but I still wanted to keep it as a separate item for emphasis in practicing the Golden Rule, to do onto others as you would have them do to you.

Other keys to successful manufacturing:

1. Flexibility. A subcontractor without his own product needs to be able to react to sudden changes in customer requirements. We used as much universal (flexible) tooling as possible to meet these changing needs in the market. We also emphasized being

adaptable to our employees' and customers' needs and to able to work with a customer's desire to have suitable products for their customers.

An excellent example comes from a Japanese company, Komatsu Dresser, and what they did in the 1990s. The company closed down their Chicago manufacturing facilities, which was the plant that was the heart of their manufacturing capabilities at that time. The plant was then moved to Poland. They then took their previously "Made in Japan" products and started building them at their plant in Peoria, Illinois.

2.  Information Technology. This field has exploded in the past twenty years and is almost as necessary as breathing.

3.  Training. This has to be constant and continuous. You may be training some to leave and start their own business, or more likely some will gravitate to larger companies. In fact, one former personnel manager for a local Fortune 500 company bragged to me about all the hourly people he had hired, and was directed to do so, from small firms after they received good training. This will be a constant, but do not fret. By the late 1980s, The Lincoln Electric Company had trained some fifty thousand people, most of whom had moved on to other companies.

4.  Total employee involvement. I used to hand out Golden Rule Awards at our biweekly Friday meetings, as mentioned previously. The idea was to raise any job performance more than 10 percent. These were handed out to recognize anyone who had come up with an idea or action that was a help to company productivity. After doing this for several meetings, it would be commonplace for employees to come up to me during the day to tell me of the good things someone else had done to help others in the business. These persons became secure and confident in themselves and their associates.

It is fairly obvious to those who follow economics that the United States has lost a significant part of its manufacturing base. Charles Day, former editor of *Industry Week* magazine, on August 20, 1990, stated that US manufacturing had been 22 percent + or – 1 percent of our gross national product (GNP) since the early 1950s. Manufacturing has been in a steady decline since 2000, down to about 12 percent of Gross Domestic Product (GDP) in 2010.

But this doesn't have to be the case if we choose to reverse this decline. Our United States Congress needs to offer better incentives again to motivate Americans to be willing to take business risks that have rewards like lower taxes, less government involvement, and less spending of our money to let business adventurers gain fair rewards for their thinking and efforts. I maintain that for us to enjoy the high prosperity we have, we need to get back to manufacturing, one of the three legs an economy grows on besides farming and mining.

CHAPTER 33

# Five-Way Partnerships

For a small company's manufacturability to be maximized, the client company's interests in their suppliers' quality, engineering, marketing, planning, and accounting abilities needs to be encouraged. And the supplier needs to look at the client at least as rigorously. This approach has the best chance of resulting in the clients' customers buying their products.

So what is manufacturability? One manufacturing corporation defines it as "concurrent product and process design for cost effective manufacture of quality differentiated products that provide the best value for our customers." This is a huge mouthful for saying the firm wants to put out better products than any of their competitors.

To me, manufacturability can be best accomplished in client firms by encouraging and supporting supplier efforts to improve their flexibility, reliability, process and product simplification, and total cost effectiveness. The clients need to walk into their subs' factories to observe their work and make suggestions for possible improvements. The best way to do this is for client engineers and buyers to make frequent visits to the folks making the parts since both parties should have sound ideas for process and product improvements. It's what teamwork is all about. This will go a long way toward reducing risks at both places but mostly at the suppliers because they don't have the cash reserves to absorb setbacks like their clients can.

Making sure the supplier understands what is expected of him early in the relationship prevents the subcontract company from getting too far in front of the project schedule because of his desire to serve the client and keep a happy customer. The small business person has a tendency for action and to leap out ahead of the pack because that's about the only way he was able to get started and keep his company going when he first began operations.

Often for the convenience of the client and for the security of the supplier company, large packages of work are subcontracted out to the smaller supplier company. On the surface, this appears to be an excellent contract situation for both parties. But my observations and experiences have been that these big package opportunities are in reality big package headaches. Why?

The single biggest opportunity for the companies involved is to know how to understand where each party is coming from in their dealings. The purchasing manager may have many millions of dollars in annual subcontract purchases under his responsibility, and letting out a package worth 10 percent of his total purchase budget, say a $10 million package, is significant to him. But it is really no big thing as compared to how the supplier sees the same package. For instance, for the small firm, a $10,000,000 piece of business could be half of his yearly sales. This would be an opportunity the small businessman feels might help him realize his long-term goals sooner than he planned. Also, the client and supplier might each have so much faith in the other party that they probably didn't have time to figure out the pertinent details before signing on the dotted line.

Then after the first deliveries are scheduled to arrive, the big problems start surfacing. Both parties get irritated with each other, with a bad case of finger-pointing following. However, there is a way to prevent this kind of regrettable problem.

Why not have the five partners get together at the conceptual stage to reveal the major problems and at least address them before any final product design work is started? Then when it comes time to negotiate or submit firm bids, there are fewer surprises and certainly no big, unpleasant ones.

## Partnership Categories

These Five Way Partnership categories and their key functions are as follows:

1. Marketing. This is where the client company has contact with their customers in the field to see what will satisfy the customers' needs. For if a customer isn't going to buy your product, there's obviously no reason to invest further time and money into the project. I call this *market focus.*

2. Engineering. Can the customer's needs be economically designed? Can the part even be built? What is a better way to make the part that gives the highest value? For example, will the needed parts fit on an existing vehicle satisfactorily, etc.? I call this *product focus.*

3. Quality Assurance. What new or different standards will the ultimate buying customer want? Are the needs compatible with the client's policies, etc.? What quality initiatives should there be? I call this *quality focus.*

4. Purchasing. The people who coordinate the partnership and keep it on track need to be sure it fits into the client's corporate guidelines. These buyers need to be knowledgeable not only about their own products but about the suppliers' capabilities as well. They also would make any recommendations for changing those guidelines. They might raise such questions as: How should cost reduction profits be shared? What is a reasonable profit for the supplier to have? In what ways will the supplier be evaluated for his work? What training costs are involved? What about any tooling costs incurred? What is purchasing's commitment to the partnership? What is management's commitment to the partnership? I call this *customer focus.*

5. Supplier. What are the incentives, if any, to make the part cheaper with the same quality requirements? What special needs are there? The formula I've used to determine value is: *value = low price + best design + flexibility* to *manufacture.* I call this *manufacturing focus.*

The greatest impact on the ultimate buying customer is in engineering design and development:

> Design it right and avoid problems heaped upon problems later in the chain of customers. ... In marketing, the opportunities lie in an expanded view: Not just sales revenue, but looking into tight alliances with customers who prefer to deal with firms that are on a course of continual improvement.[21]

## Examples

Here are a few examples where a five-way partnership would have saved time and money for our clients and ourselves:

1. Use same size metal plates in a fabricated bracket in small runs to make for plate part nesting for laser cutting instead of several thicknesses.
2. Highest value part shape. Should it be square, a triangle, T-shaped, or a ring? Knowing the answers to these simple questions have cut the part cost in half without losing any structural integrity on some work done at Seaberg Industries.
3. Making gussets from bar stock rather than laser cutting out from shape saves material and flame-cutting time when making parts in quantity.
4. When using carbide inserts to machine a part, the design people could use a 0.0794mm (1/32-inch) radius instead of a square corner in order to accommodate industry insert practice and save quoted manufacturing costs.

Another phrase that could be used for describing what we are talking about is employee involvement. As a five-way partnership, we could more easily move in the total quality realm from certification to robust design to employee involvement.[22]

---

21  Richard Schonberger, *Building a Chain of Customers,* The Free Press, NY, NY, 1990, (City, State: Publishing Co., Year), page 9..
22  Ibid. page 71.

# Implementation

To get started, a simple implementation plan would be:

1.  Purchasing and the supplier negotiate a win-win contract that gives value for services rendered and ensures a long-term relationship. All too often the buyer is rewarded in his personnel reviews almost exclusively on his price reduction achievements. I feel he should be rewarded by his own company for the *value* he brings to the company based on the equation in the *manufacturing focus* section. During the contract negotiations, the supplier should know the entire scope of the project and the schedule requirements. The stability of the schedule also needs to be frankly stated because it will help the supplier know how to plan for his cash needs, which are almost always there.

2.  Client and supplier team members meet initially at each other's facilities to see how best to work with each other's equipment and finding out the best ways to communicate between the teams. This phase can even be done before any firm contracts are let. Ideally, this meeting should be done before any product design has been completed. Items such as IT commonality, the appropriate communication format (email, Twitter, phone, etc.), and the proper contact persons would be discussed.

3.  When the teams return to their facilities and the client has decided what project to pursue, they can then start using the agreed-upon best communication medium with relative ease since team members have already gotten to know each other. After a relatively short time, the pace of the work will speed up as both companies' personnel become more familiar with each other.

4.  As work progresses on a project, the teams could meet occasionally in the field where previously built equipment is operating to better understand mutual problems/opportunities. Field work can be very revealing to team members. It points out system defects that couldn't have been very easily thought out in the office.

In most present-day large companies, there are unions to do the manufacturing work, and engineers are not allowed to get their hands on the work as per the collective bargaining agreements. This is one place where engineers are handicapped because they can't work on the floor in a union shop. The small supplier doesn't have this kind of problem. Why not let the recent graduate engineers work closely with the supplier in his shop, on the shop floor running machines doing real work? There would probably be too many problems with this kind of customer-supplier arrangement to list them all here.

Or why not share co-op undergraduate engineers for two semesters or two years? For the first period, the co-op would be employed by the supplier doing real hands-on work. He would be operating various simple machines to get a better grasp of what manufacturing engineering is all about at the operations level and get to know who his in-plant customer is. Then for the last period, he or she would be employed by the client to learn manufacturing engineering at the design level.

In the long run, wouldn't the large client company have more capable engineers and wouldn't the small company have access to that creative brainpower because client engineers would be working "hands-on" to help develop better products? I believe that over a several-year period the idea-to-product-to-market time frame would be greatly reduced as a result. For the supplier company, there would be a "closer to the customer" atmosphere among their employees because they would be working on the shop floor right next to their customer's employees.

The net result of a five-way partnership would be an increased response to the end buyers' needs, with improved quality for the products produced. It would be another win-win situation.

What I've just described was promoted by Dr. Deming in 1950 and what the ISO 9000 Series (international standards organization) for design control, as developed by Great Britain, was all about.

I believe this system was proposed to some extent between large US companies in the 1950s. I've seen it used successfully among large companies on defense contract work in the 1980s because no one company was big enough financially or physically to complete all the work or had the expertise to do a complete B2 bomber project.

There is a cultural difference concerning magnitude of size that isn't easily understood by either party because neither party has worked in the other's environment. What a small company takes for granted in making normal changes in plans is seen by employees at large companies as "lightning quick." On the other hand, small companies aren't used to the thorough kind of planning and staff support that a large company brings to the party.

CHAPTER 34

# The Fourth Level of Management (Everyone a Manager)

Much of the current management discussions in business are about how to best flatten the organization chart. In the 1990s, I think some of the companies in Silicon Valley even threw away the chart because they wanted all of the employees to be independent managers. Unfortunately for Enron, Mr. Lay encouraged every employee to be a creative manager without accountability, and that was a leading cause that bankrupted the energy company.

In the Midwest, one soap manufacturer had their two hundred-person night shift running very well (meaning profitably) without anyone who was there in a supervisory position. In the steel business, USX (formerly US Steel) went from seventeen to three or four management levels and was said by Peter Drucker to be among the best steel manufacturers in the world from eight years ago being near the bottom..[23]

These are enlightening stories, but the only problem with this kind of talk is that what I consider the most important manager level is usually not included as a management level: the individual worker at the bottom of the production chain who does the direct revenue-producing work. In the 1990s, if these bottom management level people couldn't be taught how to manage more work better than they did before 1990, such a company would cease to function altogether. Thankfully the trend of

---

23   Peter Drucker, *Managing for the Future* , Truman Talley Books/Dutton, NY, NY, 1992, page 141.

driving management to the bottom and largest layer of workers has continued on into the twenty-first century.

It's a matter of mindset whether we include this crucial layer of people as managers. Sure, they don't manage others, but in the present and especially future business climate, we will need to require all our employees to work more intelligently, responsibly, and independently than ever before. Because smaller businesses cannot afford the overhead of their larger neighbors, they will continue to be driven to improve their productivity this way. Understandably, small manufacturing firms have narrower margins for error because they don't have the cash to absorb very many relatively small mistakes. A $100,000 purchasing error is catastrophic in a small firm. However, the same amount at a Fortune 500 company would be unfortunate but hardly the very serious situation it would be at a small enterprise.

Each person was valued and significant at Seaberg Industries because each was an individual cost center who positively or negatively affected company performance, much like it is in most nonunion small businesses. The janitors, or perhaps more accurately called cleaning techs, are at the lowest rung of the organization chart but are by no means less thought of by the owners. These techs affect personnel attitudes by the quality of their cleaning and hygiene in the buildings under their responsibility. If this work was sloppy and inconsistent, it would eventually make the rest of the rank and file think that management was sloppy and uncaring about the other workers' welfare.

I called this lowest level on the organization chart at Seaberg, and the one with the most personnel, the *fourth level of management.* I arrived at this designation by calling the first level the one that the president occupies. I chose to go from the top down in level designation because I was the one who took the heat from the bank, our customers, and suppliers when things would go wrong. Since most companies do not use such a classification, I thought it would be easier to say the owner level would be called the first level. I also had the overall responsibility for meeting the payroll and in general, for the company's success. Being at this level certainly didn't make me any better than anyone else in the firm. If anything, I needed to practice even more the way Jesus, the ultimate manager, showed respect and Christian love to those around Him.

The second level of management consisted of those who reported directly to me: the vice president of manufacturing, sales manager, quality assurance and training manager, and office manager. The present owners have titles at this second level as follows: vice president, controller, operations manager, purchasing and training manager, and quality assurance manager (a nonowner position).

At the third management level, I had those who reported to the second-level managers designated as the following: team leaders, maintenance manager, and manufacturing engineering manager. The chart below illustrates the management structure.

Seaberg Industries Organization Chart
President

Sales Mgr., VP of Mfg., QA and T Mgr., Office Mgr.

TLs, Mgrs.                    Inspection Techs          Office Techs

Techs, Machine Operators, Machinists, Welders, Apprentices

This last level of management is neither a panacea nor an appeaser of feelings for the fourth or plant operations level of managers. To save any confusion, we still referred to them by their job description of machine operators, welders, etc. At Seaberg we expected everyone at a minimum to successfully manage his or her work and do all necessary coordination to best accomplish the work that was part of his or her job.

We did not believe in using highly detailed job descriptions because such job adjectives tended to become restrictive in scope. For instance, if some item was left out but was a necessary part of the job of satisfying the customer, a negative-thinking employee might say, "It's not part of my job." And in our kind of work with newer and newer technological advances being constantly introduced to the company, we wouldn't be able to keep up with writing the changes. The far better way was to say, "You are responsible for this profit center and all that happens there. Now, what can I do to assist you in satisfying our outside customers' needs?"

Working this way not only gets the task done at lower cost but also has a great psychological benefit. A simple example of how this worked was when Cheryl Wedra, a buyer, did most of the purchasing for our firm. But she willingly put aside that job to help organize our advertising for an upcoming trade show, a job that normally wouldn't be part of what she did. She had the talent for this task and was the most available person at the time to lend a hand to this project.

Not everyone could handle the amount of freedom they earned at our company. In those few cases, we tried to retrain the new employees to think as we do. And if they weren't able to work productively in this environment, they usually terminated themselves because they couldn't perform to the standards of the rest of the work force. We tried to prevent this kind of problem from the happening by hiring people with the same outlook on life as we think the other employees had in the first place. As I was preparing to leave the company in 2006, we switched to using employment agencies to review all job applications to eliminate those who would not be qualified for employment and to save managers from having to do that first step of personnel processing.

One of our new hires in the 1990s worked for a Fortune 500 company for over twenty years before the plant where he worked was closed and moved to another state. He was earning two-thirds the wages at Seaberg that he used to earn. But Jerry Sturms kept telling me, "It doesn't seem like work to be here," or "The day sure seems to go so fast in this job." He did an excellent job for us and had almost total control over how he went about getting our tool crib work done. He enjoyed what he did. We were sorry to see him retire because of the good example he set for us.

Perhaps the key to higher productivity was that people wanted to feel that what they did was significant and to also have total control over the way they accomplished their individual tasks. Then they felt that they won while the company won. When we hired people, one of the criteria we used was an opinion of how well that person could work independently after learning how to safely operate his or her assigned equipment. It's an old saw, but if someone needed a supervisor to tell him what to do all the time, then the company could certainly do without him or her.

In 1985 our twenty-two-person company was organized in the manufacturing end like this:

President—Vice President—Mfg. Mgr.—QA Mgr.
—fifteen technicians, machine operators (MOs), machinists, and welders

We were barely profitable, with about $50,000 sales/employee/year. Rejects were 6 percent of sales. When I was the only employee in 1974, I had a reject rate of 0.1 percent.

Two years later, in 1987, out of desperation I hired a management consultant to come in to see if he could find ways for us to operate more efficiently. He was originally used as a way to get our employees out of their "stinkin' thinkin'"[24] attitude. He also was a conduit for every employee to express his ideas about how to improve productivity. This idea of hiring a consultant worked out quite well. The most significant idea was to eliminate the bottleneck of everyone in the shop having to get instructions from Craig, our vice president of manufacturing.

After considerable discussion, some of it rather heated, we came up with a new organization. I was one of the early foot-draggers because I was continually fighting to reduce overhead, and adding a level of supervisors seemed to be increasing rather than decreasing costs. By 1987, we had grown rapidly from twenty-two to a sixty-person company, which now operated as follows:

President

Vice President,                QA Manager

42 technicians, MOs, machinists, welders

During this time, the QA office was a very busy place, with production employees having to help with QA inspections. It was like "busy-busy" without a whole lot of forward progress even though we were working very hard to do good work for the clients. The good news is, because of the added supervisor and QA help, production went up to about $58,000 sales/employee/year and rejects declined to 4 percent of sales. More efficiency and better quality: music to my ears!

However, the added business still left a bottleneck in the QA office/laboratory. There, parts spent way too much time in inspection, and

---

24  A "stinkin' thinkin'" attitude refers to a negative, can't-do-the-job way of thinking, versus an I *can* attitude that gets the work done.

machines were idle and not making chips because people were waiting for approval to proceed with their production work. Also, final decisions about whether to ship questionable parts were in Craig's hands. And I was in the background demanding that production meet client schedule needs. It was easy to see that we shipped some parts that we shouldn't have. My bad!

Then we made two changes that dramatically improved quality and sales. The first one occurred in the fall of 1989 when we re-organized our sixty-person manufacturing organization as follows:

Pres.—VP Mfg.—eight supervisors—thirty-eight techs, MOs, machinists, welders

      —one Maintenance Mgr.

      —one Mfg. Engineering Mgr.—two technicians

—Quality Assurance and Training Mgr.—one inspector

—Office Mgr.—four office technicians

—Sales Mgr.

Unfortunately, our sales/employee/year figures declined for a short time, not from any productivity losses but rather from a sudden and drastic general sales decline in the Midwest that couldn't have been foreseen.

The second good change happened in January of 1990 when I went back out into the shop to work as a machine operator for four hours a week on second or third shifts, helping to make parts. I wanted to use this as a way to try to figure out how to improve our efficiency. I hadn't made parts in over six years, so I started with the easiest work, like any new employee. I don't think *anyone* welcomed me. But after my fellow employees realized I was truly enjoying myself and their companionship and making their work better, we had some dramatic results. Productivity improved almost 30 percent to about $65,000/employee/year, and the 1990 reject rate dove to 0.46 percent by that fall! I was a happy guy again!

Later we changed the concept from having supervisors to creating a **team leader** concept. This was more like being a teammate and heading up a group of fellow workers, whether it was managing the third shift or helping the first-shift welders and fabricators get their assigned work done. The concept meant that the team leader gave the employees for whom he was responsible the direction they should go by furnishing any necessary coaching and training they needed. The team leader then went to work at his production task, rather than watching over others to see if they were doing productive work. Working this way was much more fun, more profitable, had better built-in quality, and definitely had more satisfied clients and fellow employees. It was a total *win-win-win* situation for everyone in the process.

## What Can Happen When a Worker is Given a Chance to Prove Himself

A story further showing what can happen when people are given the freedom to manage their work is about a friend of mine, Richard Sabo, who I mentioned previously when discussing The Lincoln Electric Company. After graduating from college, Dick became a high school teacher and football coach near Erie, Pennsylvania, in 1965. One day after practice, two of his just-graduated players came by to visit. In the course of their conversation, one of the young men said, "Hey coach, take a look at my paycheck."

These teenagers were working at The Lincoln Electric Company and were earning triple what Dick the teacher was earning! He was astounded by what they showed him. As the family wage earner, he thought about their wages and told the boys that if their company needed an old man (he was thirty at the time) that he also might be interested in working there.

One year later, the company made an offer to Sabo that he accepted. So in 1966, Dick Sabo began his career at The Lincoln Electric Company. This was a little unusual then since the company rarely hired anyone older than thirty. His first job as an hourly employee was to operate a machine called a rotor turning lathe in the motor department as a piece-rate worker. This is a job where one's pay is determined by how many pieces one produces during one's work shift. After two months on the job, his foreman noticed Dick's good work ethic and abilities and asked him if he would be interested in working on a more difficult project. He said he would be happy to do so.

The company had recently bought several stator winding machines, and they were not operating to their specified performance levels. Being an inquisitive guy, Dick thought he had an idea of how the machines could be made to run better. He was then transferred to an hourly day rate status (this is where one is paid by the hour without regard for pieces produced) so he could work on solving this troublesome problem. Dick's foreman gave him the freedom to roam about the entire unrestricted plant manufacturing areas to find the solution to the slow machine rate project. He was able to go into the tool room and run any of the machines there to make the parts he needed to increase the stator machines' productivity.

He related to me that the best part of all this was that the other machinists welcomed him to use the tool room machines once he demonstrated his competence. And they knew that in this small way, they and the company would benefit financially from his efforts. Well, he did, and they did, and the stator winding machines were operating as planned within six months. And as of 1991, they were still running as originally projected to run without any major modifications after Dick finished working on them.

If Sabo would have had to get four or five levels of approval to give the project to "someone more qualified," as most large companies do, it probably would never have been done in the best way. And the work would certainly not have been done in a time frame anywhere close to what happened.

From that small beginning, Dick rapidly advanced throughout the company, mostly because he was given the freedom to manage his job to the best of his ability. There is no doubt that Dick Sabo and The Lincoln Electric Company had a *win-win* situation.

This same kind of story has been told to me more than a few times by people who worked for a large manufacturer before coming to work at Seaberg Industries. Only the difference was that it would seem to take a committee to decide to let someone qualified follow a good machine productivity suggestion to completion. Doing projects at Seaberg took a fraction of the time and a fraction of the cost to complete a worthwhile project versus how it was done at most large employers, a large employer being defined by the US department of labor as a company with over 450 employees.

Speaking at the American Executives for Manufacturing Excellence meeting in Chicago, on May 10, 1991, Michael Spiess, executive vice president/COO of Wallace Company, the 1990 Malcolm Badridge Small Business Award Winner, said, *"Wallace quality win* means to create an atmosphere where the employee can reach his or her full potential." This is exactly the same way Sabo's company treated their personnel.

Another of my friends working for a Fortune 500 company saw that while many of his coworkers were happy in their work, there were quite a few who seemed to lead lives of quiet desperation. This became that much more apparent to him the closer a person got to retirement. He made it a point to observe his fellow workers, and most were desperate to get out of what they thought were stressful, unfulfilling jobs.

Another close friend took early retirement from a business where he had worked for some thirty years because he could just barely get out of bed in the morning to go to work because of his dissatisfaction with his job and where he worked. This man was the kind of person who made a contribution wherever he went in life. Harold Paget came to work at Seaberg and stayed until he was sixty-five and thoroughly enjoyed coming to work every day as our maintenance manager.

This was sort of like when Bill Russell and Larry Bird were NBA All-Stars for the Boston Celtics, Bill in the 1950s and '60s and Larry in the 1980s and '90's. They made others around them want to work harder and better at their skill positions. Their teammates always seemed to try harder when these guys were in the game. And it didn't matter if they were on offense or defense because they made outstanding *team* plays. Winning all those NBA titles was no accident when they played but the result of intelligently working with and encouraging their teammates to be winners.

I've tried to make my management style somewhat similar to the popular perceptions I've read concerning Japanese management thinking. When I was working on a project affecting others, like what machine to purchase to make a new client product or what effect a new marketing venture should have on our business strategic plan, etc., I sought employee feedback before I made a final decision. Initially, I wanted many questions, objections, and discussions on the subject. But as the decision time got closer, there were fewer and fewer arguments, and a consensus started to form. Then when the final decision was made, the agreement usually was unanimous. Unfortunately, this wasn't always the case. But when we did go about our decision-making this way, the final choice was normally a good one and the decision more than likely would not be the same as the one initially proposed.

## CHAPTER 35

# The New Professionals

When I was CEO at Seaberg Industries, the new professionals were those who willingly, and enjoyably, took on more responsibilities. Consequently, they were given more authority to control the work they did. This new professionals concept was built on having a positive attitude toward serving the customer by giving him the best quality, delivery, price, and flexibility to needs he was able to do.

Part of what this meant was investing more money in fewer people who did the same amount of work as the earlier larger number of workers. In the front office, we went from a support staff of four to two doing the same amount of work. Along the way, the smaller staff developed a simple steel analysis program that showed our best quantity to purchase and also helped with quoting and inventory control. As I was selling the company in 2006, we started to buy our steel in a negotiated pricing structure proposed by our chief customer in machined fabrications that was even better because of the higher tonnage of steel the customer required versus what we needed.

Another example of this professionalism is the charting of weekly reject costs I used to do. At first my efforts to track and plot the costs only seemed to help increase those costs. However, when our quality assurance and training manager saw the need for showing reject costs, he decided that he wanted to do the charting. He talked to the shop personnel and explained how he wanted to follow the cost reductions we would be making. As a result, the reject costs began plunging. This charting for all employees to see has since been modified, as the accompanying picture taken in 2011 shows.

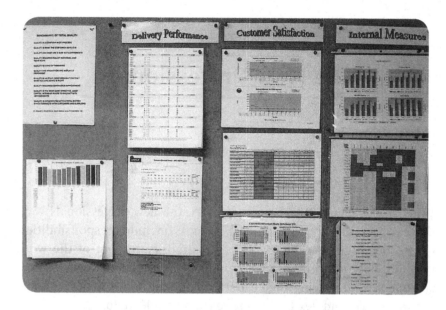

**Some of the weekly charts in the conference room showing, at a glance for the managers, the status of customer Delivery Performance, Customer Satisfaction, and Internal Measures of quality.**

When we first started using the charts, my "infinite wisdom" was perceived as a punishment tool to show how poorly we were doing rather than as a transparent help for everyone. The QA and T manager came to the rescue and presented it in a positive light to the people making the parts. Same chart, different perception—much different results.

Part of the new professionalism of the employees at our small machining and fabricating company was shown by the QA and T manager's priorities that he developed:

1. Teach Seaberg Industries quality standards to all employees. This included the benchmark standards at the time of ISO 9000 Series compliance.

2. Teach Seaberg Industries quality standards to our major manufacturing subcontractors like grinding, heat treat, and

painting shops. After all, these fine companies wanted to know the standards required of them.

3. Be the QA standards setter and interpreter in our business.

4. Coordinate all process data necessary to aid and increase company productivity.

These basic priorities are simple and common sense, but it takes this simple and direct thinking to get all the involved parties to pull in the same direction—to satisfy client needs.

Craig Kinzer, our VP of manufacturing then (he later became president) did a good job of designing and encouraging others to come up with innovative, inexpensive, and flexible tooling for making parts. And this was done before computer-aided design systems but rather by the old tried and true pencil-and-paper method with a good deal of intelligence thrown in the mix. Shortly after this in the 1990s, we installed Visual Manufacturing System software that is still functioning properly with the latest updates in 2011.

A small aside is that in 2010, I started a national First Teen Challenge robotics course at a local high school. At another local high school, the ninth through twelfth grade students routinely made 3D files (a.k.a., engineering drawings) that small manufacturers only dreamt about making at the turn of the century. They are also self-taught IT programmers. Using computer training seems to be on a space rocket pace where three months is all the time we need for major computerized engineering changes to become available to far-seeing companies.

Seaberg people also standardized both hard and perishable tooling needs. Hard tooling refers to items like clamps, tool holders, and universal devices that help hold machining and fabricating work in place. Such items like a special clamp for a prototype part would then become a production device that should last for years. Soft tooling refers to one-time-only tooling that is discarded after only one use, like making an experimental part to see if its function will be adequate for a project.

Perishable tooling includes drills, taps, and cutting inserts. As an example of new professionals' thinking, Jerry "Doc" Sturms, a machinist and tooling technician, developed a new way to grind our center drills that enabled one of the vertical machining centers to go from needing daily center drill sharpening to requiring sharpening only once a month. What happened as a result was no drill removal and machine downtime to insert a new drill and no necessity to re-sharpen center drills frequently. That was a classic case of what intelligent employee involvement in processing does.

Dick Vogel is a very valuable employee and one of our laboratory QA inspectors who has been at Seaberg since 1984. He has an orderly, positive attitude about his work and how he goes about doing it. Somewhere around 1990 when he was a machinist, he found new meaning to the work he did. This increased interest in what he was doing was because he *knew* that his production accomplishments each day were helping make a big difference in the financial outcome of the company. This, in turn, increased his pride in being a significant part of Seaberg Industries. Back then he shared with one of our managers, "Not just anyone can get a job here anymore." That was a priceless comment.

## Using the Pareto Principle in the Office

Perhaps the most cost-effective project we did in 1990 was to investigate our work process flow through the company. We first discussed this in one of our weekly material review board meetings where the president met with the quality, manufacturing, and manufacturing engineering managers to talk over all subjects relating to manufacturing quality: tooling, equipment processing, new work, rejects, training, and personnel. We usually did not include office efficiency here. We used the Pareto Principle 80-20 Rule, where we concentrated on the biggest cost reducers: 20 percent of the plant work affects 80 percent of our company costs, 20 percent of our customers give us 80 percent of our sales, 80 percent of an equipment budget comes from 20 percent of the equipment used, etc. Because of this mindset, Jim Merten, our office manager then and controller now, was able to reduce the number of office personnel 25 percent in a year while supporting the same company size and sales output.

Reducing process flow time and the related costs of an already effective system we already used looked like it could have a substantial return on investment (ROI). The manufacturing engineering manager, Anton (Tony) Alvarado, agreed to head this assignment. What he came up with was a very creative and fun game for finding solutions to a nebulous, and possibly boring, project. He had free rein to involve anyone in the company he felt could contribute to solving the challenge.

I first saw Tony do something similar to this when he was taking an MBA course at the local St. Ambrose University where he was the student plant manager looking for the best way to manufacture an assigned product. I was serving on the mock board of directors at the time and was quite impressed with the thoroughness and organization of his presentation. After his presentation, I recruited him to further his engineering manager career at Seaberg. He did this so well that he is now one of the owners and vice president.

At Federal Express, one of the largest package deliverers in the world, the delivery drivers' motto was, "Delivering a package is the company's payroll." This was related by Dianne Miller Stokely, regional vice president at the May 10, 1991, conference of the American Executives for Manufacturing Excellence that I attended. This is similar to what the mailman used to say to me when I was a youngster growing up in Moline, Illinois.

Compare the above statements to what a steel mill executive who spent seventeen years working in Gary, Indiana, mentioned. *Each day* he would go to work wondering if what he did that day would count for anything significant for his company. He told me this after he left that company and found real fulfillment at another, smaller, steel company. Statistically, 80 percent of Americans are not satisfied with what they do to earn a living, especially at the top management levels, so this was not surprising. I am very thankful I have never had that problem.

## Key Indicators

What are some of the key indicators I used to help see how well our business was doing? First of all, I only skimmed the daily sales and production figures because the time frame was too short to give a very reliable picture of how the company was performing, but it did give me a feel for how the plant was operating. There were still times when I might have a special project in the shop that took weeks to produce, shop, and invoice. Because of instances like that, I felt I would be chart-chasing without having anything worth using in our decision-making process.

For a weekly quick check, I used five figures: weekly sales, scheduled sales, backlog sales, rework costs, and machine hour loading. Weekly sales was that work invoiced that week. Many times we shipped late on Friday and didn't invoice until Monday. If Friday was the last day of the month, on the following Monday we sometimes would back date the invoices to Friday to have a truer Seaberg picture of how we did the previous month. This practice had no effect on our clients since most of them started counting their payment schedules from receipt of our invoices. Once again, this was only an internal aid to Seaberg.

Scheduled sales were purchase orders, purchase releases, etc., that called for shipment of goods within the next ten weeks. We used ten weeks to allow us time to order special materials, castings, or forgings. For most first-run orders of potential later work, it let us have sufficient time to create the work process for manufacturing, let quality assurance look for any potential problems, and build necessary gages and tooling. Doing our work this way allowed for the 10 percent of the time when we had the inevitable one- or two-day rush orders.

Backlog sales were for any work projected to be done after ten weeks. As you might expect, this was a somewhat unreliable figure to use because of forecasting uncertainties. With the 1990s' emphases on flexibility and speed, this figure became fuzzier and fuzzier compared to its usefulness to me in the 1980s, but it still did give me a feel for how to coordinate future sales work.

Rework costs answered many questions: 1. How well were we were doing our present work? 2. Did we need more training in certain areas of the plant? 3. How good was our preventive maintenance? 4. Were we too far out of our market niche for a customer to make the level of quality he wanted? We all liked to think we were on top of our responsibilities, but figures don't lie if the costs were too high for what we allowed.

All I looked for here was just a very general feel for how well the shop was balanced and loaded with work. Most of the time the work went through the plant too fast for those figures to be very accurate. But the trade-off of some inaccuracy with high speed work processing versus a low throughput of work and greater machine hour load accuracy was worth noting.

The monthly figures I relied most on were: sales, profits, Z score, sales/employee/month, inventory turns, and jobs shipped that month. Other figures I used were training dollars, maintenance costs, and suggestions/employee/year. These topics have already been covered in chapter 8. "Success Isn't An Accident."

For a short time, with the emphasis on JIT by our clients, it looked like we were going to get into an inventory storage trap: expense to us, short-term savings to the client. However, we became more innovative and were able to lower our work in process and raw material inventory. But I still watched it closely just to help keep it in line. (There's that old false idea among some of our production personnel that seeing a lot of inventory in the racks gave them job security.)

Another thought about having a positive professional attitude was that excellence isn't a goal. Rather, it's an exciting journey throughout your career that never ends but goes on and on.

A suggestion one of our new professionals made to best describe our positive attitude was to say, "We're not the company we once were, and we're not the company we're going to be."

CHAPTER 36

# Retire? Retirement? Retired.

## Retire?

In 1992, I was almost forced to default on my bank loan and declare bankruptcy. As part of my loan agreement, I had to put up our home as collateral. Even though I had a company net worth of (negative) $389,000, I knew I would never declare bankruptcy and have creditors suffer for my mishap, even if it took the rest of my life to pay back all the debts.

At the bank's urging (meaning I had no choice), I hired a banking consultant to help me work out of my dilemma. After I voluntarily reduced my own wages to a bare subsistence level, I was told I had to reduce everyone else's wages 10 percent in order to keep the doors open. As you can imagine, these were unhappy times for everyone working at SI. The blessing to me was that only one or two people bailed on the company.

The day I announced the pay cuts at an employee meeting in the shop, one of my senior employees loudly told everyone that we were going to go out of business because he had experienced this same thing at a previous company where he worked. Thankfully the good news is that Dave stayed at Seaberg, and as of 2011, he was still helping the company produce good parts.

Something happened that is amusing now but wasn't very funny at the time. A land survey crew hired by the bank came to our home to make sure the site survey matched the lot documents filed with the bank.

My next-door neighbor, Harry "Duke" Pelton, was in his backyard when the two-man crew arrived to first speak with me, and then they unloaded their measuring instruments. During the entire time the survey inspection was being done, Duke stood in the same place with his hands hanging limply at his sides, his jaw literally hanging open, and not saying a word. He just stared at what was happening in my yard. Duke knew that things were not going well in Seaberg-land, but he was still surprised to see the seriousness of our situation. After the crew packed up and left, without saying a word, Duke silently walked into his house.

In the end, when the bank saw how hard I was working and knowing I would fight any bankruptcy proceedings, they forgave $150,000 of the loan, and happily for both parties, they let me turn to another bank for a renewed loan. But the former bank made me carry a life insurance policy for fifteen years at a $1,000 annual premium to cover that forgiven amount in case I died during those fifteen years. It was a very happy time fifteen years later when I walked into the bank and told them I had made my final payment.

During 1992 I spent a lot of time on my knees asking the Lord for guidance. Years later, my good friend, Don Martin, told me the only way I survived the situation was by spending the first hour in the morning in prayer, Bible study, and meditation. It got to the point where I asked the Lord to help me make "just one decision today," as I was incapable of handling much more due to the stress I felt I was under.

The humiliation of being forced by the bank to ask my Uncle Charley, brother-in-law, Phil Trissel, and wealthy friend and advisor, Ray Brown, each for a $10,000 loan was hard to swallow. These men sensed that I did not want them to do it, and thankfully, each graciously turned me down. Along with Jesus Christ walking with me through much prayer, I had my wonderful and loving wife staying by my side.

After our restructured loan was made with a new bank, I was too exhausted to continue as an owner of a business, so I started thinking about how to go about selling the company, hoping to get ten cents on the dollar for it.

At this point my fine son, Tom, talked to me about wanting to join the firm when I told him I was going to sell the company I had owned for eighteen years. This was a terrific shot of adrenaline for me since he had a very good job as a quality engineer at the local plant of Alcoa in Bettendorf. He told me he had always wanted to own and operate a small manufacturing company like Seaberg Industries.

Well, Tom expressing his interest was certainly an instant energy restorer. I was no longer tired! So I called off my first "retirement" and had my enthusiasm for being CEO of Seaberg Industries restored once again. I will be forever grateful to Tom for being my perfect catalyst and re-energizing me to keep the ownership of Seaberg Industries in my and the new owners' hands instead of it being sold to strangers.

## Retirement?

In early 1993, Tom resigned from Alcoa and started work at Seaberg with the blessing of his wife, Ann, who he married in 1988. Even though he had helped in various company locations since he was in seventh grade and co-oped as an engineering student from the University of Iowa, we agreed that he should start a seven-month training program going through most of the jobs in the plant with his last jobs being a technician in engineering doing quoting, fixture design, and part processing before ending up as an inspector in the quality lab. The idea here was that he would then transition to become the quality assurance manager for an unspecified period of time.

He enjoyed getting to renew his acquaintances again and being involved in company operations. Once while going through his training, he found a way to improve a process in the welding area for about a cost of $500. I told him to go and complete his project. It was completed within a week. Afterward he came to me and said that a simple job like this would have taken three months just to get the paperwork approved where he had previously worked.

Then, on January 1, 1995, he moved into my office as assistant to the president. That was one of the most fun times I had at the company as I worked with Tom as he was transitioning into becoming president of the firm. During this time, our desks were next to each other so we could have close communication. We discussed business daily and traveled together to introduce him formally to our clients throughout the Midwest.

In the early summer of 1998, to my great delight, he became president and I became CEO/chairman and started to move some of my personal effects out of the plant so he could have the president's office alone.

In August of that year, I had a formal retirement party for some 450 shop friends, suppliers, and invited guests from as far away as Utah and Arizona. I paid for this event with a matured executive insurance policy that the company no longer needed. We had a beautiful night, cruising the Mississippi River on the *Celebration Belle*, a dinner-cruise paddle wheel boat I reserved for the evening. The evening ended with my personally thanking the guests and giving each of them a small gift as a remembrance of the occasion.

I was quite happy to leave the office and let Tom take the helm of the company. I went into building furniture at home for the family and supervising the building of an addition onto our home in Riverdale, Iowa, on the banks of the Great River.

But being a company president wasn't meant to be for my son. In 2000 I asked him if he wanted me to come back and resume control because he didn't enjoy what he was doing. I gladly obliged because I love him dearly. To his everlasting credit, he owned up to the fact that he didn't feel comfortable in his job, and he made a good decision for the company and for his family.

When I returned, it took me two years of working hard to catch up with what the company was now doing and feel competent in my job again. Tom went back to being quality assurance manager, and we soldiered on from there. I was never very comfortable in this replacement leadership position, but I was at peace with what I was doing.

In 2002 I made a concerted effort to find a replacement for me from among company employees. I looked at three persons from within the company to be the next president. By 2004 I finally settled on Craig Kinzer and started passing more responsibility and authority over to him. My main reason for doing this was to see if he could handle the position, even though I was confident he could do the job. It is one thing to think you can assume a higher management position and another thing to see what happens when you are given the opportunity.

An amusing incident happened during 2005 when Craig came into my office one day and politely and somewhat facetiously said something like, "Mr. Seaberg, I have been running the company for a while now." He didn't even know that I was testing him, much like Jack Welch of General Electric did when he was considering one of three men to replace him before he retired. I love Craig, but I still had to test him to see if he was going to be capable. He has taken on being CEO in a most admirable way.

By the end of 2005, I decided to offer to sell SI to six men I felt capable of continuing to grow the company long after I had left. I didn't want to fracture any cohesion of the men I chose—Craig Kinzer, Tom Seaberg, Tony Alvarado, Jim Merten, Ray Clark, and Brian DeKeyzer—so I appointed Craig to be the liaison between me and the buy group. I did this so the men would be forced to cooperate with each other and then come to me with only one voice.

A former small business owner told me it would take a year to have all the agreements ironed out, but I didn't think it would take us nearly that long. I was probably naïve to think it would be a simple transaction. It seemed to proceed well until I was told that one of the men didn't want to participate in purchasing the company from me and Tom, who was the only other original stockholder besides me.

When it finally came out that my son was uncomfortable with the proposed ownership, I was a little surprised. That was the start of the most difficult year of my life. I was trying to protect my wife's future as well as put together a separation package that was fair to my son and a plan that was fair to the managers I had chosen to sell the business to. Surprisingly, the most turmoil I had was in dealing with Tom because I didn't know his true intentions until after we were well into the negotiations. He has since moved on to a very fine position with a Fortune 500 company.

I hurt my only son emotionally, and I was hurt in return. I would not wish that kind of a situation on anyone. If you ever want to get into a squabble with all your emotions being strung out, try negotiating one of your children's financial future involving a family-owned business.

In the buyout negotiations, each party had little details that were brought up that threatened to derail the buyout train. One occurrence I remember well was when I worked very hard and wanted to keep the logo I designed and copyrighted. The men were right in coming down hard on me with a flat *no* to that idea.

By that fall, all the details had been worked out where all the parties were as satisfied as they could possibly be:

1. The successor bank was selected and approved.
2. The business and equipment were bought.
3. The building and land were to be leased for five years with a loosely agreed-to purchase price for it at the end of 2011.
4. Tom's buyout was settled.
5. The lawyers and accountant wrote up, examined, and approved all the legal documents.
6. October 1, 2006, was set as the transfer date.

Then we signed the necessary agreements and transferred ownership on October 1, 2006, with the building lease payments to begin on January 1, 2007, for five years. At the end of 2011, I hoped to have the building sold to Seaberg Industries or to any other interested party.

A nice touch has been that I had the freedom to visit the company whenever I wished to do so. After all, these now-former employees were still like family to me.

# Retired

I am now officially retired and enjoying other pursuits. I feel there is so much one can do in retirement that it wasn't possible to do when I had responsibilities for being CEO of a company.

My wife and I can now spend more time with the six of our seven grandchildren who live in the Quad Cities. We can go to school events during the day, babysit on short notice in the morning, have lunch with a granddaughter, help my son coach a junior high basketball team, and support grandkid sporting events ranging from soccer to basketball to track to wrestling or anything the grandchildren do.

A highlight for me was to take a genuine second honeymoon in 2010 where Sue and I were not responsible for anyone but ourselves. This hadn't happened since the day we were married on August 29, 1961. The trip was a casual two-week driving vacation around most of Ireland. We first went to Ireland in a tourist group several years previously and fell in love with the Emerald Isle. This time we used a travel agency to buy the plane tickets, rent a car, and arrange for us to go clockwise around Ireland from Shannon, on the west coast. The itinerary included reservations at bed and breakfast homes, hotels, and castles. Hands down, this was the best trip I had ever experienced. The only driving surprise was not driving on the left side of the road but maneuvering roads that were so narrow. The hedges at the edge of the pavement hung over the pavement so that many times the passenger side mirror was turned into a hedge trimmer.

Other special travel events we did were taking each grandchild, when he or she reached his or her tenth birthday, on a trip wherever he or she wanted to go in the contiguous United States. This began in 2005 and will continue until 2012 when we run out of ten-year-olds.

One of the joys I have had was started one year before my final retirement. It was helping start a Bible study with mixed martial arts men and writing a weekly summary of what was discussed. After six years, it is still going strong with some changes in members making up the group. So far, the emailed newsletter is still going to friends and acquaintances on every continent on the globe, except Antarctica.

The very best thing for me is that my married life, after I passed the seventy-year mark, has gotten to its best phase, much like the song I wrote, "Seek the Holy Lamb." Thank you to my best friend, Sue, my wife of fifty years.

In 2007 Sue and I went on an Alaskan cruise and heard well-known Christian speaker Chuck Swindoll speak on *"What kind of Legacy do you want to leave?"* He mentioned six rewards of a life well lived in integrity that spoke to me in my retirement. My comments are noted in parentheses.

1. Sustained cultivation of exemplary character. Have Christian teachings for our offspring into the fourth and fifth generations.

(This is what I have concentrated on, mostly since retiring. Our children probably aren't aware of this, which means that I'm not trying to shove it down their throats, but I want to give a godly example in whatever I do so our descendants will have a Christian direction to follow for *their descendants.)*

2. Having continued relief of a clear conscience. (Have no overtly sinful regrets where I have sinfully and willfully hurt someone.)

3. Having the personal delight of an intimacy with God. (This is a wonderful constant for me.)

4. Having the priceless inheritance of a lingering legacy. (This causes me to think about my Grandpa Severin Seaberg and his gentleness toward me in his last years.)

5. Having the rare privilege of being a mentor to our offspring and others. This is the highest echelon of a relationship. (This happens on an infrequent and random basis.)

6. The crowning reward of finishing well and strong.

In regard to finishing well and strong, I wrote a song called, "Seek the Holy Lamb," and had it copyrighted. It has been a highlight of life after retirement. I never expected to do such a thing. I had been listening to a song written by David Downs for the music group Celtic Woman named "Green the Whole Year 'Round" over and over because I enjoyed hearing it so much. I gradually starting singing along with the music with my own words, and before long I realized that this old engineer had a song to write. My song speaks about the four phases of life a married Christian passes through before going to heaven:

1. Being a small child, growing up, and getting married.

2. The joys of raising a family.

3. Becoming "empty nesters."

4. The best phase, which is spending the last years with your spouse and offspring.

As an aside to keep me in my place, one of the choir directors at my church wrote three excellent songs for the church in the space of six months that has me in awe of such talent because I'm not wired that way. She explained that she reads her Bible each morning from 3:00 to 6:00

a.m. and prays about putting a song together. The upbeat music Tewanta Lopez writes is very beautiful and meaningful, with a good message.

Another thing I did that has given me much personal satisfaction was becoming a member of our city's volunteer fire department. I didn't feel I would be safe because I was over seventy to crawl into a burning house as a fireman. I did the next best thing by becoming a federally certified first responder to the Riverdale Volunteer Fire Department. I attended a course taught by a paramedic and a Scott Community College professor of health and safety. This consisted of taking a night course curriculum of 126 actual classroom hours, meeting once a week. Counting my study time to learn human anatomy, I averaged thirty hours a week for the six weeks of the course and then took time to take and pass a national exam. It was a challenging task for me but well worth the effort.

I did this because I wanted to pay back the city for protecting my family during those years when I was running a company, and this seemed to be the most appropriate way to do it. One of my firefighter friends told me there were no financial rewards, but the words of thanks and the look of gratitude in someone's eyes who you just helped are priceless. Dale had it right on both counts.

In retirement the additional activities I've been privileged to do include writing a monthly interview of older members of our former church; planning a book about a much-decorated Korean War veteran; starting a high school robotics club at a local school; serving on various charitable organizations; and most of all, enjoying being with my best friend and wife of fifty years, Sue.

# Appendix A (from Chapter 8)

Seaberg Industries, Inc.
Annual Planning and Forecasting

One of five topics (time, cash, space, skills, equipment) dominate the below-shown categories of the annual plan that are the highest, or only, category to be considered for planning purposes.

## Planning

1. The purpose is to help assure financial success by enabling management to determine the following business needs.

|  |  | Category |
|---|---|---|
| A. | Highest Quality Service Possible | SKILLS |
|  |  | TIME |
| B. | Adequate Cash Flow and Sales | CASH |
|  |  | TIME |
| C. | Work-In-Process | CASH |
|  | 1. Payroll | TIME |
|  | 2. Unsold Work | SKILLS |
|  | 3. Spare Parts | EQUIPMENT |
|  | 4. Raw Material |  |
| D. | Inventory and Inventory Turns | CASH |
|  | 1. Raw Material | TIME |
| E. | Marketing, Sales, and Advertising | CASH |
| F. | Personnel and Education | SKILLS |
|  |  | CASH |

G. Tooling and Machines                                     EQUIPMENT
   1. Marketing Decisions
   2. ROI of less than one year
   3. Poke Yoke (Mistake-Proofing)

H. Facilities                                                    SPACE
   1. Time                                                        TIME
   2. Review Quarterly—April 1, July 1, October 1
   3. Rough Draft—December 3
   4. Final Plan—December 27

# Forecasting

Unscheduled, periodic meetings through the year of the president with the VP of manufacturing, sales manager, office manager, QA and T manager, manager of manufacturing engineering, and maintenance manager, usually on a one-on-one basis.

Review YTD performance vs. YTD objectives considering the following:

1. Marketing and sales as a *world-class manufacturer*
   A. Market conditions and the economy
   B. How well are we meeting client needs?
   C. Int'l market penetration: Quad City Development Group, Iowa and Illinois departments of commerce
   D. National market penetration
   E. Regional market penetration
   F. Local market penetration
   G. Competitors' ability to meet market demands
   H. Pareto Principle 80:20 Rule—80 percent of the market is held by 20 percent of the companies
   I. What didn't we do that could have improved our business, or what we did do that caused our business to exceed our forecast?
   J. Who are our competitors, and how well are they meeting market demands?

2. Productivity (efficiency + effectiveness) as a *world-class manufacturer*

   A. Building *a chain of customers*—what are we doing *outside* and *inside* the company to serve our customers?

   B. TPM—total productive maintenance: maintenance personnel are suppliers to operators; proper maintenance tools at the pertinent machines

   C. EI—Employee involvement: training of our employees (do we use 2 percent of sales for training?); how do we achieve the high level of commitment of *all* employees to reach company objectives?

   D. TQC—Total Quality Control: process is under complete control, from marketing through sales, order receipt, part processing and ordering, manufacturing, shipment, billing, and check receipt.

      1. Rejects goal achieved

      2. Activity-based costing—what are we doing to get here? Do we need to do this?

      3. Inventory turns to twenty-five-plus per year (it was twenty-two-plus in 1990)

   E. JIT—delivery on time, when needed.

   F. Kanban—keeping waiting lines short. Are we overlooking obvious improvement areas?

   G. SPC—statistical process control. Ability to confidently predict and ensure the best process results; implementation of poke yoke.

   H. What could we have done for our fellow employees to bet better productivity (i.e., education vs. equipment acquisition vs. debt pay down)?

   I. Did we follow our ROI objectives of one year payback?

   J. What poke yoke ideas did we use? What was the best one?

   K. Would we achieve better results by promoting from within for office, production, QA, or manufacturing engineering needs?

If our entire market goes up 20 percent and our sales improve 30 percent, what are the right things we can continue to improve in order to keep the momentum?

We need to independently analyze our strengths and weaknesses and determine how we can improve our company's performance. (This should be done throughout the year.)

By the October 1 meeting, we begin the process of sales forecasting, considering all the issues that have been listed thus far. The managers have several years of sales, profit, and expense history at their disposal for reference as they prepare their forecasts for discussion at that meeting.

Once I determined the most realistic (*plan*) forecast, I then estimated the *best* sales forecast. The *worst*-case scenario was usually the current year's sales figures.

I then prepared the company forecast on a spreadsheet. At this stage, all managers were involved in meetings during which we determined the percent of our annual business we would achieve in each month of the year. This was determined by reviewing the percentage of monthly contribution for the past three years and the current year, analyzing trends, and projecting the monthly spread of business for the forecast year. Once this was determined, monthly forecasts were prepared, and monthly figures were kept current so we could monitor our achievements vs. our thought-out goals.

After the sales and income objectives were stated, we prepared our expense objectives. When we prepared expense objectives, *every* expense had to be justified or we discussed the feasibility of eliminating or reducing it and every expense increase that was forecast must be justified (i.e., buy equipment on a one year ROI).

We were then ready to develop our *annual plan*.

## Annual Plan

Checklist for making the annual plan.

Clients in our current sales.

1. Inventory
   a. Inventory levels for JIT, Kanban.
   b. Minimum and maximum inventory turns (target eighteen to thirty/year)
      i. Steel—daily releases
      ii. Castings—determine specific lead times
      iii. Other materials—each treated separately
   c. Seasonal changes (i.e., tractors in the spring, combines in the late spring, Dec. and July slowdowns, etc.)
2. Sales staff
   a. Individual objectives—inside and outside personnel
   b. Sales training programs
   c. Sales tactics for each client
3. Advertising
   a. Format
   b. Media to use
   c. What image do we want to develop—continuity is important
4. Guarantees and warranties
5. Pricing strategies

New Sales Clients

1. Inventory
   a. Inventory levels (twenty-two-plus turns per year target)
   b. Minimum inventory levels required to meet the demands of our best (spring) and lowest (summer) selling three-month period.
   c. Restrictions to low WIP (work in process)—waste, client requirements
2. Sales/marketing staff
   a. Establish individual objectives

    b. Sales training programs, if necessary

    c. Sales strategies

3. Advertising

    a. What message do we want to present, and how do we plan to achieve continuity and recognition?

    b. Trade show benefits analysis

4. Sales promotion plans

5. Pricing strategy

## Finance Department

1. How can we develop and maintain good financing sources? We get feedback on our needs from our banks and CPA firm.

2. Personnel development

    a. Training (goal is 70 percent hourly, 30 percent salary expenses)

       1. In-house training

       2. Apprenticeship course

       3. Seminars

       4. Client schools

       5. College courses

       6. Other—joint venture with another firm

    b. Pay and incentive programs

3. Product/market development

    a. Financing

       1. Bank

       2. Leasing company

       3. Venture capitalist

       4. Other

    b. Insurance—degree of liability (i.e., safety conditions, such as nuclear)

    c. Leasing of equipment

    d. Ways to continue to reduce interest expenses

    e. Service contracts

    f. Client guarantees (i.e., floor plan for distributors)

Total Company Operation

1. Financial requirements     CASH
2. Personnel requirements    SKILLS
3. Equipment requirements   EQUIPMENT
4. Facilities requirements     SPACE
5. Timing of schedules       TIME

After these questions are addressed, we are ready to fill our Appendix B and combine it with A to complete the *annual plan.*

# Appendix B (from Chapter 8)

Solution to productivity problems is *an attitude of constant and continual improvement.*

1. Quality: follow annual quality improvement plan
2. JIT ordering of materials coordinated better between scheduling/ mfg/mfg eng/purchasing
3. Improve *processing.*
   a. More accurate quoting of work
   b. More accurate process steps (kanban, poke yoke, sequence, correct data, proper processing times)
   c. Seek the best *process* (i.e., For Job C142 machining, have right coolant mix, speeds, and feeds.)
4. *Preventive maintenance* improved
   a. Operator training (machine tool schools, grease and oiling points, coolant testing)
   b. Better machine checklists
   c. Machine manuals up-to-date
   d. *Process capability studies* current
5. *Scheduling* improvement
   a. Accuracy of process for machine loading
   b. Improve machine hours loading (plan vs. actual)
   c. Use a systematic approach (i.e., have a goal to improve ten jobs/week)
   d. Fewer emergencies to address
6. *Tooling* improvement
   a. Job trays always current, with sharp and proper tools

b. Are we ordering enough of the right tools in advance? Too much in advance?

c. What new tooling do we need?

7. Ways for plant personnel to spend more time making parts, training, or process analyzing instead of emergency maintenance.

8. Training for employees (QA, SPC, apprenticeship, maintenance, etc.)

9. Waste elimination—time, space, overproduction, distance

10. Marketing: do what we do best, what's new out there for us in manufacturing of machined and fabricated products.

# Appendix C (from Chapter 9)

Decentralized Process Card System

## Advantages

1. Eliminates repeated production of plastic job jackets, as had previously been done. Making job jackets involved re-copying drawings and printing process sheets every time a part was processed again. Now three-by-five job cards are used instead and accompany tubs, pallets, or cartons of parts wherever they are sent, both in-plant and/or to subcontractors. These have been effective for over fifteen years, even in an age where everything seems to be paperless.

## Typical Job Card

---

Work Center: Job No. Quantity
Press Brake 05-C891-1 14

Operation: FORM 87.9 deg BEND Step 30

---

DATE |    |   |   |   |   |   |  

PERSON     |   |   |   |   |   |   |  

Total Pieces

Finished |   |   |   |   |   |   |   |  

Rejected |   |   |   |   |   |   |   |  

Revision Date: 05/12/2011

---

2. The cards eliminate process change/edit lag time through operator ownership of the previously used process sheets, which were also too cumbersome to keep with the containers carrying the parts. Whereas it used to take days to put into process any print or process changes, it now takes a maximum of one hour to fully implement process and/or print changes.

3. Operator search time for prints and processes is reduced. Masters are kept in three locations in the company manufacturing area. If they are not in these files, they are in use at a specific machine.

4. Cost accounting is improved for each run. There is less wasted time and errors between job completion and completed costing.

5. Improved simplicity and effectiveness of internal engineering changes.

6. *Much less paper is generated.* The only new issues for each job are the job cards in the new system versus the old way of having new prints and process sheets with new job release numbers put on all the documents. Now the company uses about one-tenth of the amount of paper as was previously used.

Disadvantages—relative to the former method of processing work? *None.*

# Appendix D (from Chapter 12)

## To: All Employees

Re: *In-House Customer Survey*

We all help manage Seaberg Industries to the extent that we want our customers to keep coming back for more service, and we want to make a profit doing it.

Each one of you is also my customer at one time or another. I want to know what I can do to serve you better. By this survey, I want to avoid any of the major causes of management failure as listed by the American Management Association:

1. Arrogance
2. Insensitivity toward co-workers
3. Misuse of confidential information
4. Excessive ambition, at the expense of the company's interests
5. Failure to delegate tasks and cultivate teamwork among subordinates
6. Inefficient staffing

Enclosed is a list of items I would like to have you look at and comment on. Please sign this when you are done so I can ask you any additional questions if necessary, but you don't need to sign it if you don't want to. Please turn your suggestions in to me by the end of August.

—George Seaberg

Note: The below survey was done once, but after it was done, the employees felt it to be unnecessary because they felt they were already being heard fairly by management.

Please circle the answer you feel is the most correct for you.

Quality

Do you have enough gages and templates for your work?     Y     N
If not, what kinds do you need more of to do your work? I would appreciate your being specific with the job numbers.

Do you get the assistance from QA that you need, when you need it?
                                                        Y     N
What about SPC charts? Do they help you?                Y     N
What more would you like to have the QA manager do for you?

Manufacturing Engineering

Are the prints clear enough for you to use?              Y     N
Do the process sheets give you the latest data you need?  Y     N
What are the most common problems you have with the process sheets you use?

Do the process sheets lack anything?                    Y     N
If yes, what do they lack that would help you?

Do the fixtures or any other tooling do a good enough job for you?
                                                        Y     N
When you ask for engineering help, do you get a prompt response?
                                                        Y     N
What can manufacturing engineering do to serve your needs better?

Scheduling/Purchasing

Do you usually get your process sheets and prints on time, or are things usually in a panic?
            PANIC                OK              ON TIME

Do these persons usually try to fill your productivity needs?  Y     N
If not, what can they do to help you?

How well do they work with company suppliers and clients for you?
            POOR         OK              GOOD

Accounting

Is everything related to your pay, health benefits, and/or 401 (k) retirement plan answered to your satisfaction?       Y     N
If not, what would you like to have accounting do better to serve you?

## Maintenance

Do you get the support you need to do a high-quality job?  Y  N
Are your blue maintenance card requests answered promptly?  Y  N
Does maintenance need to conduct more preventive maintenance training on the equipment you operate?  Y  N
If yes, which machines?

## Tool Crib

Are there any other tools needed for the tool crib that would help you do your job better?  Y  N
If so, what would they be?
What are we lacking for supporting your productivity efforts in the tool crib?

## Team Leaders

Is your TL doing a good enough job for you?  Y  N
Does he do a good enough job of keeping you informed on matters that affect your job?  Y  N

What would you like to have him do to better serve you?

Management Support. Management experts say that 85 percent of what goes wrong in a business is caused by the managers because they are poor communicators, don't provide good employee training, or some other such thing. I agree. The purpose of this section is to zero in on where George needs to improve what he does for you. He also wants to know how his managers—Craig, Jim, Rhett, and Tom—can do a better job for you.

Should the office personnel operate any production machines for training or improved communication purposes:  Y  N

> One week/year on second or third shift?  Y  N
> Two weeks/year on second or third shift?  Y  N

Is George doing a good enough job for you?  Y  N
What does he need to do better?

What do you want him to quit doing?

How much confidence do you have in your management?
George    NONE    SOME    OK    GOOD    A LOT

Craig, Jim, Tom, Rhett   NONE   SOME   OK   GOOD   A LOT
Team Leaders   NONE   SOME   OK   GOOD   A LOT

Waste

There is always room for more elimination of waste: time wasted waiting; poor work layout; too much traveling between processes; too much inventory; poor processing; poor maintenance. In other words, is there anything that does not work toward satisfying your customers' needs?

Is the present plant layout good enough for you?         Y    N
In your opinion, what could we do to reduce the waste in our company?

Building a Chain of Customers

Your customer is the next person in the process who receives your work. What can the company do for you to better serve this very important person?

What poke yoke (mistake-proofing) ideas can we help you use to best serve him?

What do you feel could be done better to improve productivity between the shifts?

George has noticed much better cooperation among all company departments, from sales to accounting to engineering to first step processing to welding to machining to shipping. What do you feel could be done better to improve productivity between departments in the plant?

Training

Do we need more *building a chain of customers* classes?    Y    N
Do we need classes in problem solving?                       Y    N

Maintenance training?                                        Y    N
Math classes?                                                Y    N
Geometric tolerancing?                                       Y    N
Quality assurance theory?                                    Y    N
Any other? If so, what additional training would you like to have?

Discipline

In well-run organizations, this is something that needs very little mention. Even though we are a better than average company in terms of talent, we still need to discuss this important part of successful living. Our normal steps in our disciplining policy for violators of our rules is a verbal warning, written warning, one day off without pay, and then dismissal.

Do you feel that we deal fairly in any discipline matters?  Y    N
Do you feel we need to be firmer in handling any discipline problems, such as starting late, being absent without calling in, continued quality problems, or verbally abusing a fellow employee?    Y    N

What would you recommend that George do?

Environment

What would you like to see in the way of physical facilities to help us maintain our manufacturing leadership?

Finance

We cannot create something from nothing. But as we continue to work toward making a profit, George wants to return as much as he can to the employees. What suggestions do you have for him?

Do you like the bonuses that we get now (quarterly no lost time accidents, quarterly profits, reduced health care costs)? Note: Before my final retirement, Craig Kinzer came up with a formula for administering bonuses that has proved to be fair to all.

George will show the results of this survey to all employees.

Thank you for taking time to help him do his job better.

Signed (optional) _____date

Those who sign their survey will receive a copy of it back.

# Appendix E (from Chapter 31)

First Year

Mathematics
The Number System
Fractions and Mixed Numbers
Decimals and Fractions
Powers and Roots

Print Reading
Design to Product
Visualization
Various Views
Reading Drawings
Special Views
Materials and Processes

Machine Tool Technology
Basic Machine Arts
Safety
Layout Tools
Micrometer
Vernier
Dial Indicators, Sine Bar
Surface finish
Setup Tools
Screw Threads
Taps and Dies
Grinders
Cutoff Machines

Second Year

Mathematics

Fundamentals of Algebra
Ratios and Proportions
Gearing and Shop Formulas

Print Reading and Machine Tool Technology
Drilling Machines
Lathes
Lathe Tools and Setup
Cutting speeds
Center Drilling
Lathe Chucks
Precision Machining
Reaming, Boring
Taper turning
Thread Cutting
Turret Lathe

Third Year

Mathematics
Algebraic Expressions and Radicals
Geometry: Lines, Angles
Geometry: Postulates, Proportions
Geometry: Triangles, Quadratics
Geometry: Circle
Geometry: Area, Volume

Print Reading and Machine Tool Technology
Milling Machine
Cutters and Holders
RPM and Feed
Milling Procedures
Indexing Head
Spur Gears
Cam Milling
Digital Readouts
Shaper Operations
Grinding Wheels
Precision Grinding
Cylindrical Grinding

Speeds and Feeds
Sharpening Tools

Fourth Year

Mathematics
Right Angle Trigonometry
Oblique Angle Trigonometry
Shop Trigonometry

Print Reading and Machine Tool Technology
Cutting Fluids
Cutting tools
New Machine Technology
Numerical Control
Metal Classification
Carbon and Alloy
Heat Treatment
Special Hardness
Hardness Testing

As one can easily see, the first-year course work was quite easy, while the fourth-year work was quite rigorous in trigonometry and geometry. I felt that what we had was better than any junior college course I had seen for teaching people to be professionals in industrial manufacturing.

The following table lists the on-the-job training hours required for an apprentice to complete to become certified.

| Fabricator | | CNC Machinist | |
|---|---|---|---|
| Deburr | 100 | Deburr | 100 |
| Saw (Hor. and Vertical) | 200 | Saw | 200 |
| Drill | 300 | Drill Press, Natco | 200 |
| Milling Machine | 300 | Vertical Mill | 800 |
| Flame Cutter | 300 | Horizontal Mill | 700 |
| Tooling use and care | 40 | Blanchard Grinder | 400 |
| Press | 2500 | Lathe | 1000 |

| Forming, Template Layout | 2000 | Fixture building | 500 |
|---|---|---|---|

Equipment Maintenance 80
Inspection Procedures 80
Statistical Process Control 20
Weld and AWS Certification 2000
care 120

TOTAL HOURS 8000

Inspection Procedures 80
CNC Lathe, or CNC Mill
Programming 80
Tooling use and

Operation 3720
Statistical Process Cont. 20
Equipment Maintenance 80

TOTAL HOURS 8000

### Machinist

### CNC Machinist-
### Plasma Cutting- Punching

| Deburr | 100 | Deburr | 100 |
|---|---|---|---|
| Saw | 200 | Saw | 200 |
| Vertical Mill | 1300 | Vertical and Hor. Mill | 100 |

| Horizontal Mill | 1300 | Blanchard Grinder | 20 |
|---|---|---|---|

Blanchard Grinder 300
Lathe 2700
Bench Work—Assembly 600

Whitney
Programming 40
Tooling use, care 60

| Equipment Maintenance 80 | Operation | 6700 |
|---|---|---|

Tooling use and care 420
Inspection Procedures 80
Fixture Building 500
Statistical Process Cont. 20

TOTAL HOURS 8000

Press 200
Inspection Procedures 80
Equipment Maintenance 200
Statistical Process Cont. 20

TOTAL HOURS 8000

# Index

International Harvester 3, 60, 74
International Harvester Company
112, 139, 167, 190
inventor xv, 28, 31, 157, 190, 205
INVENTORY 164, 166
Inventory Turns 138, 247, 257
Ireland 220, 254
ISO 9000 229

## J

James Lincoln, Sr.. *See* Lincoln Electric Company
Japanese xv, 129, 130, 131, 132, 133, 137, 160, 161, 171, 178, 181, 189, 195, 222, 240
Japan Inc. xv, 137
J.C. Penney xvii
Jesus Christ 5, 21, 22, 86, 249
J.I.Case 191
Joseph of Arimathea 22

## K

Kanban 110, 157, 259, 261, 264
Kataras, Tom 134
Kelleher, Bridget 192
key indicators 245
Keystone Kops 48, 195
King Hezekiah 31
Kinzer, Craig xii, 4, 6, 82, 95, 104, 108, 243, 251, 252
K&K Hardware 95, 184
Klondike Gold Rush 183

## L

Leach, Jim 23, 26
Lebron James 81
Lincoln, Abraham 104
Lincoln Electric Company xvii, 24, 44, 75, 76, 102, 106, 213, 217, 218, 222, 237, 238
Lincoln, Jim 217
Lincoln, Jim Jr 76
Lincoln, Jimmy Jr. 218

Lincoln, John C. 217
Lombardi, Vince. *See* Green Bay Packers
Lopez, Tewanta 256
Love 79, 83
Lubick, Ron 141
Lund, JoAnne 205

## M

Madoff, Bernard 181
Malcolm Baldridge Award 67
management xvii, 37, 43, 64, 66, 70, 73, 78, 87, 88, 89, 104, 117, 118, 120, 171, 187, 189, 190, 191, 196, 211, 212, 213, 217, 219, 231, 232, 233, 235, 240, 245, 251, 257, 268, 270
Management By Crisis 75
Management Chapter of the Bible 20
Manseuer, Dan 6
manufacturability 42, 224
Manufacturing xvi, 57, 63, 64, 73, 105, 108, 116, 120, 157, 166, 212, 219, 222, 233, 235, 239, 243, 244
Manufacturing Focus 226
Market Focus 226
MARKETING 142, 226
Marti, Gary 26
Martin, Don xii, 18, 19, 135, 249
Mason, Ron 112
Massey, Morris 11, 153
MATERIAL HANDLING 165
Matthew 7
12 20
Matthew 19
19 175
McCormick, Cyrus 3, 190
McDonald's 80
McDonnell-Douglas 173
Meiji 130
melding pot 171
Mensa Society 14
Merten, Jim 244, 252
military 13, 23, 45, 57, 58, 78, 85, 87,